MURDER is my business

MUR

DER is my business

William Foster Hopkins

THE WORLD PUBLISHING COMPANY
NEW YORK AND CLEVELAND

Published by The World Publishing Company
2231 West 110th Street, Cleveland, Ohio 44102

Published simultaneously in Canada by
Nelson, Foster & Scott Ltd.

Second Printing—March, 1970

Library of Congress Catalog Card Number: 74-115796

Printed in the United States of America

Verses on page 59 are from "My Madonna" from *The Collected Poems of Robert Service,* published by Dodd, Mead & Company.

WORLD PUBLISHING
TIMES MIRROR

WITH DEEP LOVE I DEDICATE THIS
BOOK TO ANNE, MY WIFE;
AND TO THE GOVERNOR AND HIS LADY
—MY FATHER AND MOTHER

"There I stood. What else could I do?"

—MARTIN LUTHER

preface—and a creed

Josiah Quincy's father was dismayed when, in 1770, his son undertook the defense of the hated British soldiers who had massacred colonists in Boston. Yet the son, along with John Adams, accepted the defense —and both were the immediate targets of brutal and salacious attacks by the public. Quincy's father wrote a letter:

My dear son,

I am under great affliction at hearing the bitterest reproaches uttered against you, for becoming an advocate for those criminals who are charged with the murder of their fellow citizens. Good God! Is it possible? I will not believe it . . .

I must own to you that it has filled the bosom of your aged and infirmed parents with anxiety and distress, lest it should not only prove true, but destructive of your reputation and interest; and I repeat, I will not believe it, unless it be confirmed by your own mouth, or under your own hand.

Your anxious and distressed parents,
JOSIAH QUINCY

His son replied as follows:

Honoured Sir:

I have little leisure and less inclination, either to know or to take notice of those ignorant slanderers who have dared to utter their "bitter reproaches" in your hearing against me, for having become an advocate for criminals charged with murder. But the sting of reproach, when envenomed only by envy and falsehood, will never prove mortal. Before pouring their reproaches into the ear of the aged and infirm, if they had been friends, they would have surely spared a little reflection on the nature of an attorney's oath and duties—some trifling scrutiny into the business and discharge of his office, and some small portion of patience in viewing my past and future conduct.

Let such be told, Sir, that these criminals, charged with murder *are not yet legally proved guilty*, and therefore, however criminal, are entitled, by the laws of God and Man, to all legal counsel and aid; that my duty as a man obliged me to undertake; that my duty as a lawyer strengthened the obligation; that from abundant caution, I at first declined being engaged; that after the best advice, and most mature deliberation had determined my judgement, I waited on Captain Preston and told him that I would afford him my assistance; but, prior to this, in presence of two of his friends I made the most explicit declaration to him of my real opinion on the contests (as I expressed it to him) of the times, and that my heart and hand were indissolubly attached to the cause of my country; and finally that I refused all engagement, until advised and urged to undertake it, by an Adams, a Hancock, a Molineux, a Cushing, a Henshaw, a Pemberton, a Warren, a Cooper, and a Phillips. This and much more might be told with great truth; and I dare affirm that you and this whole people will one day REJOICE that I became an advocate for the aforesaid "criminals" *charged* with the murder of our fellow-citizens.

I never harboured the expectation nor any great desire that all men should speak well of me. To inquire my duty, and to do it, is my aim. Being mortal, I am subject to error; and, conscious of this, I wish to be diffident. Being a rational creature, I judge for myself according to the light afforded me. When a plan of conduct is formed with an honest deliberation, neither murmuring, slander, nor reproaches move. For my single self, I consider, judge, and with reason hope to be immutable.

There are honest men in all sects,—I wish their approbation; there are wicked bigots in all parties, I abhor them.

I am, truly and affectionately, your Son,

JOSIAH QUINCY, JR.

contents

CHAPTER 1
by way of introduction...

I walk out of the Hamilton County Courthouse, descend the worn stone steps, and—in the noonday sun of summer—walk south on Cincinnati's Main Street to my office, several blocks away. For fifty years, as a practitioner of criminal law, I have strolled this same thoroughfare: fifty springs, fifty summers, fifty autumns, and fifty winters. I have mushed along this street through snow three feet deep, have encountered thundershowers there, have sought half a century of shade from half a century of sun, and unless nailed by an infernal motorbike, I might just hang around a few more handfuls of the swiftly changing seasons.

The street is more modern than it used to be. The unlovely thoroughfare of Cincinnati's yesterdays was dirty but less dangerous. Where teen-agers now speed without majesty astride noisy two-wheelers, horse-drawn wagons once clattered over cobblestones, and serene cable cars moved in silence and slow motion. Now I can see the summer sky. But back then, telephone lines by the thousands blotted out the sun. From each long-ago smokestack of each building black smoke once blossomed to paint the brick-red city grim. Ladies—bless them—tripped along, hobbled by hobble skirts, and any man worth his salt watched carefully for the sweet glimpse of a forbidden ankle.

Good-bye, though, to yesterdays. The city streets have been bulldozed clear of yesteryear. The wrecking ball has reduced my once red brick city to memories which have been hauled away—where?—by dump trucks driven by what seem to be only children. All that remains of the nineteenth century is a building that the wreckers have forgotten—and me, now dodging dump trucks heaped with yesterdays.

As I walk along Main Street I am aware that people—some who are friendly and some who are not—look in my direction. In the eyes of the public, of which you are a part perhaps, I seem to be a puzzle. Why? Because I am a criminal lawyer and because my clients happen to be those whom society—via headlines, prosecuting attorney, and tearoom talk—condemn. But I practice criminal law the way criminal law should be practiced. Mine is not a gangland affair. I have neither Mafia contacts nor known criminals on retainer. Most of my clients have no previous criminal records at all.

On my journey along Main Street I entertain myself by looking into store windows. For fifty years I have stared into such windows and have seen stare back at me generations of lonely and angry men. Through the years the reflections in the windows have changed. Where, for instance, is the law student once reflected there? He helped pay his way through law school by serving, at times, as a professional pallbearer. That was when the University of Cincinnati Law School on Ninth Street was across from a funeral home. When the funeral director had sudden need of spare pallbearers, he put a white glove in his window as a signal. We fledgling advocates earned three dollars apiece by putting on derby hats, frock coats, white gloves, and solemn faces—disguising ourselves as grievers for the unknown dead. En route to the cemetery we were prim and proper and pseudo-sad; coming back in the empty hearse, we set our derbies at a rakish tilt and shot craps. Now all I see reflected is a tall creature who looks back at me with doubt and dignity.

All lives, I suppose, when reduced to notations are simple. Mine is. I know that only too well. Example: I was born in 1899. Lived in Norwood; Newport, Kentucky; Cincinnati; and Indian Hill—in that order. Went to Hughes High School. Then to the University of Cincinnati. While in a Saturday night crap game in the army, won a banjo. Mastered it. Passed the bar. Became a lawyer. Became a bridge champion. Married. Have purchased a crypt. Will someday die. But are these notations me?

People—some angry and some pleased—have attached a variety of adjectives to me. I have been described as old-fashioned, modern, corny, evil-minded, irritating, too polite, too curt, corrupt, bland, sentimental, distinguished, dignified, too neat, dogmatic, a free spirit, and a bunch of other things. When the flag goes by, I get a lump in my throat. Draft-card burners make me seethe. I like the dignity of the courtroom. I like the dignity of man. I suppose who I am depends on who you are. That is true of each of us in our relationships with all others.

A car passes, honks, and the driver, who is a prominent businessman with a solid gold reputation, waves at me. I wave back and, for one brief moment, I can see in his eyes the flickering of fear. He's worried. He's heard that I'm writing this book and he wonders if he will be in it. Years ago—or was it months ago?—the same gentleman sat across from my desk, with tears in his eyes and his soul trembling. He hadn't meant to get involved, or so he said. But when the police found him, he was with another gentleman in a men's rest room and they were involved in an activity better described in sordid paperbacks. Could I hush the matter up? I am no judge and I am no jury. I am only a defense attorney. *Will* he be in this book? At this point I don't know.

I *do* know this: that the book will be more than the telling of one sordid adventure after another. True, I am a criminal lawyer and true also, in these pages you will meet many frightened souls, but you will also meet others of my acquaintance, people who are sheer and beautiful delights. Example: you'll meet my Uncle Oscar, who looked and dressed like General Grant, who gave fierce piano recitals on player pianos, and who—on his breakfast grapefruit—always poured cream.

More store window reflections, but where is the high-school boy who once stared back at me? And where are the 1913 dreams he dreamed? Dreams of the Olympics in Berlin and of pole-vaulting there. Even the newspapers had written of his dreams. I can remember him on hot summer nights, practicing, practicing, practicing, trying to reach the sky as astronauts now reach for stars. His mother had promised him an honest-to-goodness bamboo pole—provided he cleared seven feet. At thirteen, he had cleared eight feet, one inch. And there the dreamer stood that long-ago twilight, panting, all five feet four inches of him, all 107 pounds of him.

And where is the football hero I used to see reflected there? The one who played on the Hughes High School team that four years straight won the interscholastic championship. Left halfback was his position. So was fullback. The player they called "Wee Willie" on the University of Cincinnati freshman team that clobbered the varsity, who busted his nose three times doing it. Then went on to the army and learned to play the banjo. Then vanished, his reflection gone forever.

Carefully now I cross the street in the wake of younger men in a hurry. To be seventy is to be no longer fleet. To be seventy is to see the traffic cop grow young and the newsboy grow old. It is to pass vacant lots where buildings used to be. It is to feel the winds of winter on an Indian summer afternoon. It is, at times, to have known too many people and to have known too many who have cried. But criminal law is my chosen work. My stock in trade is fallen sparrows. I visit the unvisited. I comfort the damned. To you who have watched "Perry Mason" on television, may I suggest in all kindness that there is more to the practice of criminal law than that? Come along with me in these pages and live fifty years of the real McCoy. See a man die in the electric chair. No acting. He dies for real. Visit with me the drab little cages that contain lonely souls accused of crime and hear with me their melancholy songs. Stand at my side before juries and—when things go astray—try not to scream or drown. Forget the fat fees. In this book, we'll visit another side of criminal law. For instance, come with me to the morgue. I have witnessed too many times the final ice-cold congregation of slabfuls of nameless stiffs. I have watched—half sick—autopsies performed: naked murder victims scientifically gutted in search of justice or a bullet. Don't cringe. Listen, during those early autopsies I learned what little girls were made of. There's nothing sexy about a butchered female.

Give me ladies who smile and walk and talk! Ah, the ladies in my life! You'll meet on these pages three wonderful married ladies who have been and still are quite essential to my well-being. First is my wife, Anne. Second, my secretary, Mrs. Ginny Heuser. Third, my mother. Without Anne I would have no cave into which to crawl when at times the world breaks my heart. Before Anne came into my life, my life was a string of lonely days. Because of Anne, Henry Luhrman —her son—became my son, too. He has grown up to be a fine young man and one of New York's better publicity agents. Thus, via Anne, I am doubly blessed. Ginny Heuser is the smartest and nicest legal secretary who ever took two hours for lunch. She can do everything well: analyze a jury, make coffee, interview witnesses, collect bills, type briefs, and—when she's right and I'm wrong—tell me off. With Anne looking out for me at home and Ginny doing the same at the office, I have been turned into a damned Boy Scout, reduced to standing on street corners and helping old ladies across.

The third married lady in my life is my mother. My father courted that charmer during the gay nineties. She bubbled with love and life, all of which she lavished on her family—us—along with mashed potatoes and homemade pies. She wasn't a quiet person; hush was not her mood. Silences did not occupy her days. Strong-willed and wonderful, she always had her say. Her name was Lillian Roberta Foster Hopkins but we all called her Lillie.

Where the Carew Tower is now, the Manhattan Restaurant used to be. Once a month my father and my mother took my brother and me there to live high off the hog: two bits paid for a roast beef dinner complete with soup, salad, and strawberry shortcake. My father used to tip a quarter for the crowd. After dinner we'd sit in the balcony of the Keith Theater and watch great acts—including that of Sophie Tucker—performed on the vaudeville stage.

My mother's folks came from Virginia—over the mountains in covered wagons to their Ohio farm in Adams County. This was in 1832. First they built a log cabin, then a frame house—with one fireplace in the great living room and another in the kitchen for cooking. I remember that house well, the ticking of its grandfather clock and the moan of the winter wind. I remember its fireside benches and rocking chairs so small only children could rock in them. My mother loved that house of her ancestors. After I became a lawyer, she and

I used to drive out on weekends to the farm and the house so full of memories. My maternal grandparents had been married in that living room; so, on November 27, 1895, had my parents. My maternal grandmother and grandfather had been buried from its living room. But the house is no longer there. Six months after my mother died, the house died, too. It collapsed, crash, bang, and that was that.

The death of the house was one execution that I could not stay.

The house, now gone, is—as criminal lawyers around here are— an item of the past. How many criminal lawyers are in this area? Too few, and each year our number grows less. Termites nailed the house. Your attitude and the attitude of most law schools have nailed the profession of criminal law. Only a few seek my path. As my mother used to say, "There are no more 'taters in those hills." Fledgling lawyers haven't the time or patience for the drudgery of the craft.

There's Fountain Square—or rather, where Fountain Square used to be. Now we have a sleek modern plaza surrounded by brand-new skyscrapers.

Although I have had several offices around town, my present office is in the twelve-story Mercantile Library Building on Walnut Street, built on land that city founders set aside as part of a square in which religious, governmental, and educational facilities were supposed to blossom. A medical college once stood on the site. Also a law college. Ralph Waldo Emerson lectured here. So did Wendell Phillips, William Makepeace Thackeray, Henry Ward Beecher, Bret Harte, and the English novelist John Galsworthy. The library, a private affair, is on the eleventh floor. My offices are on the twelfth. A special elevator operates between the lobby and the two top floors. Thus its passengers are those seeking solace both literary and legal. Those accused of murder have often shared the elevator with those accused of writing poetry.

I suppose that every community has a trial lawyer who tries most of that community's criminal cases. But in Cincinnati—thank God— there is a difference: no syndicate business. Even when we had the policy business here, we had not one but seven outfits in the numbers racket. What keeps the syndicate out of Cincinnati? Our Cincinnati police. We've had some great police chiefs here. The one we have now, Jake Schott, is the greatest. He's a real straight shooter who came up through the ranks, earning the honest respect of the officers under him as well as the honest respect of just about every one of us on the right side of the law. But cops are human and that is also what some of this book, and my life, has been about. Criminal lawyers, it is said, police the police. Also, we police the courts. Every time we try a person, we are trying—and defending—more than the accused. We're defending you, that lady down the street, and the Bill of Rights. But nonetheless, criminal lawyers are controversial figures. We try to get justice for the ones you or the newspapers have labeled bad. But we can sleep nights, because we're the ones who hold the state to the ground rules you and our legislators have established. We're the ones who see to it that society doesn't convict a person who shouldn't be convicted.

Look around my office and you'll see, perhaps, what I mean. Over there is a glass case, the sort found in old-fashioned dry-goods stores, and in it is a collection of guns. Each gun in that case killed someone. And I defended the ones who pulled the trigger. The hammer in the glass case? It's not for nailing pictures to a wall. The hammer was used to hammer a person straight into the hereafter. The broken Coke bottle? Used for the same purpose. Because of those dozens of death weapons in that old-fashioned case, dozens of people have died. Dozens of prosecutors have cried for justice. Dozens of juries have searched their souls. And after each trial I have returned to this office, each time a hundred years older.

And the pictures on the wall? Row after row of glum-looking people, all of whom have sat in that chair—the deep leather one in front of my desk—and sung their songs. That lady? She blasted her husband to Kingdom Come. Her song was a sorry tune. You'll hear it in this book. That pretty girl? A real charmer, isn't she? But deadly with a pistol. That shy-looking, pinched-faced little squirt? More deadly than a floor crawling with rattlesnakes. They've all been here.

But know this: for most of them, life had been ordinary until they got involved one time—and one time only—with murder. Tomorrow your picture might stare down from my office wall, and tomorrow that revolver you keep—for prowlers, you say—might be in my little museum, the result of having blown the face off your spouse. So whatever we do, let us not look smug. Each of these lost souls has gone through the twists and turns of that dance we call a trial, a stylized dance that has evolved its pattern from the Bill of Rights and centuries of human pain, a minuet that seeks justice and the truth. Someday you too might be involved in the patterns of that dance and have need of a criminal lawyer.

It is as in that song "Valse Milieu" from *Irma La Douce* where the man points out the dregs of Paris nightlife and says:

> *This is a world you forget or forgive.*
> *Sinner or saint, we have all got to live.*
> *So don't turn away your face—*
> *There but for God's good grace*
> *You might be in their place . . .*
> *Dancing the Valse Milieu.*

So, my friend, let me take you by the hand and let us tour the memories of this beautiful—and dread—profession.

CHAPTER 2
the redheaded widow

I probably was the only lawyer in the United States who could have saved Wesley Belcher from the electric chair.

Before branding me a braggart it might be well to hear me out, and then I will leave the decision entirely up to you.

Following a Guilty plea for one Tom Murphy before Judge Darby, criminal cases had been few and far between. With the exception of another court appointment and one appearance in police court on behalf of a neighborhood boy charged with disorderly conduct, my activity in the practice of criminal law had practically come to a standstill.

It was tough, nearly impossible, to get a foothold in the criminal practice, for it was 1923 and we had in Cincinnati seven crackerjack criminal lawyers practicing at the bar. They were all good and, of course, among them blanketed the criminal trial field.

It was six o'clock and I was still at the office.

In those days I did my own typing and I had been drawing several bills of particulars representing suits for unpaid accounts long past due my client, our family grocer.

Over the rattle of the keys I heard someone speak, but I could not distinguish what was said. I swung around and saw a woman standing in the doorway facing me. She was tall and erect. The nondescript hat she wore did not conceal her neatly combed gray hair, which was pulled back on either side and secured in a bun. Her hands appeared worn and I noted a thin gold band on the third finger of her left hand. Her dress was a cotton print which had never graced a merchant's rack. She bore the unmistakable stamp of the mountains of Kentucky.

"I'm terribly sorry but I didn't hear you," I said.

Her clear blue eyes focused directly on mine as she answered, "I says, be you a lawyer?"

"Yes, ma'am, I am. Won't you come in?"

"Don't mind if I do set a spell, I'm near tuckered out," she said as she sank into a chair and faced me across the desk.

"And what can I do for you?" I asked.

"I got in here," she said "from Parksville, Kentucky, at five o'clock this morning and I ain't stopped since. I've got a boy up here in the jailhouse. His name is Wesley Belcher. Out of seventeen young'uns he's the first to shame the Belcher name. The jailkeeper was right neighborly to me. He's got some kinfolk down near Parksville and he let me and Wesley talk for nigh onto an hour. Then I went out and tried to hire Wesley a lawyer. I talked to Judge Fricke, William Thorndyke, Froome Morris, Raymond Radcliff, and three others but nary a one will take Wesley's case."

"What did your son do?" I asked.

"He's charged with killing a man," she said.

It didn't make sense to me that seven criminal lawyers would turn down a murder case unless she had been unable to pay the attorney fee.

"You know," I said, "you can get lawyers appointed by the Court if you are financially unable to hire one."

"They didn't even mention money," she said. "They just told me they were too busy to take the case."

I knew I had heard the name Wesley Belcher someplace but for the life of me I couldn't remember when or where.

"Well, how did you happen to come to me?"

"A boy running an elevator told me you might take the case," she answered.

"Who did your son kill?"

"A man by the name of William Bond," she said.

"Not the policeman?"

She looked at me with the childlike stare so common to mountain people as she slowly nodded her head.

So that was it. Since 1907 seven policemen from the 4th District alone had been murdered and the jury verdicts in each case had been Guilty of murder in the first degree, which made the death penalty mandatory.

Just recently a policeman from another district had been slain and his killer had met the same fate.

Bill Bond had been a popular policeman. According to the press, he was fifty-six years old and had been on the police force for some twenty-seven years. While on duty, Bond had heard some shots and pursued two men to a third-floor room on Richmond Street where he demanded that one of the men (later identified as Belcher) surrender his gun. Instead of complying, Belcher, it was charged, shot Bond twice in the stomach. He died one hour later, but not before making a dying declaration and positively identifying Belcher as his killer.

It was easy to understand why no one wanted the Belcher case. It was a cinch he was headed for the electric chair, for jurors in our community didn't grant mercy to cop killers and no lawyer wanted a death case.

I was young and inexperienced and I was scared.

A federal judge once told me that if you didn't want a case you needn't disclose that fact to your potential client, but merely name a fee out of his reach.

I looked at Mrs. Belcher and with a deep breath said, "I would have to have one thousand dollars to defend your son."

It was with resignation and disappointment that she answered me—"We'uns ain't got that kind of money. I'd been mighty proud to have you be Wesley's lawyer."

She stood. For a moment our eyes locked and then she bade me good-bye and I heard the outer door close as she departed.

It wasn't that I was a coward, but I just wasn't quite equipped yet to shoulder the awesome responsibility of a first degree murder case, a human being's life in my hands.

Actually I was doing Mrs. Belcher and in particular her son a favor, for I knew the court would appoint two lawyers to represent Belcher who, regardless of their identity, would have far greater experience and know-how than I.

There would be a trial and Belcher would be convicted and sentenced to death in the electric chair. His case would be appealed to the higher courts but eventually the death sentence would be carried out and he would become a statistic supporting the axiom that the wages of sin are surely death. This was all unfortunate but there wasn't a thing I could do about it.

Three weeks passed and then, one afternoon, the receptionist announced that a Mrs. Belcher was waiting to see me.

Attaching no significance to her visit I walked to the door. There, attired in the same dress and wearing the identical hat, was Mrs. Belcher, standing in the outer office with a boy at her side. He appeared to be about fourteen and was wearing a checkered shirt, open at the throat, and faded overalls. He was toting a bag and he was barefoot.

"Wal, here we are, lawyer," was her greeting as they followed me into my private office. "I told you I'd be proud to have you be Wesley's lawyer."

Before I could make any comment she continued, "Son, put that bag on Mr. Hopkins's desk."

With some puffing and blowing the boy deposited the bag on the top of my desk where, at her command, he proceeded to open the fastening and, with the aplomb and finesse of a magician, pour out its contents. Believe it or not, one thousand dollars, mostly in small coins, which I later learned had been collected in the mountains of Kentucky and Virginia, came tumbling out with a continuous jingle which surely would have brought delight to a money changer's ears.

I was speechless and I was demoralized. It had to be a nightmare, but I knew it was for real. There was no backing out now.

I had my first murder case and Belcher, God help him, had the handicap of counsel.

My father, however, was proud of me. He had become a conductor on the Norfolk and Western Railroad and impressed upon each and every passenger between here and Norfolk the greatness of his son, the criminal attorney. You see, years and years before, long before my time, on court days lawyers used to "ride the circuit." Court, then, was a show that came to town. Everyone and his brother would head straight for the courthouse. Those who couldn't crowd in, crowded around outside and listened through the open window which, no matter how cold the weather, stayed open during court. In the summer, those outside would sprawl on the courthouse lawn, listening to the great oratory that poured forth from the window. My father, as a boy, would be sprawled on the grass, or straddling a cannon, listening. There, he conceived an ambition to become a lawyer himself, but my grandfather lost his shirt in business in Morrow, Ohio. College was not in the cards for my father. Instead, he went to work for the railroad and gave his beautiful dream to me. As far as my being a "great lawyer," though, he and my mother had more confidence in me than I had.

Mrs. Belcher oozed confidence too, both in me and in the Lord, but Wesley couldn't have cared less. While he was struggling with the officer, so the report went, a witness used the officer's pistol to beat such a tattoo on my client's head that his brains were addled. They say that after his arrest, he spent most of the night in Central Station jail, praying and shouting, until he dropped off to sleep. Most of the time I was associated with him, he stared vacantly, blinked a lot, and his mouth hung slackjawed. The plea, obviously, was insanity. His own mother had confessed that when her Wesley was ten he had been hit in the head with a stone and "hadn't been quite right since."

In other words, the conversations with my client before and during the trial were not exactly helpful; they left much—in fact, they left *everything*—to be desired.

I don't suppose in the recorded history of criminal cases there has been one tried with less know-how and finesse and more enthusiasm than I demonstrated in the efforts I put forth on behalf of my client, Wesley Belcher.

Of course I didn't have much opposition. Charles S. Bell, prosecutor of Hamilton County and later to become a justice of the Ohio Supreme Court, and Nelson Schwab, who shortly after the Belcher case was elected to the Common Pleas Bench, were the prosecutors.

As trained practitioners they tried the case in a smooth and efficient manner.

I, on the other hand, due to my inexperience, spread havoc and utter confusion throughout the entire trial.

My unexpected and unprecedented maneuvers were unique and unorthodox to say the least and at times left my opponents, and for that matter, the court, at a loss when attempting to determine what, if any, retaliatory measures should or could be taken.

The trial should have been stopped in the first round as a mismatch, but Judge Fred Hoffman, a hardnosed and veteran jurist, refused to intervene.

In those days each side had sixteen peremptory challenges, and it was not uncommon to consume two weeks in obtaining a jury in any given murder case. In the five days which had elapsed since the trial's beginning, the state had used nine peremptory challenges and I had challenged seven jurors.

The challenges are exercised alternately beginning with the state and followed by the defense. At each turn the side having the privilege must either challenge a juror or pass. In either event, the right to challenge once again reverts to the opponent. This may go on until a total of thirty-two challenges has been exercised. If either side should pass a challenge and this is followed by a pass by the other side, the jury is then complete although any number of challenges remain unused.

As the jury was now constituted, there were two men and one woman I intended to challenge. The men weren't too bad, but the woman had to go.

She was a redheaded widow who was old enough to be my mother or grandmother depending upon how charitable the appraiser happened to be. She must have had some great disappointment in her life, for from the very first day of the trial she seemed to hate everybody and I was, at least temporarily, number one on the hate parade.

She made no effort to conceal her feelings toward me and my client, and it was evident to all that there was present an unmistakable animus—of unknown origin but sufficient intensity to disqualify her as a fair and impartial juror.

It was my challenge but I had nine challenges left. I wanted to save the redheaded widow until last, and besides I was in no hurry, for I wanted her to feel safe and secure until the moment of truth.

It was with great anticipation and, I must confess, sadistic delight that I awaited the moment of triumph when I would stand and, in a thundering voice, banish her from the courtroom. I'd teach her to mind her manners.

On two other occasions I had passed and the prosecutor had challenged a juror. I knew I was taking no chances, so I passed again. I was beginning to think that I was cleverly outmaneuvering the state at every turn and playing with the prosecutor as a cat might with a mouse. Renewed strength flowed through my veins. I was an advocate. And then it happened.

The prosecutor stood and addressed the court. "We also will pass. We are satisfied with the jury."

"The jury," said the court, "will stand and be sworn."

The bailiff administered the oath and the jurors resumed their seats in the jury box.

The prosecutor favored me with a big grin and the redheaded widow just sat looking at me, shaking her head. I was demoralized and frightened. I had made a colossal ass of myself but it was too late to do anything about that.

Through my own stupidity and egotism I had lost one juror already and we hadn't even started the case.

Witness after witness came to the stand. One was a nine-year-old moppet who lived on the second floor of the building in which the shooting had taken place. That urchin conquered the courtroom the way Shirley Temple later conquered the silver screen. A cute little lass, squirming and full of fidgets, she seemed lost in the witness chair. Her voice, when she spoke, was hardly above a whisper. A tremendous witness.

Unfortunately, she was a witness for the prosecution.

Her testimony placed my client at the scene of the murder.

Another prosecution witness was the policeman's widow. She had been called for the distasteful but essential task of proving that prior to the shooting her husband had been alive and that, indeed, he was the one who had been killed. When the prosecution held up her husband's bloody uniform to be identified, his widow broke down, sobbed, and could not go on.

That was all right. I was too choked to cross-examine her.

Actually, I added little to the scene but worry, ignorance, and sweat. Each day found the courtroom more humid than the day before.

And the entire Belcher clan, headed by Mrs. Belcher, sweltered in the second row of seats, panting, wiping foreheads, fanning themselves, not missing a single second of a single session. Each night when court adjourned, the Belchers en masse would descend upon the defense table, pat me on the back, and say how well I was handling Wesley's case. There I was, punch-drunk with Shirley Temples and wailing widows, hanging on the ropes, and beaten legally to a pulp, but they—the Belchers—thought I was the greatest. I felt like a prizefighter who has sustained a beating in the first round and when told by his manager that he has his opponent on the run, climbs through the ropes and announces he is going home while still winning.

I, too, would have liked to call it a day; but the trouble was they were playing for keeps and I couldn't get loose.

The defense didn't take long. Mrs. Belcher testified that her son, when ten, had been struck on the head with a stone and "hadn't been quite right since."

A woman named Beulah Campbell took the stand and testified that Belcher had lived in her house in West Virginia and at that time "was diseased both in mind and body."

Belcher took the stand in his own defense and testified that on the day in question, he was suffering from a toothache and had taken some liquor to ease the pain.

"Did it help your toothache?" I asked.

"I don't know," he answered. "The next thing I remember I woke up in jail."

The defendant under a grueling cross-examination by Bell consistently denied all knowledge and participation in the crime. After two hours of hammering, during which time Belcher steadfastly insisted he had no memory of shooting the policeman, Bell advised the court he had no further questions and Belcher left the stand.

According to one newspaper account:

> Only twice did his [Belcher's] countenance light up with ordinary human intelligence. Once when he identified his mother

in the courtroom and the other time when questioned by Prosecutor Bell.

"Have you any children?" Prosecutor Bell asked him.

"Why yes," he said with a smile and a sudden lighting of his otherwise dull eyes. "I have two."

He was unable to say just how old they were or where they and his wife were now.

"It's been quite a spell since I seen them," he said, and standing up in the witness box, indicated the height of the older. "I don't recall how old they are, but one was just about this high," he said, indicating a three- or four-year-old child. "The other one was littler."

Both sides rested and court was adjourned until the following morning when final arguments would be made.

I made my *first* final argument the next day to the mirror in my bathroom. The argument I made was one that even Clarence Darrow would have envied. The jury—including the redheaded widow—had tears in their eyes. The judge, awed by my eloquence and my grasp of the law, gaped with ill-concealed admiration. Both prosecutors listened, angrily at first, but soon I swayed them too. The audience that filled the courtroom wept without shame and, when I concluded my ringing speech to the jury, the audience stood and cheered. So did the judge. So did the jury. So did the prosecutors.

Then I finished shaving and went downstairs. The pretense was over.

When I arrived at the courthouse the Belchers—loyal to the end, which was coming up fast—sat, waiting for me to do my best.

The redheaded widow, fanning herself in the jury box, was waiting for me to do my worst.

The judge and the prosecutors, concern in their eyes, waited too. They hoped I would not make any more hash of jurisprudence than I had up to that point in the proceedings. The pained looks in their eyes seemed to be saying, "Foss, why don't you go back to the world of music. As a lawyer, you're great on the banjo. And your shimmy isn't bad, either." I only imagined them saying that, but I did not have to imagine the butterflies in my stomach. They were real—and working overtime.

Schwab led off for the state. He was convincing. As he reviewed the tons of damaging evidence which had been introduced, the jury listened intently. He contended that the state had proved the defendant guilty of killing a police officer and, in his impassioned voice which impressed even me, he demanded a verdict that would send Belcher to his death in the electric chair.

Then, wiping his forehead dry with a clean handkerchief, he sat down.

Well, I must be honest here. Following his masterful plea, it was a badly scared and shaken lawyer—with damp palms and trembling knees—who arose to deliver the final argument for the defense. I was no longer facing the bathroom mirror. I faced a jury that played for keeps. I cleared my throat and began.

If it had not been for the redheaded widow I might have done reasonably well, but her glares threw me for a loss. My mind refused to function. I could not recall nor would my lips even form those shining phrases with which I had dazzled the mirror.

As I write this narrative, I have before me the original Belcher file, now yellow with age, containing my handwritten argument which I had intended to deliver to that long-ago jury. For a first effort it was pretty good, but any similarity to the argument I delivered was coincidental.

Then, my defense was over. I gaped at the jury, the jury gaped at me, and—knowing my effort had been a fiasco of catastrophic dimensions—I resumed my seat at the defense table. I listened, numb, to Bell giving the state's final argument. He needed no bathroom mirror to make him great. He was an excellent prosecutor and an orator of note. As he admonished that jury—in his enraged voice—to "extend the same mercy he [my client] bestowed on Bill Bond when he shot him in cold blood," I became convinced that Belcher was headed straight for the chair.

The redheaded widow glared at me from the jury box as if to say, "I told you so!"

Judge Hoffman began to read his charge to the jury but didn't get far. The heat of the courtroom had proved too much for one male juror. Right in the middle of the judge's charge, the juror fainted and confusion reigned. Through it all sat the redheaded widow, fanning herself and glaring at me.

Finally order prevailed, the judge finished reading his charge, and the jury—wearing a collective death mask—filed by the defense table and into the jury room. The courtroom spectators didn't move. They stayed in their seats. They felt, as did the rest of us, that the jury would be quick about condemning Wesley.

All felt that way, that is, but the Belchers. They crowded around me at the defense table. They were so lavish in their praise and so optimistic, they made a piker of Pollyanna.

"Don't you worry, lawyer," said Mrs. Belcher, wringing my hand. "With you and the good Lord on Wesley's side, we got us nothing to worry about."

"No," I said.

"Yes," she said—and wrung my hand some more.

I didn't have the heart to tell her the handwriting was not only on the wall but had been on the face of every juror. The Belchers had faith in me they shouldn't have had.

So began the wake, the first of many I would endure.

There wasn't anything for me to do but sit, feel sorry for myself and my client, and wait for the ax to fall. Every minute that passed was an hour and, as I sat at that defense table, every hour became a century. I waited only for one thing: the sound of the jury buzzer which would herald their verdict of death and end the Belcher's faith in me.

Somehow two whole hours passed, much to everyone's surprise, and there had not been one peep from the jury.

"What's holding them up?" a clerk complained.

For a moment, no one could answer.

Then Charlie Stagnaro, the criminal bailiff, winked at me and said: "They must be having a hell of a time electing a foreman. Don't you think so, counselor?"

I made no comment.

"Aw, cheer up, counselor," Charlie said with compassion. "I mean it. You can't win 'em all."

At six-thirty the jurors, escorted by the bailiff and two deputies, adjourned to a hotel, where arrangements had been made for their dinner.

When the jury returned at eight-fifteen, I caught a glimpse of them as they straggled along the corridor. They had not been cheered by dinner. Their faces left no doubt as to the seriousness of their mood.

They were herded back into the jury room, the door was closed, and that was that.

Once more I slid into my seat at the defense table. My mouth was dry. My hair was soaked with sweat. My clothes clung as if plastered to my frame. I ached to unbutton my vest, but didn't. Dignity, you know. But I couldn't sit still. I got up, left the courtroom, and began to pace the corridor outside where, moments before, the jury had straggled by. By then the corridor was empty.

Buildings have moods. By day the courthouse mood is people, paper, and telephones ringing. By night, with corridors dimly lighted, long, and empty, the courthouse dances to a sadder tune. Only the janitor sweeping slowly belongs. Through an open window in some unattended office I heard a river packet's deep cry of farewell to the public landing.

I paced back and forth. I looked at my wristwatch. Ten o'clock. I wiped more sweat from my face. I peered into the courtroom where, still assembled, the professional onlookers lingered.

"He'll burn," I heard one say.

"I smell flesh burning already," I heard another say.

To them justice was vaudeville.

But Bill Morris, dean of the courthouse reporters, stepped out and stood beside me.

"How are you, counselor?" he said. His voice was gentle.

"Dying by inches, Mr. Morris," I said.

"You'll get used to it," he said. "My first two murder cases upset me. But I've learned to take them in my stride."

There was actual compassion in his eyes.

"You have to remember," he said. "You didn't pull the trigger that made this show begin."

I shook my head. "I'm never going to get used to it," I said. "This is my last murder case."

He was silent a moment.

"Maybe you'll change your mind," he said finally. "Listen, they can't all be against you in that jury room—or they would have come back long ago."

"Do we really have a chance, though?" I said.

He shrugged. "What do you say we find out? Have you ever heard a jury deliberate?"

"But that would be unethical," I said. "Wouldn't it?"

He gave me a look I couldn't read.

"Come on," he said. "Let's go down to the press room. It's more comfortable there."

We did.

But as we entered the press room, he did a strange thing. He locked the door behind us. Then he said: "You probably would like to use the rest room. But be sure to close the door."

After making this incongruous statement, he went to his desk, sat down, busied himself with papers, and ignored me.

As directed, but still confused, I went into the little rest room the press room contained. I closed the door. I ran cold water over my wrists and wiped my face with a cool damp cloth. That felt good. But as I raised my hand to open the door and leave, I heard muffled—and angry—voices coming eerily from somewhere above my head. The voices were both men's and women's. They seemed to drift out from the air vent five feet above the sink. As I listened the voices grew louder and angrier, but I couldn't tell what they were saying.

I stood, suddenly dumbfounded.

The press room was adjacent to the courtroom, and it was possible that the room in which I stood was connected directly to the air vent in the juror's rest room.

Evidently one of the jurors had left the door ajar, and through the air vent to my cramped quarters poured the voices of the jurors themselves. The temptation was too great to resist.

I climbed carefully up onto the washbowl, thrust my fingers through the vent, and pressed my ear against its screening.

A battle seemed to be raging. Though I couldn't understand at first any particular statement, I heard words like "chair . . . policeman . . . no mercy." Finally a male juror's voice rose above the others. He must have struck the jury table two blows as he bellowed for the attention of the jurors and—of course—for mine.

"I want to say," he shouted in a commanding voice, "that I'm not going to make a career out of this case!"

Having got their attention, they became silent, and he went on in a lower voice but one that carried so I could hear every word.

"I've got a living to make," he said. "Now I've been voting five hours for the chair, but we're not going to convince these five to vote our way. I'm willing to change my vote to mercy if the rest of you are. If we don't, this jury is going to be deadlocked and the case will have to be tried again. It costs us taxpayers money to try these cases and I personally don't think this one is worth it."

Silence.

Then I heard a woman's voice and recognized its owner: the red-headed widow.

"All right," she screeched, fed up about something. "All right, all right, all right! I'll change my vote but I'm going straight to Judge Hoffman as soon as we report our verdict. There ought to be a law passed stopping such incompetent lawyers from representing people in murder cases!"

If she had hit me with a brick the impact could not have been more severe.

Shocked, I tried to disengage myself from that precarious perch but my foot slipped and I fell. In falling I grabbed the shower curtain, which broke the force of my fall, but down we both went into a heap upon the floor. There, with the shower curtain for a shroud, I reached the breaking point. Exhaustion and despair consumed me. I unbuttoned my vest and sat there, bawling like a baby.

It was ten minutes before I regained composure enough to leave that room. Then I returned to the courtroom and the defense table, sitting down just as the buzzer sounded.

A minute later the bailiff announced to Judge Hoffman that the jury had arrived at a verdict. A few minutes after that, a deputy sheriff arrived with Wesley Belcher, who sat beside me at my table. The jury filed in. The judge ascended the bench.

The foreman handed the written verdict to the clerk, who looked at it, looked at it again as if surprised, then read:

"We, the members of this jury, find the defendant Wesley Belcher Guilty of murder in the first degree as he stands charged in the indictment—" there was an agonizing pause "—but we do recommend mercy."

"Praise the Lord," Mrs. Belcher muttered.

The judge thanked the jurors for their services. The court officially adjourned.

Mrs. Belcher was first to reach the defense table. As she hugged me there were tears streaming down her face.

"I told you, lawyer, I told you," she said, "I told you that you'd save my boy's life. You're the only lawyer that could have done it . . ."

Over the years as I have analyzed the Belcher case, I have come to the conclusion that Mrs. Belcher was one hundred percent correct in her last statement, although for a different reason than she supposed.

The following morning lawyers and courthouse attachés congratulated me on my "victory" in the Belcher case. One morning newspaper ran a headline, YOUNG LAWYER SAVES COP KILLER, which must have made the redheaded widow pause in disbelief. I have never been so embarrassed in my life. Every time someone would shake my hand or pat me on the back I felt as phoney as a three-dollar bill. All day long I wanted to hide, for everywhere I went the redheaded widow's words "There ought to be a law passed" haunted my every move. But there was no relief. The redheaded widow became my constant companion: a jealous and demanding mistress who wouldn't let me call my soul my own.

CHAPTER 3
the valley of
the shadow of death

That redheaded widow on the jury in the Belcher case—thanks to my imagination—became my constant companion. Banjo-playing and the mashed potatoes my mother heaped nightly upon my plate during the days following the Belcher trial could not drive the redhead away. Sometimes at dinner, in the midst of a conversation about the Cincinnati Reds or the weather, I would fall silent because, in my mind, I had heard that widow say again, "There ought to be a law passed . . ." One morning while shaving the answer came.

I knew if I was to continue to practice criminal law I would have to accept the redheaded widow's challenge and attempt to become a criminal lawyer capable of trying murder cases.

I figured that after my exhibition in the Belcher case there was only one way for me to go and that was up. I had nothing to lose and there was always the outside chance that I might succeed.

I took an oath that morning that I would dedicate the balance of my life to becoming a good criminal trial lawyer. No stone would be left unturned, nor would any sacrifice be too great in attaining my goal.

I had to show that redheaded widow that *I could* try a case.

A philosopher once stated that behind every successful man stands some woman who silently and unselfishly aided and assisted him in his climb up the ladder. Most successful men acknowledge this fact and pay tribute to their wives or mothers. I want to pay tribute to a redheaded widow.

It is true she was not reticent nor unselfish but her evaluation of me and her ridicule reignited the spark of ambition which she had extinguished and which under any other circumstances would probably have lain permanently buried in the deepest recesses of my body.

When I stumbled or faltered, her tongue-lashing drove me inexorably on, and when I was victorious, her silence was beautiful music to my ears.

I hurried to the office that long-ago morning, eager to get started. The office I was then associated with contained an array of legal talent, with me (and my vest) at the bottom of the heap. Howard Bevis, later president of Ohio State University, was there. So was Stanley Struble, judge of Common Pleas Court. So was Charlie Tatgenhorst, later United States Congressman. A few rungs above me in the fledgling department was David Attig, who, one morning after my great decision, greeted me with: "Well, how's the big-shot criminal lawyer today?"

I ignored his remark. Instead, I said: "Do you want to see a man die in the electric chair?"

He got serious fast.

"You have to be kidding," he said.

"No," I said. "If I'm going to try men for their lives, I should know what happens if I lose."

I showed Dave a copy of my letter to the Ohio State Penitentiary requesting that I, together with an associate, be allowed to witness an execution. When Dave put the letter down, his face was white. Before he could say a word, I handed him the reply from

Columbus. It said that an execution had been scheduled two weeks hence and gave us instructions as to the exact time and place.

We arrived in Columbus about 6:30 P.M. We headed for a restaurant to eat our evening meal, which Dave morbidly christened the Last Supper.

I shall never be able to forget what we saw during that trip to Columbus. Though I had always been opposed to capital punishment, I became doubly convinced that it was vengeance based upon the edict of an eye for an eye and a tooth for a tooth, an edict promulgated before the arrival of Christ upon our earth. After that, I could never erase either the redheaded widow's sneer or the execution I had witnessed. Nonetheless, for a quarter of a century after the Belcher case and witnessing that execution, I had almost managed to learn to live with myself—until the day Fred Arwood entered my life. In those twenty-five years my practice as a criminal lawyer had been soundly established.

Ginny Heuser—who was by then my secretary—and I were in my office, preparing a brief, when we were interrupted by the telephone.

"It's Fred Arwood's sister," Ginny said. "She wants you to represent her brother."

I sighed and shoved aside the yellow legal pad on which I had been scribbling. Here it comes again, I thought.

"Well?" said Ginny.

"You know the answer as well as I do," I said.

She nodded and murmured some words into the telephone.

Fred Arwood had been accused of killing his wife. The testimony of witnesses and the police and of Fred Arwood conflicted; but that his bride, tied nude and spreadeagled upon her bed, had been stabbed to death was a fact.

What right had I to refuse Fred Arwood the benefit of counsel? To have said no would have marked a no vote for courts and law and justice. We are a civilized people who have come a long way from the caves. Civilization lays obligations on us. No matter what we may personally think of those with whom fate requires us as lawyers to associate, the right of any man—which tomorrow could be you—to a fair trial must not be tossed away.

In this country, as in England, we employ the adversary system

—a system based on the idea that truth will emerge out of a struggle between two contesting parties presenting their case to an impartial tribunal. Harris B. Steinberg in the American Law Institute's book *The Problem of a Criminal Defense* stated it best. He said, "Each man's lawyer will do his best to establish a case for his client and destroy the case that his opponent is trying to make. The system is a commitment to the notion that the right result will emerge out of the conflict. Such a system will work only if the two contesting parties are relatively equal . . ."

And so Ginny and I once again made that trip to the jail atop the Hamilton County Courthouse. There we were closeted in the little conference room where, in silence, we waited for the appearance of our client, Fred Arwood.

Outside, down on the streets, newsboys cried the latest of the crime that had occurred in a sleazy Third Street rooming house. As I heard their faint shouts, filtered through the prison walls, I thought of the magic that the street near the river had once possessed. Third Street had been Cincinnati's own Wall Street—host to sixteen of our city's two dozen banks. But those stone and brick buildings—architectural valentines—had long ago turned sour. Some had become noisy and foul-smelling red brick cauldrons that contained scores of dimlit cubbyholes peopled by the poor and the drunk. Yet, along Third Street, Rutherford B. Hayes had practiced law, and so had Salmon P. Chase. Here Frank Duveneck had painted, Jenny Lind had sung, and on mellow summer evenings, John James Audubon had strolled. Here, too, had been the Woodruff House, a five-story hotel that boasted Cincinnati's first roof garden. And around the corner had been the Sycamore Theater where Hamlet's lament had been answered by a river packet's melancholy cry.

Now, along Third Street, all was gone save misery—and there, dominating the jailhouse conference door with his huge bulk, Fred Arwood stood, peering at me. He must have been at least six feet four. He had dark bushy hair. His hands, massive and powerful, were twice the size of mine. I guessed his weight at 220 pounds. He reminded me of Luis Firpo, the Argentine strongman, but he smelled of stale beer, sweat, and prison soap, and of the electric chair.

"Sit down, Mr. Arwood," I said.

He did—and made the tiny room seem smaller than it had ever seemed before.

I cleared my throat and began.

"Mr. Arwood," I said, "I want to get one thing straight. A lot of people call me and think because they pay money that they can buy their freedom. Well, that's not true. I have been practicing law for a long time . . ."

I let Fred Arwood tell his side of the story without interruption. He spoke in a slow drawl, seemed anxious to cooperate, but denied knowledge of stabbing his wife. He did admit that whenever she sassed him, he would slap her around. Also, he admitted that he had been convicted in Chattanooga of killing a man. On another occasion, he told us, he had been found Guilty of assault to kill and had, again, been sentenced to the penitentiary.

"What about the day your wife was murdered?" I said, when he had finished his story.

He said he had been drinking heavily. But, he added quickly, he could remember nothing until someone told him that his wife was dead.

Newspaper accounts said that Arwood's wife had been found tied, nude, on the bed in their crowded one-room flat. When the police had arrived, other people had been found jammed into that little room, but they were all too drunk to tell—coherently—what had happened exactly to cause the lady to meet her end. The police had hauled everyone off in a paddy wagon and the body of Mrs. Arwood, bride of three months, had been removed to the morgue, where it remained, unclaimed by any kin.

"Well," said Ginny, who had then only been with our law office a year, "you've got a mean one this time, haven't you?"

"They're all mean," I said. "Would you rather work on my brother's side of the business, doing estate work?"

"No," she said.

"I will suggest, though," I said, "that our client smells of death. If we can pull this one off . . ."

I didn't finish. And Ginny didn't ask me to.

The grand jury indicted Fred Arwood for first degree murder. His trial was set for December 1, 1946.

We impaneled a jury of nine women and three men, the same ratio as the Belcher jury twenty-three years before.

The prosecutor stated in his opening address (and later established during the course of the trial) that for two days prior to the death of Mrs. Arwood her husband had kept her tied naked on the bed, and during this period had beaten her severely.

Most damaging was the testimony of one witness, a lady who had known Fred Arwood for several years. When he invited her to his room that fatal Sunday, she had accompanied him, but found the door padlocked. He unlocked the door, swung it open, and there on the bed his wife was tied. She said that Arwood, then drunk, proceeded to introduce the two ladies to one another.

After that, the witness said, she and Arwood sat around the room, drinking.

You could see the horror register on the faces of the jury, but there was nothing I could do to stop her testimony.

The witness testified that Arwood's wife had pleaded for her clothes, saying she didn't like lying around that way in full view of company, but Arwood had told her she didn't need clothes.

"Then he got mad," the witness said, "and started to beat her. He kept hitting her—about thirty or forty times. I couldn't count them . . ."

As I sat at the defense table beside the huge bulk of Fred Arwood I felt the courtroom seethe with hatred for my client.

The witness testified that after a while, she and Arwood went to a coffeehouse, leaving his wife in that room, whimpering helplessly. While the two were out, they met the witness's husband and another man from the same building. Arwood invited them all back to his place to drink.

She testified that the four crowded into the room, drinking, and that Mrs. Arwood moaned for a glass of water.

"Arwood," the witness said, "told her she could have a beer."

She said that the men got into a fight—she couldn't remember why—and then left to get more beer. That was when she saw Arwood with the knife, she said.

The prosecutor showed the witness a butcher's boning knife. He placed it in evidence as the weapon that had ended Mrs. Arwood's nightmare because, according to the witness, Arwood had said: *"I've nailed her to the bed as Jesus was nailed to the Cross!"*

By the time the state rested its case, there was no doubt in anyone's mind that the state had proved my client Guilty, and that the jurors who had already professed belief in capital punishment would return a verdict sending Fred Arwood to the chair.

As for the defense, I succeeded in establishing only one fact: when he killed his wife, Arwood had been intoxicated.

The situation became so tense I wouldn't have been surprised if they had brought the electric chair into the courtroom and dispatched Fred Arwood there.

"Things look bad, don't they?" Ginny asked me during one recess.

"When there's a burning case," I told her, "you can feel something in the courtroom you don't feel any other time. Have you noticed how we're going about our business? Look at us. Can't you sense it?"

She nodded.

To sense death in a courtroom is a hateful ability that fills each participant with a special—and private—despair.

The judge and the rest of us were suddenly playing our roles too politely, drenching ourselves with ritual in order to ease the pain. Our voices, when we spoke, acquired a hollow and metallic sound. We seculars of the law had become life-size marionettes from some Javanese folk tale. We quarreled stylized quarrels, wore the masks of civilized men, but all the while our nostrils smelled the stench of burning flesh. The jibes and jokes with which lawyers and judges and clerks cheer one another had become too forced or—for the most part—had vanished from the script. Even the jurors began to show the strain. The solemnity of their faces registered the hopelessness of the defendant's cause and the futility of it all.

In this atmosphere of doom and finality, the prosecutor rose to address the jury.

He drew a parallel between Christ nailed to the Cross asking for water and being tendered wine by his tormentors, and Mrs. Arwood, beaten and tied to her bed, pleading for water and being offered beer.

He compared Arwood to Jack the Ripper; you could sense the jury nodding.

He extolled the jury to "remove this cancerous growth from our fair city."

The jury winced—and even I shuddered—at the enormity of Fred Arwood's guilt and at the persuasiveness of the prosecutor as he thundered on.

"Arwood tells you he doesn't remember what happened. But you and I know he lies to save his neck. When you go back to the jury room, remember above all else his statement following the murder of his wife—'I've nailed her to the bed as Jesus was nailed to the Cross!' I suggest—*demand*—that you give Fred Arwood the same mercy he extended to his wife on the day he plunged a boning knife through her heart!"

The prosecutor sat. He had strapped Fred Arwood in the electric chair. All the jury had to do was, by its verdict, administer the coup de grace.

Because it was four in the afternoon, court was adjourned until the next morning. Fred Arwood returned to his cell atop the courthouse, the courtroom emptied fast, and I—avoiding the spectators—went out among the Christmas shoppers, flagged a cab, rode back to my office, and once inside my office twelve floors up, collapsed into the chair at my desk.

Twelve floors straight down a Salvation Army trumpet tooted brassy praise up to where God was. This trumpet sound mingled with the noise of the evening rush hour: autos honking, the clang of trolley bells, and the wailing of the newsboys who, as town criers, shouted of the courthouse drama of the day.

"Aren't you going to light a light?" Ginny said.

I hadn't heard her come in.

"Later," I said. "You go home."

And there I was, alone in the office gloom, engulfed in a lawyer's loneliest hour.

Usually, I told myself, in a murder case there is someplace to hang your hat. But in the Fred Arwood case, where was that? Ever since I had been retained by Fred Arwood's sister, I—along with a young legal assistant—had tediously but unsuccessfully searched to uncover a mitigating fact or circumstance which might have been sufficient to save Arwood's life.

We had turned up absolutely nothing.

The trumpet had been replaced by a Salvation Army chorus, the twilight by night, and the rush-hour noises had dwindled to the unrushed ordinary sounds of the street. I sighed and turned on the desk lamp.

"Why defend a guilty man?" one of the spectators had asked during a recess, and I had turned away without answering. But the question came back. I could hear it being asked all over the city. Some lawyers will do anything for a buck. Only a few know better. Why defend any guilty party? Because it is not the job of a lawyer to be the judge. OK, so I can't lie to the court, I can't bribe witnesses, I can't suborn perjury. What good can I do? Help my client—if I can. He may not know about things like venue and jurisdiction. These items are my meat. He may not know much about mental illness as a defense. I read once that "there are a great many things that are immoral about which men may feel a twinge of conscience, and yet, these immoral acts may contain only four out of five of the necessary and essential elements of the crime charged." The accused has to have a lawyer in order to avoid unwittingly discarding any of his constitutional rights. Why defend a man who is guilty?

Because I am a lawyer. Simple as that.

But as far as Fred Arwood was concerned, I felt helpless all over again, the same as in the Belcher case.

Voluntary drunkenness, I realized, was not a defense in Ohio but, on the other hand, when a defendant is intoxicated at the time of the killing, this fact is usually considered by a jury determining whether or not mercy should be extended. I shook my head. No, because of the circumstances of the Arwood case, no jury would take Arwood's drunkenness into consideration. I would have to think of something else.

But what? There was no answer anywhere.

"Goodnight, Mr. Hopkins," said the building watchman. "Have a good night's sleep."

"Everybody is a comedian," I said—and pushed through the revolving doors out into the midnight streets of downtown Cincinnati.

I slept little that night. At home I read—and reread—the transcript of the trial. I sought, with little hope, a fact or circumstance that I might use in my argument the next morning.

No such item existed.

At four in the morning, while the city slept, I shoved the transcript aside. I had failed. My client was going to the chair. With the exception of the intoxication angle, which I knew the prosecutor could tear to shreds, I was helpless.

I had racked my brain for something—anything—to say on Fred Arwood's behalf. I had not come up with a single thing. I crawled into bed and stared at the ceiling.

"There ought to be a law . . ." the redheaded widow was saying, over and over and over.

And finally, sleep came.

A few minutes before ten that morning I arrived—exhausted—at the courthouse and made my way through the crowds to criminal courtroom Number 2. I had just joined Fred Arwood and my young legal assistant at the defense table when the jury marched into the room, settled itself in the jury box, and sat back, waiting.

The courtroom itself was packed. Spectators occupied every available inch of space because the word was that Fred Arwood had to burn. They had foregone their Christmas shopping so they could be in on the kill.

Promptly at ten the judge ascended the bench and the bailiff opened court.

The judge's eyes sought mine.

"You may proceed with your argument," he said.

Under any circumstances to make a defense argument in a first degree murder case is difficult. You are making a pitch for the life of a fellow human being. One slip—however slight—can make the difference between his life and his death. When you have something concrete to say in that man's defense your summation is, nonetheless, still difficult. But to have to face a jury as I did that morning and have nothing to say . . . I was in deep trouble.

As I fumbled with the papers on the defense table, my young assistant—frightened—could contain his question no longer.

"What *are* you going to say?" he whispered.

I kept a poker face.

"I'll be damned if I know," I muttered—and stood to face the jury.

"If your Honor pleases," I began. "Gentlemen of the prosecution, and ladies and gentlemen of the jury . . ."

The jurors, who had been staring straight at Arwood—hate shining in their eyes—turned to stare at me as if I were an unwanted intrusion. Some of the hate spilled over on me. I could sense the intensity of their animosity and indignation at the crime my client had committed. I sensed that they resented the fact I stood before them to insult their intelligence by arguing a case which their hate had already determined.

"All right," they seemed to say. "We know you have a job to do, but get it over fast."

I mentioned the presumption of innocence to the jury. I explained the legal definition of that magic term "reasonable doubt." I cautioned them that they each must have an abiding conviction amounting to a moral certainty of the truth of the charge before they could convict my client of first degree murder. I discussed intoxication and the effect it would have on premeditation and deliberation which, I said, the state would have to establish before the jury could find my client guilty. I talked twenty minutes but the jurors had become restless and inattentive.

The jury was doing the best that it could, but the hearts of the jurors just weren't in it.

One juror squirmed. Another shifted continuously in his seat. Some stole glances at the judge. Others glanced at the table where the prosecution sat. Others looked at Arwood and a few stared at the gray winter day outside the courtroom window. There I stood, completely alone, daring to raise my voice as the one dissenter to an edict of death shortly to be decreed by them.

The jury and I, however, had two things in common. We were both uncomfortable. We both had a wild desire to be somewhere else.

As I stood before them I realized that I had failed.

I was unable to hold the attention of these nine women and three men, much less convince them that mercy should be extended to my client. There was nothing more that I could say in behalf of Fred Arwood; I had said it all—and it had not been enough.

I closed my eyes. My mind raced to capture anything to add to my plea for Fred Arwood's life. But nothing could be found.

Then, as I stood there, the last friend Fred Arwood would have on earth, I heard from somewhere the redheaded widow's voice saying: "... *There ought to be a law passed stopping such incompetent lawyers from representing people in murder cases.*"

My mind flashed back to the Belcher trial and to the execution that I had witnessed. I could still see that transaction with death unfolding before my eyes. But the jury had no conception of what it was like to decree a man's death. They had no idea what happened between the reading of their verdict and that moment of truth when Fred Arwood would be killed as they had decreed.

The judge's voice brought me back to reality.

"Mr. Hopkins," he was saying, "are you all right?"

I opened my eyes. The courtroom was silent. I don't recall how long I had been standing there, but the jurors and the prosecutors were staring at me with perplexity.

I found my voice.

"I'm all right, your Honor," I said. "I was weighing a matter before proceeding with my argument."

I turned and faced the jury. I had a job to do. Once again I was an advocate with a mission and a message.

"Each of you," I said, "on your voir dire examination when you were being qualified as jurors, under oath, stated that if the State of Ohio proved Fred Arwood Guilty of first degree murder beyond a reasonable doubt, and if you felt under all the surrounding circumstances that mercy should be withheld, you could and would return a verdict which would send Fred Arwood to his death in the electric chair.

"At the conclusion of the arguments and the charge of the court upon the law, you will retire to your jury room and eventually decide the fate of my client. If you do not exercise your prerogative and grant mercy, your verdict will be one condemning Fred Arwood to his death.

"Following that verdict you will be discharged by the court, and shortly thereafter you will return to the normal routine of your life that was interrupted by your service upon this jury. You ladies will resume your household duties and social activities and functions. You will plan meals, supervise the running of your house, perhaps attend your bridge club or the P.T.A. and do those thousand and one things which are necessary to be done in the complexity of your life. You gentlemen will likewise return to your homes and businesses and through necessity become engaged in the multiplicity of tasks which must be met head-on and accomplished in our individual struggle and pursuit of the almighty dollar. You, too, on weekends will probably play golf or perhaps bridge or poker with your friends, squire your wife to a movie or social function, and on Sunday attend the church of your choice. All of you ladies and gentlemen will again live as you formerly lived and, as far as you are concerned, the case of the State of Ohio versus Fred Arwood is ended . . ."

As I spoke, I could see some of them already relishing those sweet moments the future held for them. I could sense a relaxing.

"It may be some years hence," I went on, "that you pick up your morning paper and there, for all to see and read, is an account of Fred Arwood's death. It will be somewhat different from the usual obituary, but you will be advised that at 8 P.M. on the evening before, Fred Arwood had been electrocuted at the penitentiary. You will find the paper carries a box score stating exactly when the electricity was applied and how many minutes it took to complete the kill.

"Do you ladies and gentlemen know or did you ever consider what would happen following a death verdict at your hands? Let me tell you . . ."

One juror stopped short his sweet anticipating. He frowned at me —hard.

"Within three days following your verdict," I said, "I, as Arwood's attorney, will file a motion for a new trial. In due time this motion is set for a hearing and the matter is argued before his Honor Judge Schneider. You can take my word for it the judge will rule— correctly—that our motion is not well taken because there is no error present in the record and he will overrule the motion. Then Judge Schneider will call Arwood before the bar.

" 'Fred Arwood,' the court will begin, 'you have been found Guilty by a jury of the crime of first degree murder. Have you anything to say why this sentence should not be passed?'

"Well, of course, there isn't anything to say, for you have said it by your death verdict. And so the court, in slow and measured tones, will pronounce the ritualistic sentence of death decreed by your verdict. The court will have no other choice because your verdict will have made the death sentence mandatory. The death sentence, by the way, is brutally frank in phraseology, leaving no hope or prayer of misinterpretation. It is couched in such terms that a child could understand that Fred Arwood has been sentenced to his death in the electric chair.

" 'It is the sentence of this court,' the judge will say, 'that you be taken from this courtroom and by the sheriff of this county delivered to the warden of the Ohio State Penitentiary where on the twentieth day of May a current of electricity be forced through your body of sufficient intensity to cause your death, and may God have mercy on your soul. . . .' "

Where there had been coughing among the spectators in the courtroom that morning, there was silence.

I paused, then proceeded with my awful task.

"The deputy sheriff will then grab Fred Arwood and he will be hustled out of the courtroom. Within a few minutes he will be deposited in the county jail, where twenty-four hours later he will be delivered to the warden of the penitentiary, who will assign him to temporary residence in death row.

"Meanwhile I will make every legal move I can to save Fred Arwood from the electric chair. A notice of appeal will be filed and served upon the prosecuting attorney. The official transcript will be typed. Assignment of alleged errors together with briefs will be filed with the Court of Appeals, who will grant Arwood a stay of execution while his appeal is being perfected. The case will then be argued by the prosecutor representing the state and by me as Arwood's attorney. And again—you can take my word for it—the lower court's judgment will be affirmed, for there is no legal error present in the record.

"We file a motion for leave to appeal with the Supreme Court of Ohio. More briefs are printed and filed in Arwood's behalf and more arguments are made—but once again his appeal is turned down.

"I attempt to get into the Supreme Court of the United States. I file on Arwood's behalf a petition for a writ of certiorari. Again I am successful in obtaining a stay of execution but the justices fall into line and turn thumbs down upon our appeal and issue a mandate to the Supreme Court of the State of Ohio, directing the authorities to carry out the provisions of the original sentence.

"I next make application for a clemency hearing before the Ohio State Pardon and Parole Board. Within a short time, a hearing is had. Arwood's sister and other relatives beg for his life and I, as his attorney, plead for mercy, pointing out to the board that, because of Arwood's intoxicated condition at the time of the slaying, he was not in full possession of all his faculties and, in my opinion, should not be held to the full measure of punishment.

"Here again it has been a futile attempt. A week later the board recommends to the Governor of the State of Ohio that the original sentence of death, as ordered by your verdict, be immediately carried out. The Governor grants us an audience but, because of the board's recommendation, refuses to intervene. We, at long last, have reached the end of the road . . ."

The jury no longer stared about the courtroom or out the window at the winter's day.

I didn't want to go on, but I had to.

"For weeks and for month upon month," I said, "Arwood has been occupying a cell on death row. His only companions have been other men who, like him, have been condemned to death in the electric chair by a jury of their peers. He has a calendar on the wall of his cell. A date has been circled on it in red. It is February 24. It is a very important date to Fred Arwood for it is the day set by the Supreme Court for his date with death. It is now February 22. All days of the month prior to the twenty-second have been checked off on the calendar. Time moves quickly. The twenty-second and twenty-third pass and are checked off and here, at last, is the day of doom.

"On his last day on earth the State of Ohio is very kind and considerate to Fred Arwood. We who are about to kill him grant him his every wish. He may order anything he may desire for his last meal and he may have company at this last repast of his own choosing. We supply him with cigars and cigarettes. We give him a new white shirt. In our generosity, we even give him a haircut. Of course, it is a trifle short at the rear of the top of the head, but otherwise it is a first-class tonsorial effort.

"His left trouser leg is cut to the knee, resulting in a peculiar flapping sound as he walks. To complete his ensemble, we add a pair of cloth slippers so that as he walks his last mile, he will not disturb God.

"We supply him with a deck of cards, a checkerboard, and a chaplain. The chaplain spends the last few hours with Arwood, either in prayer, checkers, conversation, or poker, depending entirely upon Arwood's mood and desire.

"Let me take you by the hand and lead you to the warden's office where you and I have made arrangements to witness Arwood's execution. As we open the door to the warden's office, we find the air heavy and blue with tobacco smoke. The room, you see, is filled with thirty other individuals who are also here to witness Arwood's death. We present our credentials to the warden. There is an open book on his desk. He asks us to sign our names, indicating that we have witnessed Arwood's death. You and I advise the warden that we prefer to wait until after the execution to subscribe our names. But he finally convinces us that we had better follow his advice. After some misgivings, we affix our signatures to the witness sheet. A moment later, the clock in the office strikes eight . . ."

I closed my eyes again. I was back in the warden's office. I wanted to cleanse my soul of the memory, but I couldn't. I opened my eyes and every juror was looking straight at me. Their eyes were filled with the pain that my soul was enduring.

"The warden stands in the middle of his office," I go on, "and in the most peculiar voice you've ever heard says, 'Gentlemen, will you follow me?' So you and I and the rest of the morbidly curious follow the warden out into the night, across the prison yard, and to the building which houses the execution chamber, the chamber which the inmates call the 'dance hall.' After a short walk, we enter the deathhouse itself.

"There, resting on a slightly raised platform in the center of the room and facing us with its uninviting arms spread wide and ready for a lethal embrace, is the chair.

"The pictures on the wall of the hundreds of men—and three women—who have been sentenced to death in that chair are mute testimony to the efficiency and deadliness of the chair.

"You and I are seated in the front row. The warden takes up his position directly behind the chair. To his left and to his rear stands a standard hospital bed on wheels.

"There is a green door, as you have read about. And as you and I wait, all eyes are focused on that door through which Fred Arwood must enter on his way to the chair.

"The green door swings open—wide—and two penitentiary guards step into the chamber. Directly behind the guards walk Arwood and a minister. You will hear the minister's voice: *"Yea, though I walk through the valley of the shadow of death, I will fear no evil . . .'*

"And that quickly, the guards, who are well trained and proficient, have Arwood strapped into the chair.

" 'Fred Arwood,' inquires the warden, 'have you anything to say why the sentence of the court should not be carried out?'

"But Fred Arwood doesn't answer because he and the minister are reciting the Lord's Prayer: *"Our Father who art in Heaven, Hallowed be thy name . . .'* and his voice becomes muffled and indistinct as a guard forces a black hood over his head and face. You will hear, *'Thy Kingdom come, Thy Will be Done . . .'* as the warden raises his right arm and drops it to his side.

"A concealed and ready hand, in compliance with the warden's signal, drives home the switch and high on the wall a red light appears.

"You will hear a humming sound not unlike a thousand hornets on the prowl—and Fred Arwood will jump toward you like something possessed.

"A step from the chair with his eyes closed and his head bowed stands the minister. Above the hum, you hear *'Lead us not into Temptation, but Deliver us from Evil, for Thine is the Kingdom, and the Power and the Glory, forever, Amen.'*

"The room will have become dim. The chair will creak and groan. The straps holding Arwood will strain and snap as his uncourted partner embraces him in a wild and grotesque dance of death.

"What is going to fascinate you are his knuckles. They are fiery red and will, of all things, remind you of red flashing lights. It is almost as if someone were shouting, *'Stop, good God, Stop!'* But they don't stop. This man must be killed because you have decreed it.

"Seems like it goes on forever. You try to tear your eyes away from Arwood's tortured and jumping body but some hypnotic force beyond your control has taken command.

"And then a sickening thing happens. You smell flesh burning. And for the first time you see white smoke rising from the back of Arwood's head and spiraling slowly toward the ceiling.

"Yes, we burn them in this state.

"At last the warden gives the signal and the death switch is disengaged. Arwood slumps in the chair. A doctor, in a white coat, steps forward. He pulls Arwood's shirt aside, exposing his chest, and places a stethoscope in the region of his heart. The doctor listens. Then he says, 'I pronounce this man dead.' We look. The light on the wall is out. You and I have seen a man meet his maker.

" 'You are now excused, gentlemen,' the warden announces. You and I, on shaky legs, grope our way out into the prison yard. We gulp fresh air. We look up at the heavens. Then we vomit—as we have never vomited before.

"We, together with the other witnesses, make our way to the prison gate and somehow we drive home. We don't sleep well the next six months. It is impossible to obliterate the horror we have witnessed and to cast aside the unresolved guilt that we feel . . ."

I paused. I was wringing wet and emotionally drained.

I had relived—step by step—the horror of the execution I had witnessed years before.

The jurors leaned toward me; some of their faces were white, and two women appeared ill. Their expressions reflected shock, distress, panic, and horror. I could do no more for Arwood. I had gone the limit.

"I have attempted," I said, "to the best of my ability to describe for you what would happen following a death verdict at your hands. I realize and appreciate full well that any portrayal by me would necessarily fall far short of an experience as an actual eyewitness in the execution chamber. For those who have witnessed an electrocution, no words are necessary. For those who have not, no words are adequate.

"The prosecutors urge—in fact, they demand—that you return a verdict sending Fred Arwood to his death in the electric chair. But I say to you, remember that we are not operating under the dogmas of the Old Testament and the Mosaic law of an eye for an eye and a tooth for a tooth. What these gentlemen representing the state have overlooked is the fact that a New Testament has been written and a Christ has been crucified. Remember, if you will, when Christ was near death, he looked down from the Cross upon his murderers and offered a plea in their behalf, 'Father, forgive them, for they know not what they do . . .'

"If you can live with your conscience, then send Fred Arwood to his death. It is your responsibility, not mine. But before you do, I beg you to remember and heed the advice that Jesus gave to the Pharisees as recorded in the Book of Mark: 'Render unto Caesar the things that are Caesar's and unto God the things that are God's.' "

Done!

I sat down at the defense table. But no one else in the courtroom moved. There was not even a sound of breathing. Finally, the judge, in the same strange voice that the warden had used to dismiss the witnesses following the execution, addressed the jury.

"You will," he said, "at this point take a fifteen-minute recess. You may retire to the jury room."

I had been seated for a few minutes talking to Fred Arwood and his sister when *Enquirer* courthouse reporter Tom Mercer walked over.

"You know," he said, "I witnessed two executions in my lifetime. One was Anna Marie Hahn, the poison murderess, at Columbus, and the other was Fred Arwood right here in this courtroom today." He looked at me solemnly and added, "I asked Hoy why he didn't object. He told me he got carried away and forgot to."

Before I could say a word, Tom left the courtroom.

Following the prosecutor's final argument, the court instructed the jury on the law. The jurors returned to the jury room. Four hours later they found Fred Arwood Guilty of murder in the first degree, but recommended mercy, which saved him from the chair.

The courtroom was, for one brief moment, an angry hubbub. I stood, listening to the noise of it. The next day, of course, I would be denounced in the press. The *Enquirer* would say: "Only the flimsiest of defenses was offered. The defense's main reliance was on an emotional appeal to the jury, of whom nine were women. . . . It is a sad commentary upon justice that it should be so much at the mercy of the eloquence of one attorney." Another editorial would question the fitness of women to serve on juries.

Walter Radtke, dean of the Hamilton County Courthouse reporters, would write: "This proves to me they should burn the electric chair and not keep it to burn this type of criminal."

And the man on the street would look at me with hatred. I had, in his mind, cheated the public of a burning.

But that would be the next day.

In the interim, I left the courtroom, pushed my way through the crowd, ignored the angry remarks muttered in my wake, and soon was outside where fresh air was.

On my way home that evening I stopped at my favorite bar. Joe, as usual, was wiping the bar and when I invited him to join me in a toast to an old redheaded widow I had once known, he said: "But who is the broad?"

"To tell you the truth, Joe, I've never met her," I said.

"Then why the hell the toast?"

"Because she was the cause of it all," I said—and our glasses touched.

"The cause of what?"

"You wouldn't understand," I said.

"Broads," he spat out in utter disrespect for the female gender. Joe fancied himself an expert on women. He had entered the marriage sweepstakes on five different occasions and ended up a loser each time.

"Confidentially, Joe, I hate her guts."

Before he could comment I threw a bill on the counter and went out into the night.

That same redheaded widow had one other moment of glory.

One morning in the spring of 1948 I represented a client in a preliminary hearing at City Hall. I had just left the courtroom when a fellow lawyer told me I was wanted on the phone. It was Ginny and she advised me Judge Hoffman wanted to see me at the courthouse.

Some fifteen minutes later I was seated in his chambers.

"Keeping you busy, counselor?" he asked.

"I have no complaints, your Honor."

"I had an arraignment this morning," the judge said, "and there was a defendant charged with first degree murder who couldn't afford to retain a lawyer. I was wondering if you would accept an appointment to defend him?"

"I don't want to seem unappreciative," I told the judge, "but there must be many lawyers who would be glad to have the appointment and who could probably use the fee."

"That is true," the judge said, "but there is a special reason I want you to try this case."

I didn't say anything and the judge continued—"You remember the Belcher first degree murder case some twenty-five years ago you tried in my room?"

I nodded my head.

"Well, there was a woman on that jury. I think she had red hair. She came to see me the next day. She was highly complimentary of Bell and Schwab but did she raise hell about you. She told me something should be done to stop such untrained lawyers appearing in first degree murder cases and asked me if I had any suggestions. I told her all young lawyers have a lot to learn and that your performance was about par for the course. After a few minutes she left in a huff saying something about taking it up with the Bar Association. If she did I never heard about it. I never heard from her or saw her again. How many murder cases have you tried since then?"

"Around two hundred and twenty-five."

The judge didn't say anything for a moment, then—"If you will take this appointment I will make arrangements with the assignment commissioner to try this case in my room." With a twinkle in his eye he continued, "I'd like to see whether you've improved or not."

By God, the redheaded widow had kept her word! She had threatened to go to Judge Hoffman and that was exactly what she had done.

I became resigned to my fate.

I would never get this woman out of my hair as long as I lived, so I told the judge I would accept this appointment.

The facts in the new case were simple but tragic. My client was seventy-two and charged with killing a woman less than half his age.

Although married and the father of seven grown children, he had strayed from the home fires and endeavored to rekindle the dying embers of his youth.

The affair could only culminate in embarrassing ridicule or tragedy. Fate chose the latter, for the woman was shot to death by my client.

At the conclusion of the evidence the prosecutor, in his final argument, demanded the death penalty and painted a glowing tribute to womanhood and, in particular, to the virtues of the fallen sister, even comparing her, believe it or not, to Joan of Arc.

During the trial I had introduced evidence establishing that the deceased had, for some months prior to her death, been blackmailing my client, but the prosecutor, in his address to the jury, had completely ignored this testimony.

If I was to obtain a good result it would be necessary for me to remove her somewhat shaky halo and put her in her proper setting.

I was going to be doubly sure the jury didn't ignore or forget the blackmail testimony. I not only, in my argument, wanted to tear down the state's evaluation of the deceased but, at the same time, to expose the prosecutor's phoney buildup of a woman of loose morals and taking ways.

I hit as hard as I could on the blackmail angle and then, to add the icing to the cake, closed my final argument by quoting "My Madonna" by Robert Service.

The poem tells of an artist who paints a woman from the streets, hiding in his magic touch all traces of her profession, and of a connoisseur who mistakenly believes the painting to be that of a saint:

> I hailed me a woman from the streets
> Shameless, but oh so fair.
> I bade her sit in the model's seat
> And I painted her sitting there.
>
> I hid all trace of her heart unclean
> I painted a babe at her breast;
> I painted her as she might have been
> If the worst had been the best.
>
> She laughed at my picture and went away.
> Then came with a knowing nod
> A connoisseur, and I heard him say
> " 'Tis Mary, the Mother of God."
>
> So I painted a halo 'round her hair
> And I sold her and took my fee,
> And she hangs in the Church of St. Hillaire
> Where you and all may see.

At the conclusion of my argument the judge called a recess and I walked out to the hall, where I espied Detective Walter Hart* of the homicide squad.

Walter and I had been friends for years but our friendship did not diminish his enthusiasm for ferreting out a killer when I was the defense counsel. No holds were barred as we both attempted, from a subjective viewpoint, to see that justice was done.

"Well, Walter, do you think I took care of that bitch?" I asked him. Hart, without a moment's hesitation, shot back—"Personally, I like 'Trees' better."

I could understand Walter's preference, for trees are used in hanging and I was sure he felt that was exactly the punishment many of my clients deserved.

I don't know what effect Robert Service's poem had, but the jury returned a verdict of Guilty of second degree murder.

As court was adjourned Judge Hoffman beckoned to me to approach the bench.

"Congratulations, counselor," he said. "If I ever see that red-headed juror again I'm going to tell her you've improved."

"Save your breath, Judge," I replied. "She'll never believe you."

As I left the courtroom Walter was waiting just outside the door.

"Nice going, Foss," he said, "but I still like 'Trees' better."

Walter never did appreciate poetry.

* On September 21, 1955, Detective Hart, while attempting to thwart a holdup, was murdered by Lemuel "Sonny" Trotter, who was later executed.

CHAPTER 4
the court jester

Not all individuals in need of defense counsel are charged with murder, of course, and not all cases are grim. Some are quite amusing. One such example was my very first case as attorney for the defense. It began when I paid my respects to Judge Thomas Darby in criminal court. I presented the judge with one of my crisp, fresh, brand-new business cards and asked him if I might be appointed to represent an indigent defendant—*any* indigent defendant, but I didn't say it that way.

Judge Darby, formal and polite, held my card in his left hand. His right dipped into a pocket to emerge holding a stack of similar cards thick as a double canasta deck and secured together by a heavy rubber band. As he placed my card on the bottom he explained he would do "the best he could." Two weeks later I received a postcard announcing I had been appointed to represent one Thomas Murphy.

Early the next morning I arrived at the courthouse. I rode the elevator to the fifth floor, walked up another flight to the county jail, pushed a button, and waited. The jail door swung slightly open. Filling the doorway was a giant wearing a blue shirt and blue trousers and in need of a shave. Pinned over his heart was a large nickel badge inscribed DEPUTY SHERIFF.

"Whatcha want?" he said.

"I would like to see Thomas Murphy," I said.

"Come back on a visiting day," he said, and slammed the door before I could explain my mission. I got out one of my brand-new business cards and the judge's postcard and pushed the jail button again.

The door opened again and I was face to face with my adversary, only this time he was mad. "I told you—" he shouted, but quickly I interrupted.

"I am a lawyer," I said. I handed him my card and the postcard and tried to look mature—a character role. He grudgingly opened the door to allow me to enter his sanctum sanctorum.

The reverberation of the metal door slamming behind me only echoed the deputy sheriff's lack of hospitality and courtesy.

"Who's that you wanted to see?" he said.

"Tom Murphy," I said.

The deputy sheriff walked over to the wall, slammed down a lever on an intercom, and bawled, "43-A—in office."

"OK, General, one coming up," came the answer from someplace within the county jail.

Another door swung open to reveal a man in white T-shirt and faded denims. Across the chest of the shirt, in inch-high black letters, was printed PROPERTY OF HAMILTON COUNTY JAIL. He had sharp features, appeared to be in his mid-forties, and stood over six feet.

"Are you Tom Murphy?" I said.

"I am," he said, "but who the hell are you?"

"My name," I replied, "is William F. Hopkins, lawyer, and the court has appointed me to represent you."

"My God!" he said. "How old are you?" he added.

"Almost twenty-two," I said.

"Well," he said, "at least you're an improvement. The last time the judge appointed an old shyster with an ear trumpet. I had to shout so damn loud to make him hear, every son of a bitch within a mile was in on the conference and trying to give me advice. I pleaded Guilty in self-defense."

"What's the charge against you this time?" I said.

"Robbing a bank," he said. "And they've got me cold," he tossed in thoughtfully.

I wished he hadn't said that.

"Do you mind answering questions?" I said.

"I've got all the time in the world," he said.

My interview with Tom Murphy disclosed he had spent nineteen years in penal institutions and had been convicted five times for robbery and burglary. According to him, he and two companions had attempted to rob the Pearl Market Bank in Cincinnati. As Murphy, who was carrying some eight thousand dollars of the bank's money in one hand and a pistol in the other, turned to warn everyone to remain silent, he lost his footing and fell head-first through the door, his pistol skidded across the pavement, and before he could recover, two pedestrians jumped on him and held him for the police. The police took him back into the bank, where witnesses positively identified him as one of the robbers. Also, he said, they had his pistol as evidence, as well as eight thousand dollars in the bank's wrappers which was picked up beside him on the sidewalk. Also, he said, his two companions had been corralled almost immediately by the police, admitted their participation in the robbery, and named Murphy as one of the robbers.

"So, counselor," Murphy said, "you can see I'm dead. Make arrangements for me to plead Guilty as soon as possible. This is all dead time in this joint."

My next stop was the prosecutor's office, where I inquired who was handling the Thomas Murphy case. The receptionist advised me that Nelson Schwab, who was representing the state, could be found in the second office to the right. Schwab said the case was hopeless and suggested that I enter a Guilty plea.

I moped back to my office disappointed at the turn of events. I had hoped to be retained in a criminal case where I could make a commendable showing so that I could repay my parents for their sacrifices on my behalf. But it was evident that my father and mother would have to defer until some later date any payment on account of their investment in me. When I arrived at the office everyone had gone home except Howard Bevis, a professor at the Cincinnati Law School who, years later, became an Ohio Supreme Court justice and president of Ohio State University. I told Mr. Bevis about my case.

He said there was nothing to get excited about. "All you have to do," he said, "is plead your client Guilty and then make a short plea on his behalf."

"But what do I say?"

"I'll write your plea for you," he said.

A half hour later Mr. Bevis walked into my office and handed me a folded sheet of yellow legal paper.

"That will take care of everything nicely," he said.

Going home on the streetcar I took Mr. Bevis's plea from my pocket and read it for the first time. It was stupendous. Lincoln's Gettysburg Address did not surpass its poetry in prose. Here was oratory seldom, if ever, afforded a young lawyer.

True, I had neglected to tell Mr. Bevis of my client's criminal record, but that didn't seem important. When I made this plea I'd have them in the palm of my hand. I could see the headlines now—MASTERFUL PLEA MADE BY YOUNG LAWYER—IMPASSIONED PLEA SWAYS JUDGE—RECIDIVIST SAVED BY PLEA. I spent at least three hours before a full-length mirror at home, perfecting the plea I would make the next morning.

The following morning I arrived at the courthouse at eight-thirty, impatiently awaiting the opening of court. Other cases were on the docket but, finally, when the clerk called the case of the State of Ohio versus Thomas Murphy, my client left the prisoner's dock and shuffled to the bar where we stood side by side facing Judge Darby.

"If your Honor please," I said, "the defendant Thomas Murphy wishes to withdraw his plea of Not Guilty and enter a plea of Guilty to the charge of armed robbery."

Judge Darby asked Murphy if that was his desire and Murphy grunted yes.

"I want," continued the judge, "to be absolutely certain that you understand your constitutional rights. You have a right to a trial by jury or, if you waive a jury, a trial by the court. By your Guilty plea, you are admitting the correctness of the charge set forth in the indictment returned against you. Do you realize that, because of your Guilty plea, there is nothing left but for the court to sentence you?"

Murphy, who had had much more experience in criminal court than I had, grunted that he understood.

"What are the facts, Mr. Prosecutor?" asked the judge. Schwab told of my client's downfall. Then he handed the judge three sheets of paper containing Murphy's criminal record. Judge Darby was absorbed for some time in his examination of Murphy's antisocial activities. Finally, though, he gazed at us.

"Have you anything to say," he asked, "why the sentence of the court should not be passed?"

This was where I was going to thank my parents and, through technique and oratory, sway the court and impress all fortunate enough to be in the courtroom. Looking Judge Darby straight in the eye, I took a deep breath and began:

"Your Honor sits on the seat of justice. Your duty binds you to do justice, but justice tempered with mercy. We have a boy—" here Mr. Bevis had suggested I put my arm around the defendant's shoulders and I followed his instructions "—who has been judged by businessmen in the community. Their judgment is that he is not a criminal but a potential asset to the State of Ohio."

Judge Darby's eyes were wide and a startled expression came over his face. I continued the plea just as Mr. Bevis had written it, and then I reached the grand finale (Mr. Bevis had made a marginal note— "Drop your eyes," and once again I complied): "The Lord prayed forgiveness for the repentant thief. I, therefore, have no hesitancy in asking your Honor for a suspended sentence."

"My God!" grunted my client, Murphy, "we lost the judge."

Behind me I heard whispers. I looked up. There was no judge on the bench. I caught a glimpse of his judicial robes disappearing into the judge's chambers just before the door closed.

"Counselor," Murphy said, "that was the most moving speech I've ever heard. It moved the judge right off the bench."

I felt the blood rush to my face. I wanted the floor to open and drop me into oblivion. I stood for what seemed a lifetime before the door to the judge's chambers opened and Judge Darby remounted the bench. He was red of face but he was game. Looking at the defendant and not at me, Judge Darby, in a tremulous voice, intoned: "It is the sentence of this court that you be confined in the Ohio State Penitentiary for a period of twenty-five years."

And in those days that was the limit.

I was crushed, but when you're young hope springs anew and fortunately restores our ambition and confidence so that we may, along the way, cope with subsequent adversities.

Some weeks later, when Mr. Bevis and I were walking up Main Street to the courthouse, we ran into a lawyer I will call Bob.

"You look like you've lost your last friend," Mr. Bevis said. "Anything wrong?"

"I'm worried," the lawyer said, "about a case tomorrow morning. I've never been in criminal court in my life but, for some strange reason, Judge Darby appointed me to represent an indigent prisoner. I haven't the slightest idea how to proceed."

"What is your client charged with?" I said.

"Armed robbery," Bob replied, "and Nelson Schwab advises me to plead him Guilty."

"Where did the robbery take place?" Mr. Bevis inquired.

"It seems," said the lawyer, "that three men held up the Pearl Market Bank some weeks ago and took eight thousand dollars in currency. All three were captured within minutes, identified by the victims, and confessed to the robbery."

"What about your client?" I said. "How does he feel about it?"

"He admits his guilt," Bob said. "He wants to plead Guilty and get it over with. But I don't know what to say in his behalf."

I looked at Mr. Bevis. Mr. Bevis looked at me. Since we both wanted to be of assistance to this lawyer in distress, we arrived simultaneously at the identical decision.

"Bob," Mr. Bevis said, "you are the most fortunate young lawyer in Cincinnati. I was in Chicago several months ago and heard Clarence Darrow make a plea in a criminal case. I thought so much of it I had the court reporter run off a copy. I'll be glad to let you have it. I'll guarantee it will make an impression on Judge Darby."

The twenty-five-year sentence Judge Darby had meted out to my client had shaken me up somewhat but I had not lost faith in the great potential of Bevis's plea. It was so good, in my opinion, it deserved another chance; for some reason, I felt that Bob was the lawyer to give it the old college try.

The next morning I joined Mr. Bevis in criminal courtroom Number 2. Moments later Bob's case was called. He withdrew the former Not Guilty plea of his client and entered a plea of Guilty, whereupon Judge Darby proceeded with his ritualistic exploration into the defendant's knowledge and understanding of his constitutional rights which, because of the Guilty plea, he had waived and forsaken.

Schwab, as he had in my case, related the damning facts surrounding the robbery and recited the defendant's lengthy criminal record. Addressing himself to the defendant, Judge Darby inquired: "Have you anything to say why sentence should not be passed?"

Bob, as I had before, looked Judge Darby in the eye, and began: "Your Honor sits on the seat of justice. Your duty binds you to do justice but justice tempered with mercy."

A startled expression spread over Judge Darby's face and when Bob, putting his arm around the defendant's shoulders, said, "We have here a boy . . ." *that* did it. The judge's face became beet red. His eyes narrowed as he gazed toward the seats in the rear of the courtroom.

But Mr. Bevis and I had already come to the conclusion we had better leave—so we did. Our departure was unfortunate, for I learned later Bob's performance *was* sensational. It must have been, for the afternoon press reported the sentence—twenty-five years in the penitentiary.

One courthouse wag, who had heard both Bob and me make our pleas before Judge Darby, said, "That's one plea that carried conviction, if you know what I mean."

But I still like that plea. The original—written on yellow paper, discolored and faded by the years—still reposes in my desk in a private, locked file.

One December, early in my law practice, I defended a woman I shall call Jewel on a charge of shoplifting. She professed her innocence, I entered a plea of Not Guilty on her behalf, and she was released upon bond. So far, so good. But a week before Christmas I received a package containing ten expensive Countess Mara neckties—and an unsigned card wishing me a Merry Christmas. That same evening my phone rang.

"Did you get my Christmas present?" a female voice said. "This is Jewel. I hope you like them. You see, I didn't have much time to pick them out."

Before I could say a word I heard a click and the connection was broken.

There was no doubt the ties were stolen, but since they bore no identifying store label, I had no way of returning them to their rightful owner. I did the next best thing. I spread Christmas joy and good will by presenting nine court officers and attachés with Jewel's ties, saving one for myself. At Jewel's trial after the first of the year, I, as defense counsel, the prosecutor and his aid, together with the clerk, the messenger, the official shorthand reporter, the bailiff, and two deputy sheriffs, were all resplendent in Countess Mara's ties; and if one looked closely, peeking out from the judge's robe was mute evidence that his Honor had not been forgotten in my Christmas splurge.

Late one afternoon Ginny advised me over the office intercom that Freddie Hutchins was waiting to see me. In a low voice she added that, in her opinion, Hutchins was a "gay boy." I had been recommended to him by a male hair stylist who had appeared as a witness for a client of mine in a murder case.

When Freddie finally entered my office, I sensed from the way he moved that certain indefinable something so common to all womenfolk but rare to the male gender. Ginny's suspicions were confirmed when he stated his case. It seemed he had been in Eden Park talking to another young man, who, it developed, was a member of the police department and who had subsequently arrested Freddie and charged him with a violation of the statute making it an offense to solicit another for contemplated homosexual activity. But Freddie maintained he had been "minding his own business" when the plainclothes officer struck up a conversation, and that the officer had "propositioned" him. It was only after much urging, lisped Freddie, that he had agreed to the proposed assignation. "Actually," wailed Freddie, "I was seduced. I go for blonds. This guy was a brunet."

"If you want me to represent you," I said, "it will cost you one thousand dollars."

"That's no problem," he lisped. He produced a check and, to my surprise, filled it out for the entire fee.

Two weeks later, Freddie again burst into my office. He threw an affidavit on my desk.

"Look at that," he screamed, high-pitched and outraged. "I wish the goddamned police would make up their minds what I am. First they charge me with being a homosexual and now I get arrested on a bastardy warrant. They're charging me with being the father of an unborn illegitimate child. Well, I'll tell you one thing. If that Lesbian bitch ever gives birth to a baby it will be a second Immaculate Conception!"

I examined the paper he had hurled on my desk and, sure enough, one Jackie Evans had charged him with being the father of her unborn child.

The police never did make up their minds or establish in court what Freddie was, for in the first case I advanced the defense of entrapment upon the part of the police officer, and the judge granted my motion for an acquittal. Nor was the question answered by a hearing upon the bastardy warrant, for the prosecuting witness failed to put in an appearance at the preliminary hearing and the complaint was dismissed.

Freddie seemed more than satisfied at the outcome of the cases. I don't know if he ever got his identity straightened out for I never saw him again.

Some years ago I was called upon to defend a client for murder in a small town in northern Ohio.

The official court reporter was a man over seventy whose appearance and demeanor were reminiscent of a mid-Victorian character. As he sat stiffly at a table directly in front of the witness stand, I noticed he was using an old-fashioned pen, which he dipped from time to time into a small bottle of purple ink. He wore a high starched collar and his hair was parted in the middle. His pince-nez glasses rested precariously on the bridge of his nose as he prissily recorded the sworn testimony.

The state produced eight witnesses who established beyond any doubt that the deceased had once lived and was now dead and that he met his death as the direct result of four bullet wounds in the back. As each state witness finished his testimony, I indicated I had no cross-examination; and when the prosecutor rested his case, I had not asked one question.

Only by innuendo and guesswork could my client be connected with the offense, for the state had failed to offer any evidence, direct or circumstantial, establishing his guilt.

I immediately made a motion for a directed verdict of Not Guilty, and the court called a recess to consider the matter. I was seated at the counsel table conversing with my client when the official reporter passed us on the way to the hall. As he reached us he leaned over and, in an effeminate voice, dropped these pearls of wisdom: "Blessed is he that knoweth when to keep his goddam mouth shut." He was gone before I could reply.

At the conclusion of a lecture which I had delivered at an Eastern law school, a young man, who identified himself as a senior law student, approached the rostrum where I stood talking with the assistant dean.

"I wonder," he said, "if I could ask you a question?"

"Certainly," I said.

"There is a matter," he said, "which has worried me for three years. If I am appointed to represent an indigent prisoner and he tells me, confidentially, that he is guilty, how can I, in good conscience, go into court and, upon his insistence, enter a plea of Not Guilty?"

"Your worries are over, son," I said. "In fact, you have worried needlessly for three years."

"How come?" he said.

"Take my word for it," I said, "that as soon as your client learns of your attitude, he'll worry enough for both of you!"

At one time I had seventeen murder cases awaiting trial and, because of lack of time and the amount of investigation necessary for each, had assigned to an assistant the legwork in several of the second degree cases; this consisted of interviewing witnesses and, in general, preparing the cases for presentation to a jury. I had just returned from a three-day trial in Columbus, only to be notified that I had to go to trial the following morning in the Carter murder case which was to be tried before Judge Stanley Struble. This was a case I had assigned to my assistant for preparation. For hours before the opening of court, he had briefed me concerning the facts surrounding his investigation. It was a run-of-the-mill self-defense case in which, if the testimony and evidence gathered by my assistant could be established, the jury would find Carter Not Guilty.

Following the prosecutor's opening statement, I rose to outline to the jury the evidence that would be presented by the defense to support Carter's plea of self-defense. As I proceeded, a perplexed assistant prosecuting attorney stared at me in disbelief, as he periodically thumbed frantically through his trial brief.

When I resumed my seat at the counsel table, my client tapped me on the shoulder and said: "It didn't happen exactly like that, Mr. Hopkins, but I like your version better."

Before I could answer, the prosecutor was on his feet, requesting a short recess, which the court granted.

"One of us," he told me, "has to be crazy. I don't know where you got your facts but they are not the facts in this case."

I turned to my assistant. He didn't say anything but his face was red. He handed me another file. He had investigated and prepared several murder cases for trial and two of the defendants were named Carter: one Ben, the other John. Both were charged with second degree murder, both had killed their assailant with a knife, and both claimed self-defense.

The only trouble was my assistant had handed me the wrong Carter's file.

Just before I was scheduled for a kidneystone operation, I was defending a client charged with embezzlement. Off and on during the trial I had become nauseated, but it was not until the judge was about to charge the jury that I really became ill. My hands began to tremble. To no avail, I swallowed medication prescribed by my physicians. The pain was excruciating. Chill after chill racked my body. I insisted, however, on finishing the trial. The court granted permission for me to don my overcoat, which I wore as I sat at the counsel table.

As the judge began his charge, my client, sitting directly behind me, leaned forward and said: "How are you feeling, counselor?"

"I think I'm going to die," I said gloomily as I pulled my overcoat about my shaking frame.

"My God," was his agonized response, "if you die what will become of me?"

It was in May, 1964, that I, along with Paul Ziegler and Henry Sheldon, represented one Stanley Tarnoff, a sales manager for the Loral Company of New York. Tarnoff, together with Emanuel Siegel, the company's vice-president, had been indicted by the federal grand jury for the Southern District of Ohio, sitting at Dayton, Ohio, upon the charge of attempting to bribe a government employee at Wright-Patterson Air Force Base.

This was my initial appearance in the courtroom of Judge Carl A. Weinman, at Dayton, Ohio, and I strenuously objected to his ruling that counsel would not be permitted to inquire of the prospective jurors as to their individual qualifications. The judge was inexorable and suggested that if any counsel desired to submit questions to him, he would be happy to incorporate them in his questions to the prospective jurors. Much to my chagrin and over my numerous objections and challenges, the judge finally completed his voir dire examination and the jury was duly sworn. The fact that the jury, after a seven-day knockdown, no-holds-barred trial, returned a verdict finding both defendants Not Guilty in no way altered my opinion as to the right of counsel to interrogate prospective jurors personally.

It was the same Judge Weinman, some three years later, who, in a landmark decision, granted Dr. Sam Sheppard a new trial which eventually led to his freedom. On August 17, 1964, immediately after the Sheppard decision, I wrote to Judge Weinman:

HON. CARL A. WEINMAN
UNITED STATES DISTRICT COURT
DAYTON, OHIO.

Dear Judge:

Please accept my congratulations upon your decision in the Sheppard case. To deny the writ would have been so easy but you, by your monumental decision, have demonstrated to the entire country that we have at least one judge who will fearlessly render justice.

Your decision should serve as a warning to those officials and prosecutors who from time to time become over-zealous and over-enthusiastic.

Your decision may not stop but should advise certain powerful newspaper interests that such selfish and irresponsible reporting and reprehensible conduct will not be tolerated.

Your decision should serve as a beacon light for all those who come hereafter who are interested in fair play in the administration of criminal justice.

You may place small moment upon my evaluation of you and your decision but I felt that I would be derelict in my duty if I did not voice my opinion.

Respectfully,
WILLIAM F. HOPKINS

P.S. I still believe I am right about the selection of a jury.

On September 8, I received the following reply:

WILLIAM F. HOPKINS, ESQ.
1210 MERCANTILE LIBRARY BLDG.
CINCINNATI, OHIO.

Dear Mr. Hopkins:

I have just returned from Europe and I indeed appreciate your letter of August 17, 1964.

It was indeed a pleasure to have you appear in my court and to watch you operate. At least the jury was well selected.

Most sincerely,
CARL A. WEINMAN
JUDGE

P.S. If I were still in trial work I would agree with you.

When I had been invited to address a church group, the minister, in good voice, introduced me to his congregation.

"The great patriot Patrick Henry said, 'Give me liberty or give me death.' Mr. Hopkins's clients say, 'Give me liberty or get me life.' I say to you, if in trouble, get Mr. Hopkins."

His words must have struck the right chord. As I arose to speak, the audience greeted me with a tumultuous welcome.

I was once retained to represent a local man who had been indicted by a federal grand jury sitting below the Mason-Dixon line. He was charged with interstate auto theft. I, together with my client, flew to the site of the trial a day early so that we could confer with an ex-judge I had retained as our local counsel. The morning was consumed in reviewing evidence and mapping strategy, but that afternoon my co-counsel took me on a tour of the town. He showed me the old federal courthouse where we would try our case, southern mansions which housed the town's wealthy, the well-to-do neighborhood of the middle class, and the stark reality of the shacks of the poor. What impressed me was the number of churches. There must have been at least thirty-five, and all were Baptist.

"Looks like the Baptists have a stranglehold on the community," I commented.

"That's right," the ex-judge responded. "Everybody in town except the town drunk is a Baptist, but the brothers and sisters are working on him and, in due time, he will be corralled and dipped in the holy water and emerge cleansed and sanctified. Some years back an itinerant Methodist minister tried to set up a Methodist church here, but he left three weeks later."

"What happened?" I said. "Did the Baptists chase him out?"

"No," he said. "We wouldn't do that. No one attended the services. Then some of our deacons got together and tried to convert him. That did it. He just up and left town."

When the court opened the following morning my co-counsel stood and, with me at his side, addressed the court. "Your Honor, may I present William Foster Hopkins to this honorable court. Mr. Hopkins is a practicing attorney in the State of Ohio and has been a member of that bar for twenty-eight years. He is admitted to practice in the federal district courts of that state and the Federal Circuit Court of the Sixth District and the Supreme Court of the United States. He enjoys an excellent reputation and is of good moral character. I would like to move his admission to practice before this honorable court."

For a few moments after my co-counsel's flowing introduction, the judge studied some papers before him. Then he looked up. "What is your religion, Mr. Hopkins?" he asked. I hesitated. The only sound in the enormous courtroom came from high above where the twin blades of the ceiling fan laboriously bit into the hot and sultry air. Never in history was there a faster conversion. "I've been down under,"* I replied.

---

* An expression meaning baptism by complete immersion.

"Welcome to my courtroom," said the judge. "Proceed with your case, gentlemen."

As I took my seat at the defense table I did not miss the wink his Honor bestowed upon my co-counsel. The judge and my co-counsel did not know it as yet but my client, a devout Catholic, had also just become a Baptist. That left only the drunk outside the veil but, as my co-counsel said, sooner or later, he too would see the light.

Charlie Junker, the amiable warden of the Hamilton County Jail, called my office one day and insisted, as Ginny advised me later, that he talk to me personally.

"Counselor," he said, "one of my misguided sheep is desirous of an immediate audience with you. He's in a jam and needs your help. According to the indictment, he tried to shake down the Pullman Company president for fifty G's. His name is the Reverend Cadley Niles."

I was intrigued by the warden's interest in the defendant's welfare.

"Why all the personal attention on this one?" I said.

"Well, counselor," he said, "I feel sorry for the son of a bitch."

"Do you realize you're speaking about a man of the cloth?"

"My God, you're right," he said. "I'll light a candle and pray for forgiveness."

The next day I had a talk with the Reverend. Niles—Negro, forty years old, and small of stature—had two remarkable qualities. His voice dripped honey and his hypnotic eyes never left my face. He said that he had two occupations: he was a door-to-door salesman of shoelaces, shoe polish, and brushes; and he was also a clairvoyant.

According to the Reverend, the latter occupation kept him broke and had caused his present incarceration. He said he charged three dollars a reading, but since his customers were women with problems, he would make a follow-up visit to their homes and he got to know his clients almost too well. In fact, at the time of his difficulty, he was paying nine separate women for nine different illegitimate children, which, according to the Reverend, were the products of his efforts to rehabilitate his clients. When a Mrs. Hester had sought a reading it was love at first sight as far as the Reverend was concerned and, neglecting both his occupations, he courted Mrs. Hester with all the enthusiasm and ardor which might be expected of one half his age.

Jealousy intervened, however; for the Reverend, when on a visit to his lady love, observed new sheets and pillowcases on Mrs. Hester's bed. Each bore the name of Pullman. A surveillance of her apartment resulted in noting that a man named Sam Jones entered but did not for some seven hours exit. Jones was a Pullman Company porter. The Reverend, in jealous rage, wrote a letter to the president of the Pullman Company, demanding fifty thousand dollars upon threat of death, and signed Sam Jones's name; but the letter was traced to the Reverend and he was arrested.

When we tried his case before a jury in Judge Robert LeBlond's room, the prosecutor proved beyond a reasonable doubt every allegation contained in the indictment—with the exception of one. He couldn't prove that the Reverend intended to extort money from the prosecuting witness. The signing of his rival's name, Sam Jones, and the giving of Jones's address negated that assumption.

In my final argument to the jury I said that while my client was a most despicable character, a fraud, cheat, and an undesirable citizen, this did not give them a legal right to convict him of a crime not proven. As I resumed my seat, my client leaned forward and muttered sadly: "Whose lawyer is you?"

The jury, out only forty-five minutes, returned a Not Guilty verdict.

The following morning the Reverend Cadley Niles called at my office to thank me for my efforts in his behalf and to bring me to hold as collateral for my attorney fee his most cherished possession.

It was his crystal ball. To this day I have never seen him again. Perhaps if I were to look into the crystal ball . . .

In the 1940's seven policy houses operated in southern Ohio. Each had its headquarters in Newport, Kentucky, just across the Ohio River. The houses were not Mafia controlled but operated by enterprising local citizens, both colored and white. The most enthusiastic of the lot was "Skeets" Coleman. If Skeets had devoted his endeavors to the legitimate he might have become a wealthy man, but since he had a touch of larceny in his heart he chose to pursue the fast buck. No one ever knew where Skeets got the idea, but through ingenuity and showmanship he came up with a gimmick which increased his personal take tenfold and nearly wrecked all his competitors. He rented a large hall in the west end of town. On a raised platform in the center area in full view of some two hundred occupants was an over-sized purple coffin replete with white satin interior. In the casket reposed a giant Negro who wore a purple turban and was attired in a dress suit. His enormous hands, clasping a purple lily, were folded over his chest. A blue light from above played on the features of the departed brother.

At the door stood a dwarf, resplendent in scarlet bloomers, purple tunic, and a turban of white sequins. Each person entering was required to drop a fifty-cent piece in a funeral urn held in the dwarf's outstretched hands. Five days a week for over a year, exactly thirty minutes before the New York Stock Market closed, the door leading to the funeral bier swung open and within a few minutes every available seat was occupied. Somewhere from within the chamber's dim interior a cymbal crashed and, as the audience sat bug-eyed on the edges of their chairs, the "corpse" slowly assumed a sitting position.

"The winning number," thundered the now-seated corpse, "is . . . three . . . three . . . three. I said, three hundred and thirty-three!"

From bitter experience and a keen sense of self-preservation, the dwarf scampered quickly to safety, leaving the exit free and clear. At this point those assembled made a wild dash—en masse—for the door, bent on placing their wagers on the day's winning number—as touted by a messenger from the hereafter.

Not once during the years did the prediction come true, but day after day Skeets played to packed houses. It was simply an unexplainable phenomenon.

It was too bad the police did not share Skeets's enthusiasm or appreciate his theatrical talent, for during the year they arrested him fifty-seven times on myriad charges in an attempt to put him out of business. All of which provoked an outburst of New Year sentiment and good will toward men as evidenced by the New Year's card Skeets forwarded to the gambling squad. It read: "Here's wishing you a happy and less strenuous New Year."

Some ten years ago the local press carried an item reporting that Skeets had been gunned down at Saratoga. His murderer was never apprehended. His comment, I'm sure, would have been: "Just an occupational hazard."

The moments of laughter are rare. More common in a defense attorney's life are moments—and hours, and days—of "blood, sweat, and tears." Of these, there are all too many.

CHAPTER 5
a portfolio of murder

The dance has many forms but all of them are deadly. Among my souvenirs of the many dances are things—*broken Coke bottles, sordid photographs, and a tool that embalmers use*—and memories—*a man recalled from the dead, two lads dying in the chair, and my own legal inadequacies that caused them to depart this life in such a violent manner.* Having tried to lighten the mood in the previous chapter, let me with these six memories balance the account. First, the man who, though dead, addressed a jury . . .

His name: Morris Abbott.

Morris Abbott, I suppose, had he not by chance employed "Scotty" Gordon to help out on his Butler County farm, might have lived to a ripe old age, sitting on the front porch of his pleasant Ohio farm in his twilight years and enjoying the fruits of his lifelong labor. But chance—or destiny—caused him to hire Gordon. Gordon entered into an illicit love affair with Mrs. Abbott, and the lonely little drama ended when, one evening, the husband returned home to be killed by a blow on the head with a mattock. The mattock was wielded by Scotty Gordon. When the wife returned home, her lover said there had been a fight and that her husband was dead. Why do lovers so often panic? These two did. Later on in this book you'll meet another such lady, Edythe Klumpp. But for now, suffice to say the two lovers here decided to compound the deed: they placed the corpse on a railroad track and left it there. Their plan: a train would pass over the slain man, mutilating him, and thus disguise the act of murder. And so, in the pale spring moonlight, the corpse waited, unattended, for a passing train. But they had placed the corpse on the track poorly. It slipped from the rail—or perhaps God gave it a gentle nudge. Although eleven trains passed over the corpse that spring night, none touched it. It lay between the rails, low and out of reach, waiting for justice. The body was found, the mattock wound was evident, Gordon was arrested, signed a confession involving the farmer's wife, and she too was arrested. Although she admitted her illicit affair with Gordon, she denied that she had either planned or premeditated the death of her spouse.

I, together with Gus Condo (who was a close friend of Mrs. Abbott's, as well as president of the Butler County Bar), and Condo's partner, Herbert Walsh, made many efforts for a change of venue; but we were consistently overruled by the court. And so the trial began in Hamilton, the county seat.

The county was angry; it seethed. Butler County, just north of Cincinnati, is a place of industry, pig farms, and the academic. Its residents, however charming, are a mixed sort. In its towns—Hamilton, Middletown, and the rest—live mostly middle- and lower-middle-class people, the solid citizens who work shifts, drink beer, and—when angered—cry for justice. Out in the rolling countryside are the farm folk, some of whom have farmed the same land for generations; slow to anger, they are church people, and when someone traffics with any of the Ten Commandments, they react with slow rage, but rage nonetheless. Also in the county is Oxford, where Miami University and Western College for Women are located. Remote. Detached. The good people there were hardly aware that all around them the rest of the county bubbled with hatred. Simply put, to draw a jury from this county would be to stack the deck against my client, Mrs. Abbott.

Gordon, the other accused, did not help matters by turning poet. During the trial one of his attempts to be lyrical was brought forth as evidence. In one poem to Mrs. Abbott, he had written:

> I loved you in the Springtime,
> I loved you in the Fall,
> But last night on the hillside,
> I loved you best of all.

The poem, read with great relish by the prosecutor to the jury during the trial, soon became a favorite chant of urchins gathered on the Hamilton street corners, as well of as some male adults. The interest in the trial was such that the county courthouse attracted five thousand people, none of them poetry fanciers. The police had to rope off one entire street to accommodate the mob assembled. The trial lasted three weeks. When it ended, Gordon was found Guilty of first-degree murder with a recommendation of mercy, which saved him from the electric chair, and Mrs. Abbott was found Guilty of second degree murder, which in Ohio means approximately ten years behind bars. I was outraged. Why? Because where was justice? True, she had been proved and found guilty of adultery, but was this any reason to convict her of another crime—one in which she had not participated?

Carl V. Roberts reported in the Dayton *Daily News:*

> And then there are two other figures in the street below you. Talking to a tipsy man in his shirt sleeves is the man in the blue gabardine suit. He is William F. Hopkins, the lawyer. He wears glasses, a light Panama hat, and an expensive tie. He's good and he knows he is good and his services come high. After 29 years of criminal practice he has allowed himself to become interested in a client above and beyond the call of his duties as a defender —and he is angry.
>
> So at 1:30 on the morning of July 31 he has found the one citizen with "a reasonable doubt" who does not have an abiding conviction amounting to a moral certainty.
>
> The man in the blue gabardine suit, to whom seven men and five women would not listen, listens to the tipsy man who cries, "They did not convict her of murder. They convicted her of adultery."

The man in the blue gabardine suit hears this, listens, and is more angry!

Yes, because I am human I am capable of anger. But even as I drove back to Cincinnati that summer night I knew that the violence of anger—however therapeutic—would not unlock the prison doors and free my client. Only logic could do that. A mob may practice violence; civilized creatures practice logic, which, in the case of my profession, is the law and its application to human beings capable of anger and love and murder and joy. Even before I pulled into my driveway that sticky night, I was mentally laying out my campaign.

But it would be eighteen months before I could bring logic and justice into play. For those eighteen months my client sat in prison being punished for murder when her crime was adultery. First, the Court of Appeals of the First Appellate District refused to disturb the jury's verdict. I took the matter to the Ohio State Supreme Court. My point was that the original trial judge—Fred B. Cramer—had, over my objections, allowed the prosecutor to read the hired hand's 37-page confession. True, the judge was on solid legal ground because the State Supreme Court had, on several earlier occasions, handed down written opinions setting forth the law he followed. But although the judge had instructed the jurors that the confession could not be considered by them in determining the guilt or innocence of Mrs. Abbott, I maintained that the confession itself was so damning to her interests that no instructions to the jury, however well intended, would remove the prejudicial effect from their minds.

The Ohio State Supreme Court agreed with me,* the conviction of Mrs. Abbott was reversed, and a new trial was granted her. With the exception of the confession of the co-defendant, the second trial ran much the same as the first. Again the public was angry. But this time I brought in a dead man to tell the jury things I could not tell them. Said the local press:

> He [Mr. Hopkins] had Morris Abbott climbing out of the grave to advise and instruct the jury to acquit his wife and return her to their children.
> No medium in total darkness could have created a more

* State v. Abbott, 40 Ohio Opinions 228.

dramatic and awe-inspiring effect than the lawyer accomplished when he said: "Yes, as Omar Khayyam wrote many years ago, and what a sermon to each of us:

> Yesterday this day's Madness did prepare
> Tomorrow's Silence, Triumph and Despair.

Truer words were never written and how applicable to this case —'As ye sow, so shall ye reap'—and what a crop and what a harvest of sorrow and despair have grown from the seeds of deceit and unfaithfulness, cast by Marie Abbott, upon the quick-sands of shame and sin. Marie Abbott by her unfaithfulness has brought sorrow and despair to her respected parents. She has brought tragedy to the Abbott name. And she has taken her children by the hand and led them to the very doorstep of the damned. She employed passion as her yardstick in the measure-ment of her conduct instead of following and being guided by those mandatory rules of virtuous living which a woman must observe if she desires to be respected by the community and loved and revered by her husband. She has seared her soul and has rightfully been subjected to the unsympathetic limelight of public censure and condemnation.

"But because Marie Abbott has sinned, because she has been unfaithful, and because you and I and the community at large condemn her immoral actions gives you ladies and gentle-men of the jury no legal right to play God and attempt to punish her by a conviction of a crime of which she is not guilty.

"It was not my privilege to know Morris Abbott. It was my duty, however, to make an investigation of this case and that investigation disclosed that Morris Abbott was an outstanding citizen in the community; that he was God-fearing; that he was honest and upright; that he was a hard worker; that he enjoyed a good reputation; and that he was a good husband and father.

"During Morris Abbott's lifetime and shortly before his untimely death he learned from his wife that she had been un-faithful to him and that she had committed adultery. Being the man that he was he extended to her the hand of forgiveness.

"Morris Abbott is dead but Morris Abbott is at this very moment standing before you just as surely as I am standing be-fore you. He has shown you the way. Morris Abbott cannot speak for himself, but you have heard his message through the lips of witnesses and you are hearing it here and now through my lips just as surely as if it were a voice from the grave. Morris Abbott said in his lifetime and in his voice through mine is say-

ing to you and to his wife here and now, 'Marie Abbott, go and
sin no more.' For when Jesus was in the Temple, the scribes
and the Pharisees brought unto him a woman taken in adultery
and said, 'Master, this woman was taken in adultery, in the very
act. Now Moses in the law commanded us that she should be
stoned; but what sayeth Thou?'

"And at first Jesus did not answer them. But when they
continued asking Him, He said unto them, 'He that is without
sin among you, let him first cast a stone at her,' and they that
heard it, being convicted by their own consciences, went out one
by one, even unto the last, and Jesus was left with the woman.
And when Jesus saw none but the woman, He said unto her,
'Woman, where are thine accusers? Hath no man condemned
thee?' And when the woman answered, 'No,' Jesus said unto her,
'Neither do I condemn thee; go and sin no more . . .' "

Twenty hours later the jury returned its verdict. It found Mrs.
Abbott Not Guilty.

As one juror muttered, "With that message from the other side,
what else could we do?"

Yet, even today, in the backlands of Butler County, when old
women and old men are gathered on a winter's night to spin memories,
here and there you will hear murmurs that say, "But she was guilty . . .
guilty as sin . . ."

And to that I say only, "Yes. She was guilty. But guilty of *what?*"

Or is adultery too distasteful? If it is, I suggest you skip this
next entry on the dance card of the damned. For here we traffic with
perversion. Such things do occur, and not only in sleazy paperbacks.

Shortly after the awful events at Pearl Harbor, when the good
citizens were preoccupied with where Pearl Harbor was, the practically
nude body of a man was found on the ninth floor of one of Cincinnati's more respectable hotels. He was identified as George Winlack,
a guest of the hotel. His residence was listed as Canton, Ohio. Six
hours after his body had been discovered in his room, a lad named
John English walked into the police station in Middletown, Ohio, and
gave himself up in connection with the grim event. The lad was wearing, at the time, the deceased's overcoat and gloves. Later, the grand
jury indicted English on two counts: one said that the accused "un-

lawfully, purposely, and of deliberate and premeditated malice killed one George Winlack"; and to make doubly sure the lad did not escape punishment, the other charged that he did "unlawfully, purposely, and while in the perpetration of a robbery kill one George Winlack." Conviction on either count carried the death penalty.

English told me that he had met the dead man earlier in the hotel bar, had had a few drinks with him, and that when he had missed his last bus to Middletown, the dead man had invited him to sleep in his hotel room. Once there, the accused said, the man made improper advances, a fight started, and when English left, he had no idea the man was dead. When he read about the death the next morning, he told me, he immediately gave himself up to the police.

So the trial began.

In his opening statement the prosecutor pulled out every stop. He said that the state would establish by competent evidence and beyond reasonable doubt that the defendant and Winlack sat at the bar several hours—talking—and that when Winlack left the bar, he was followed by the accused to the deceased's room. There, intoned the prosecutor, the accused attempted to rob the man and, upon being resisted, beat the man savagely. On and on the prosecutor went, describing the state's interpretation of that sordid deathly drama.

As I listened to him, I watched the faces of the jurors, seven women and five men. Mine was not an easy task. Because of the homosexual features of the case, I had to be careful at the outset not to embarrass or alienate the seven ladies sitting in judgment. But it has been my experience in such cases that when sordid and obscene testimony is to be heard by ladies on a jury, once they have been made aware of the duties they assumed because of the office they hold, women jurors usually come through with flying colors. Further, I believe that since the jurors will hear this unpleasant testimony in the actual trial, it is far better for me to prepare them by giving them a short résumé of what the evidence will disclose.

Then, it was my turn to address them. I stood, looked at them thoughtfully, and began.

After telling of English's background, schooling, and employment, I looked directly at the ladies and said, "Our defense in this case is what is known in the law as self-defense. The facts are not pretty. But it is my sworn duty to present the defense of the accused. And it is your sworn duty to listen to that defense—and to evaluate it. We both would be derelict in our duty if we did not live up to our individual oaths. But since our defense has to do with sex perversion and homosexuality, I am sorry that it has to be presented to you, and in advance, I wish to apologize. Not for what I am about to say, but for the necessity of saying it.

"We will establish that Winlack was a forty-four-year-old unmarried sex deviationist, commonly known as a pervert or—if you please—in the vernacular, a queer or fairy. We will establish that he struck up a conversation with John English in the bar with one thought and only one thought in mind and that was to possess John English. We will show how Winlack plied English with drink after drink, gave him five dollars, caused him to miss his bus to Middletown, and then invited him to his room in order that he might gratify his insatiable, unholy, and unnatural lust for this boy's body.

"The evidence will disclose . . ." and I went on, detailing the drama of that ill-fated night in the hotel room. "In conclusion," I said, "after you have heard all the evidence and testimony presented and the charge of the court, it is my opinion you will have only one safe and legal verdict and that is a verdict finding the defendant John English Not Guilty. And by returning this verdict yours will be a rare privilege, because you—and each one of you—will have helped correct a terrible and despicable wrong that has been done to this young man."

The state, to prove its case, introduced a parade of patrons and employees, each testifying that they had seen the deceased and English drinking together in the bar. The bar's cashier testified that she had fifty five-dollar bills with serial numbers from J-113221101-A to J-113221150-A and that she had cashed a check for Winlack, giving him five of the bills. Sergeant Joseph Newkirk of the Middletown police testified that when English had surrendered to him, the accused wore the deceased's coat and gloves and, in addition, was in possession of a five-dollar bill bearing the serial number J-113221129-A. After other witnesses for the state had appeared, the coroner gave the finishing touches by saying, "Death, in my opinion, was due to intra-cranial hemorrhage, secondary to skull fracture."

I asked the coroner about Winlack. He said that Winlack was

well-nourished, forty-four years old, six feet two inches tall, and weighed approximately 220 pounds.

And that was the state's case.

The only witness I called to the stand was the defendant himself. He testified that he had been in the bar and that Winlack had struck up a conversation with him. This dovetailed with the testimony of the state's witnesses. Then he testified that Winlack had invited him to spend the night in his room because he had missed the bus. He testified that he had accepted Winlack's invitation.

"After you got to the room, what happened?" I said.

"I started to undress. Winlack asked me if I knew the 'score' and when I said I didn't know what he meant, he put some money in my suit pocket and said, 'Don't be so dumb. You know what I mean.' "

English said he undressed to his shorts, climbed into bed, and almost immediately fell asleep.

"What, if anything, happened next?"

"I don't know how long I had been asleep but I felt Winlack's body against mine and his hands on my private parts."

"Go on."

"I shoved his hand away and went back to sleep."

"Did anything else occur?"

"The next thing I knew I felt some heavy pressure on my legs and Winlack had his head under the covers and was trying to turn me on my back."

"Anything else?"

English hesitated, embarrassed. His face started to turn red.

Judge Bell leaned forward.

"Go on," the judge said. "Answer the question."

English, his eyes downcast and his face red, in a low but distinct voice said: "He was trying to put my penis in his mouth."

English next told the jury how he had shoved Winlack out of bed, got out of bed himself, and started to get dressed. English said that while he was tying his shoelaces, he looked up to see Winlack coming toward him. He said that Winlack wore only a short undershirt, was in a stooped position, and had a "wild expression" on his face.

"Did you notice anything else?" I said.

Again his face turned red. Again his eyes sought the floor.

"He had an erection."

"What did you do?"

"I jumped up—and when he tried to grab me, I hit him with my fist."

"Where did you hit him?"

"In the face."

"How many times did you strike him?"

"Several times. He finally went down."

"Then what did you do?"

"I finished dressing, went to the bathroom to wash my knuckles, which were bleeding, and then I started to leave. But the chain was on the door and as I was trying to unfasten it, he got up off the floor and came at me again. I hit him again and he tore my coat collar and the pockets were ripped out. He fell to the floor and I took his coat in place of mine and I left the room. He was lying on the floor when I left."

English completed his testimony by telling the jurors how, immediately after hearing of Winlack's death, he had gone to the Middletown police, turned over to them the five-dollar bill Winlack had put in his pocket, and Winlack's coat and gloves, and had told the Middletown authorities the same story he had just told the jury. Following two grueling hours of cross-examination by the prosecutor, both sides rested their case.

The state, in its final argument, stuck to its guns and contended that the evidence proved English guilty beyond a reasonable doubt of murder while in the perpetration of a robbery and urged the jury to return a verdict that would send English to the electric chair.

Some of the things that, in my final argument, *I* said to the jury were:

"Does a man have the legal and God-given right to protect his body and, by the use of force, prevent a degenerate from satisfying his homosexual proclivities and insatiable lust?

"Would a woman have the God-given and legal right to protect her body from a rapist by use of any means and any force available to prevent her attacker from satisfying his unholy lust?

"I say to you that under such circumstances the law does not measure nicely the degree of force that may be used in repelling force.

"Is there any member of this jury, or the prosecutor, or the judge, or anyone within the sound of my voice, who would have reacted differently from John English? Is there anyone in this courtroom who can point a finger at John English and say to him that his actions were not normal? What happened in this case was brought about by the unbridled and unrestrained homosexual and perverted passion of George Winlack. Just because Winlack was a homosexual did not give John English the right to hit or kill him. It did, however, give John English the legal right to protect himself and his body from Winlack's advances and to repel those advances by force sufficient to stop Winlack from successfully accomplishing his purpose.

"Courts for years have endeavored to define self-defense, but I feel it was Cicero—thousands of years ago—who gave to the world the one and only true definition of self-defense when he said, 'This is the law, oh judges, we do not learn from books, for it is embodied in each of us that if our life is in danger any means of escape is honorable. Reason has taught this law of self-defense to all learned men, necessity to barbarians, and nature to wild beasts.'

"This law of self-defense is not of recent vintage but has been the law since the beginning of time. This is so because man has demanded it be the law. It is the first law of nature and the last law man will ever relinquish. Every other law promulgated by man throughout the ages has gone through some change or vicissitude with the exception of this law of self-defense. It has remained the same, never changing, never varying, and is engraved on each man's heart; for I say to you, our laws will never be strong enough nor will our statutes be broad enough to stop a man from raising his hand in defense of his body.

"I told you in my opening statement that it was my opinion that at the conclusion of this case you would have the privilege of acquitting John English and thereby righting a terrible wrong. It is my opinion now that the time has come under your oaths to exercise that privilege —and return a verdict finding John English Not Guilty."

And in exactly one hour the wonderful jury did exactly that.

But the premise of death is not always restricted to the accused. A quarter of a century ago, Thomas A. Gallagher and I were appointed to defend Edward Reuger on a first degree murder charge— and we almost got knocked off instead of the defendant. The state alleged that fifty-two-year-old Reuger, in love with nineteen-year-old Alberta Judd, had, when she refused to break a date with a younger man, drawn her into his arms, kissed her, and shot her dead. We maintained that the defendant, despondent, had bought the pistol to do away with himself, had gone to the young lady's house to do it dramatically, and—while kissing her good-bye—had placed the pistol at his own head; there had been a struggle, and the girl had been accidentally blown to Kingdom Come. The case itself wasn't spectacular. It was the typical May-December romance that untypically ended with a gun going off.

The state, logically, brought witnesses saying that Reuger had intended to shoot the girl. A member of the homicide squad testified that Reuger had told him, "I shot her because I wanted her to die in my arms." The state also introduced in evidence the gun that fired the fatal shot, as well as the five additional bullets found in Reuger's pocket.

Reuger, the chief witness in his own defense, said that he had never said anything at all like the statement the homicide squad had attributed to him. He went on to say, ". . . I told her I was going away. I kissed her and as I did so I had a sudden impulse to kill myself. I took the gun out of the holster. I put it to my head and she grabbed me and pulled the revolver down. I had it cocked and she seemed to jam it against her body and it was discharged. I had no intention of killing her. The gun went off accidentally."

As good as his word, the prosecutor had demanded the death penalty. At one point, labeling Reuger not only a vicious killer but a perjurer (Reuger had said the bullets he carried would not fit the revolver), the prosecutor loaded the five bullets into the revolver—and they fitted perfectly.

Near the close of my final argument I asked my co-counsel, Gallagher, to stand with me before the jury. With Gallagher acting out the role of the doomed girl and me acting the defendant's role, we attempted to re-create the defense version of the young lady's demise. Dramatic.

I put my arm around Gallagher, picked up the pistol, and placed it at my head. Gallagher grabbed for the gun and, as the defense claimed, pulled it down against his chest. The trigger gave a resounding *click* as the hammer came down—and the jury seemed visibly impressed with our little drama. Gallagher resumed his seat at the defense table. As I returned the pistol to the exhibit table, a thought hit me—and I froze. I reached again for the pistol, but this time my hand trembled as I raised it from the table. I didn't want to examine it, but I had to. When I released the cylinder, my worst fear became a fact.

The gun was loaded!

Both Gallagher and I, under the trial's tension, had forgotten the prosecutor's demonstration. Only by the grace of God had I failed to kill my co-counsel—for the hammer had fallen on the pistol's only unloaded chamber.

Go on with the trial? I couldn't. I asked for a recess, the court granted it, and during the recess the bailiff said the judge wanted to see me in his chambers. When I entered the chambers, there stood a quart bottle of Old Taylor and a glass at its side. Although my hand was still shaking, I managed—during the next fifteen minutes—to slosh down four generous servings. The judge must have been almost as upset as I because on two occasions he joined me.

For once in my career I didn't complete my final argument before the jury. Anyway, there was nothing more to be said. I felt confident the jury would understand. The last thing *I* remember of that trial was the judge charging the jury . . .

A loud knocking awakened me. As I groped to the door, my head was splitting. There stood my co-counsel.

"Well, counselor," he said, "how are you?"

"I'm dying," I groaned. I looked about. "Exactly where the hell am I?" I added.

"The Gibson Hotel," he said. "Congratulations."

"For what?"

"The verdict," he said.

For the first time the events reinstated themselves and, so help me, I realized I didn't know how the case had come out.

"Well," I said, "let's have it."

"About eight last night," he said, "we poured you into bed. You'd had it. After that, we went back to the courthouse. At eleven the jury came in with a second degree murder verdict. Reuger's tickled pink and the prosecutor is mad as hell, but there's nothing the prosecutor can do about it."

All's well—said Shakespeare, whom my brother likes and I

don't—that ends well. With the headache I had, my only thought was all's well that ends. On the other hand, some power may have overruled that jury's verdict.

Within three months the defendant caught consumption while in the Ohio Penitentiary and died.

One of the most widely publicized cases I have ever tried occurred during the last world war, when an Eastern army captain was indicted for the murder of his wife, whose nude body had been found in a Cincinnati hotel-room bathtub. The press tagged the case "The Bathtub Murder." It developed into a battle, no holds barred, between the medical experts hired by the state and those hired by the defense. Undertakers and gravediggers got into the act. Before the case was concluded, I had acquired an education not only in medicine but also in the art of embalming.

The wife had come from an Eastern city to spend a few days with her husband, who was on leave from Fort Knox before being shipped overseas. The couple, evidently on the best of terms, made the rounds of the night spots in Cincinnati and northern Kentucky. But on the last day the captain called Station X and reported that his wife was dead. He told the police he and his wife had not gone to bed until eight o'clock that morning. That she had awakened about noon and, according to the captain, had told him she was going to take a bath. He had gone back to sleep. He said he had awakened an hour later, gone to the bathroom, and found his wife's nude body in the tub, her head immersed in the water. He said he lifted his wife's body from the tub, carried it to the room, placed her on the floor, and applied artificial respiration. He said that the cuts on her back and head probably had been caused by fragments from a broken Coca Cola bottle which had fallen from the dresser.

As skeptical detectives listened to the captain's story, the coroner and his assistants were performing an autopsy upon his wife's body. Three hours later, they announced that the young woman had died of natural causes.

The captain was released and accompanied his wife's body to the East, where the funeral and interment took place.

A week after her burial, an attorney employed by the parents of the deceased advised the police that his clients had suspicions their daughter had not died of natural causes. The body was exhumed. A second autopsy, performed in the East, disclosed a fracture of the laryngeal cartilage, some hemorrhage surrounding it, plus an injury to the back of the head. It was the opinion of the Eastern experts that she had, as the result of external force, sustained these fatal injuries during life. Following consultation with the Eastern doctors, the Cincinnati coroner revised his original ruling to confirm the second autopsy. The assistant coroner, however, was just as adamant in support of the original findings—and this conflict of pathological opinions set the stage for a sensational murder trial which followed the captain's indictment for the murder of his wife.

The state, supported by experts, contended that the defendant had struck his wife with a bottle and caused a cerebral hemorrhage. It said that the injury to her larynx had been caused by his choking her to death. In contrast to this position, we of the defense, likewise supported by medical testimony, claimed that all the injuries sustained by the deceased were incurred after her death: the head injury as a result of the resuscitation attempt and the larynx damage from the undertaker's instrument during embalming.

The state's medical expert was the doctor who had performed the second autopsy. He, in no uncertain terms, qualified himself by announcing that he had, during his career, performed between 12,000 and 13,000 autopsies. He said he had found several bruises on the deceased's body, which he maintained were there before death. He said he had found hemorrhage of the brain and fracture and hemorrhage of the larynx.

"I haven't the slightest doubt, sir," he said, when the prosecutor asked whether the injuries had occurred before the young woman's death.

The expert concluded his testimony saying that he had found no evidence of death from natural causes and that, in his opinion, death was caused by violence. He had made a profound impression on the jury. Unless his testimony could be torn down, the captain was as good as convicted.

For some weeks I had been preparing for the task that confronted me. Through friends in the medical profession and a client's connection with a mortician, I witnessed two autopsies and three embalmings—all performed on deceased females. The assignment was not pleasant. I became nauseated at times. But I did observe the techniques of the pathologist and the mortician. I wasn't ready for my Hippocratic oath or qualified for the down-under trade, but I had absorbed enough knowledge to make a nuisance of myself in a courtroom.

"Doctor, the thirteen thousand autopsies you mentioned yesterday, were they all your patients?" I said.

"Certainly not," said the doctor.

The smile was gone from his face, the battle was on.

"Now, doctor, in your qualifications you gave the jury a long list of medical societies in which you hold membership. Were any of these memberships invitational?" I said.

"No, they were not," he said.

"Were any bestowed upon you as a reward for some medical accomplishment?"

"They were not."

"Then, doctor, are we to assume that *any* doctor who has passed the state examination and holds a license to practice medicine could join those societies by merely paying the annual dues?"

"That is correct."

"With your vast experience, doctor, have you ever written or delivered a paper to any medical society, anywhere?" I said.

When the doctor admitted he had not, I launched into the technicalities of the mortician's trade. Resting on the counsel table where I had placed them in full view of the jury were eight wrapped packages, each concealing a standard embalming instrument.

"Yesterday you testified that the injuries which you say you discovered on the deceased's body were, in your opinion, sustained during life and could not have been inflicted during embalming," I said.

"That is correct."

"You further testified that you had embalmed some hundred bodies, did you not?"

"That is correct."

"Then it is true that you are familiar with the different instruments necessary to accomplish that task?"

After some hesitation the doctor answered yes.

Walking to the defense table I picked up one package. I unwrapped it and unveiled a gleaming swordlike instrument eighteen inches long. I handed it to the doctor.

"Will you kindly examine and then identify this instrument?"

A state's objection was promptly overruled because I assured the court I would introduce expert testimony identifying not only this instrument but the seven to follow as the tools universally employed by undertakers in embalming bodies.

The doctor could not identify either that instrument or the seven that followed. He explained that although he had witnessed many embalmings—"I never was an active participant but was merely a spectator."

It was apparent that the jury was becoming interested. Their doubting glances, forme ly bestowed on me, now were transferred to the uncomfortable expert.

"Will you admit, doctor, that prior to embalming an endeavor is made to drain all the blood from the body?"

"That is true."

"Will you further admit that it is impossible to withdraw or drain all of the blood from the head and neck?"

"That sounds reasonable," he said.

The state moved that the doctor's answer be stricken and the jury be instructed to disregard it. Once again, upon my assurance that defense experts would so testify, the court permitted the answer to stand.

"Isn't it true that the undrained blood remaining in the head and neck region would be forced ahead of the embalming fluid as a direct result of the great pressure exerted by the trocar?"

"That is true."

"Doesn't it follow, doctor, that the pressure of the trocar forcing the undrained blood through the head and neck region could stimulate the pathological findings which you say you found surrounding the injured larynx?"

After some hesitation the doctor answered, "It's possible but I don't think so."

Only the head injury now remained to be explained. The autopsy had disclosed a straight-line wound on the back of the deceased's head and the doctor, on direct examination, had said that the injury had been caused by a blow from a hard object, such as a Coca Cola bottle, resulting in a cerebral hemorrhage.

"It was your testimony on direct examination, was it not, that it is possible to strike a person over the head with a bottle hard enough to cause a cerebral hemorrhage and leave a straight-line wound on the scalp?"

"That is correct, sir."

"Isn't it true that such a blow hard enough to cause a cerebral hemorrhage would leave stellate or angular lacerations with pointed extremities and not a straight-line scalp wound?"

"Absolutely not!"

When I asked the doctor if he had any authorities to support his viewpoint, he named several medical writers who, he claimed, were in accord with his opinion.

Upon the witness stand, during the doctor's direct and cross-examination, lay a red book which, I was sure, was some medical authority. On the pretext of examining an exhibit, I made my way to a table directly adjacent to the witness stand, from where I could identify the book. It was unbelievable and fantastic but the book lying in front of the witness was entitled *Legal Medicine and Toxicology*, written by Thomas A. Gonzales. I had intended citing Gonzales as the defense medical authority but this golden opportunity was too much to resist.

"What is that book before you?"

"That," said the doctor, "is Gonzales."

"Who did you say?"

"Gonzales," repeated the doctor.

"And who is Gonzales?"

"Gonzales is the chief medical examiner for the City of New York. He is internationally famous and is known as the pathologist's pathologist."

"Would you consider him the highest authority?"

"Absolutely."

"And does Gonzales agree with your opinion?"

"Absolutely."

"Doctor, will you turn to page 110 and read the last paragraph to the jury?"

The doctor favored me with a bored glance. He reached for the volume, thumbed through the leaves until he came to page 110 and, in a contemptuous voice, began ". . . by direct impact of a hard object like a bottle against skin stretched over an underlying layer of bone. The subcutaneous layers are pulpified—" and here the doctor came to a dead stop.

"Go on," I urged.

He hesitated and then, with each word dealing his doom, continued, "and the dermis and epithelial layers are split by the blow, producing stellate or angular lacerations with pointed extremities."

The doctor's face had become pasty white. His fingers feverishly thumbed through the book as he frantically sought out some word or passage in support of his voiced opinion.

"Unless you have something to offer to the contrary, doctor, I have no further questions."

The doctor slammed the medical book shut and, without a backward glance, left the stand.

The first defense witness was a doctor, who, after being qualified, testified that in his opinion the captain's wife had died of natural causes, to wit: cerebral edema (water on the brain) and a diseased condition of the liver and spleen. This opinion was corroborated by the assistant coroner, who had performed the original autopsy. He testified that he had examined the larynx by probing it with his fingers and that he found no roughening, depression, or sharp edges present. The witness further testified that tissues are weakened during postmortem, and the injection of embalming fluid under pressure could have caused the laryngeal injury discovered by the state's witness. He stated that it was his belief and opinion that the larynx had been injured during one of the two postmortems or during embalming.

"Did you find any sign of hemorrhage in the tissue covering the brain?"

"There was none," the assistant coroner said.

"Was there any sign of hemorrhage or blood clot on the brain?"

"There was not," he said.

"Basing your answer upon your training and experience and reasonable medical certainty, have you an opinion as to the cause of death of the deceased?"

"I have."

"What is that opinion?"

"It is my opinion the deceased died of natural causes—cerebral edema and cirrhosis of the liver."

I next called the funeral director who had embalmed the body and prepared it for shipment.

"Do you embalm a body after a postmortem examination differently from the way you embalm one where no postmortem is held?"

"We do, because in a postmortem arteries are cut and it is necessary to embalm all parts of the body separately."

I had a trocar marked for identification. I handed it to the witness, who identified it as an instrument used in embalming a dead body. He demonstrated how the instrument is jammed into all parts of the body in a probing fashion to insert the embalming fluid.

Using me as a model, the witness showed the jurors how he had forced the instrument up into the throat artieries on both sides of the larynx to carry the embalming fluid into those organs.

The jury winced.

Having demonstrated how the deceased's larynx could have been fractured in the embalming operation, I called the captain to the stand. His direct questioning and cross-examination consumed some six hours but, at the end, he was still denying the prosecutor's accusations and professing love for his deceased wife.

After arguments of counsel, the case was submitted to the jury, which five hours later returned a verdict finding the captain Not Guilty.

In the mid-thirties I was retained to defend a young man by the name of William Kuhlman, who together with three other defendants was tried at Brookville, Indiana, for the murder of Harry Miller, a former fire captain of Cincinnati. The case was known far and wide as "The Head and Hands Murder."

Kuhlman had quite a pedigree. He was one of eight children. His father, a heavy drinker who suffered from acute alcoholism, had committed suicide. Kuhlman's grandfather had also died an alcoholic. His two uncles had been adjudged insane. His two aunts had been adjudged mentally incompetent. Kuhlman himself had inherited syphilis and suffered from epilepsy. Early in life he had been committed to an Ohio state hospital for epileptics and the feeble-minded, but had escaped and found refuge with his brother-in-law, who had a long criminal record. The training and schooling in crime that Kuhlman received at his brother-in-law's hands was thorough.

Kuhlman, together with this brother-in-law and two other criminals, killed and mutilated Captain Miller. The victim's head and hands were severed, encased in cement, and thrown into a lake at Carrollton, Kentucky. The torso was stashed under a culvert nearby and partially covered with stones. Approximately a week later— to hear Captain Patrick Hayes of the Cincinnati police force tell it —"Miller started talking." This was literally true. The weather was warm, and soon the sickening odor of decaying flesh flavored the air of the makeshift burial site. Several men investigated. Miller's body, minus its head and hands, was exhumed.

The coroner, who decided the situation called for immediate action, held an on-the-spot inquest. He said that the dead man was not a local citizen—nor was he known in "these parts." Having come to this conclusion, the coroner made one of the most amazing decisions in the annals of crime. He returned a verdict of suicide.

The coroner's incongruous verdict might have ended the investigation had not two youngsters, weeks later while wading, found the cement block, broken it open, and discovered the perfectly preserved head and hands of Captain Miller.

The cover to a box of folding matches advertising a café in Ohio, which had been inadvertently discarded by one of the killers at the scene, was the clue which, through masterful detective work, eventually led to the arrest and indictment of the four conspirators.

The prosecutor claimed, but never established, that the victim's sister, a frustrated opera singer, had engineered her brother's death in order that she might inherit his quarter-of-a-million-dollar estate. When one of the defendants, Heber L. Hicks, Miss Miller's chauffeur and confidant, entered a Not Guilty plea and stood trial, two of the co-defendants, Kuhlman and John J. Poholsky, confessed their individual participation in Captain Miller's demise and testified for the State of Indiana. The jury found Hicks Guilty of murder in the first degree. Eight years before, in Kentucky, Hicks had murdered a widow, stolen her jewelry, and buried her body beneath a stone slab in her garage. For this caper, he had been sentenced to life in the penitentiary but seven years later had been paroled.

Upon arraignment all three defendants, Williams, Poholsky, and Kuhlman, entered Guilty pleas to the indictment. But on Kuhlman's behalf, in an endeavor to save his life, I demanded and was granted, as provided by Indiana law, a jury trial to determine what penalty would be meted out. It was my contention that, although Kuhlman was not legally insane, he had a diseased and warped mind and was not responsible for his act because of his meager mental equipment.

The prosecutor, as he had in the Hicks trial two months before, paraded before the jury some two score witnesses who repeated their stories of the finding of Captain Miller's torso and his head and hands. Once again the prosecutor introduced in evidence a blood-stained ax, a meat cleaver, a broken block of cement which had housed the victim's head and hands and, to add the coup de grace, a four by six foot blown-up photograph of the head and hands.

Over my objection, this gruesome picture remained set up facing the jury during the rest of the trial.

Kuhlman's sister was the first witness for the defense. Her testimony outlined the physical and mental infirmities which had shadowed her brother's adolescent life. She told of their drunken father, who kicked and beat his children, and of Kuhlman's commitment to a state institution at Gallipolis, Ohio, as an epileptic when he was fourteen, and her visit to the institution some weeks later when, sickened by the treatment accorded to the inmates, she had kidnapped her brother. She related to the jury how she had hidden her brother from the authorities for over a year.

"It was all my fault," she testified. "If I had only left him there they would have cured him."

The witness went on to tell of her marriage to Frank Gore Williams and how he had put her brother through a course of instruction in crime.

Kuhlman was the last witness for the defense. In a calm voice he told the jury how his boyhood had been blighted by poverty and insanity and drunkenness in the family. Williams, he testified, appeared in juvenile court after his arrest for truancy and persuaded the authorities to turn him over to Williams upon his promise "to keep an eye on me, and to see to it that I walked the straight and narrow path." Kuhlman told the jury that Williams did not keep his word with the court but, on the contrary, trained him in crime, teaching him the use of firearms, how to "blow" a safe, how to steal a car, how to shoplift by the use of a dummy third arm, the art of mugging, the modus operandi of "laying down paper" (passing worthless checks), and an assortment of flim-flam and con games.

With the conclusion of Kuhlman's testimony the defense rested, only to have Frank Gore Williams, who was called as the state's star rebuttal witness, add the Judas touch to the proceedings. No snake in the jungle ever shot venom into its victim with more deadly accuracy than Williams displayed in his verbal attack upon Kuhlman. He denied Kuhlman's statement that he had instructed him in crime.

"In fact," said Williams, "I learned some tricks from him."

Williams testified that Kuhlman fired three shots into Miller's body on the fatal ride from New Trenton to Carroll County, Kentucky, and that Miller was still not dead. According to Williams, Kuhlman said, "I'm going to shoot the old son of a bitch once more and if he is not dead then, I'm going to get out and run."

The witness said Kuhlman shot Miller again and then he and Poholsky raised their voices in a chorus of "Sweet Violets." On cross-examination I hammered at Williams for the better part of an hour but he stuck to his story.

Williams was finally excused. As he left the courtroom, he passed close to the defense table. He and Kuhlman locked eyes. I had the feeling I was surrounded by death. A chill ran down my spine. As I arose to address the jury, death was in the air. The jurors' faces were set in hard masks. During my plea not one of them looked at me. Their minds were made up. I kept pitching in a hope that I might reach at least one of them. But the words which had sounded so well in preparation became hollow as they fell on deaf ears.

Joseph Garretson, Jr., in the Cincinnati *Enquirer,* had this to say:

> In an eloquent, impassioned plea Hopkins told the jurors that the easy thing for them to do would be to return a death verdict. He continued, "Men and women who do not think will applaud a death verdict. The cruel and thoughtless will approve a death verdict and glory in its vengeance. But, gentlemen, I cannot

believe that you can possibly, after considering William Kuhlman's life, his training, his physical and mental condition, and his complete history, fail to spare his life.

"I have said before and I will repeat it to you, gentlemen," the lawyer pleaded, "that neither this defendant's mother, nor his brothers or sisters, nor I, as his attorney, would want his release. Those closest to him know perfectly well that he should be permanently isolated from society. I am asking this jury to save his life, which is the least and the most you gentlemen can do.

"I do not know but that you would be more merciful if you sent William Kuhlman to the electric chair—merciful to William Kuhlman but not merciful to those who would be left behind. To pass the balance of his life in prison is mighty little, if anything, to look forward to.

"It would simply mean that William Kuhlman would be among the living dead. Year following year, month following month and day following day, with nothing to look forward to but hostile guards and stone walls, with the one exception that those who love him, his mother, his sisters and brothers, could perhaps see him once or twice a year and perhaps feel everything was not lost.

"I wonder if Judge O'Byrne, or Mr. Young, or Judge Lowe, or myself or any man on this jury would have, with like training, turned out any better than William Kuhlman?" . . .

As I resumed my seat at the defense table I knew that I had failed. What I had had to say hadn't been good enough.

In four hours the jury returned a death verdict.

Sixty days later Kuhlman walked the last mile at Michigan City, Indiana.

Two hours before he was electrocuted I received a telegram that read: "Thanks for everything. I'll be seeing you." It was signed, "Your friend, Bill Kuhlman."

For years before this trial I had tried to get my brother to sit with me in a major criminal trial. With misgivings Rob had agreed to sit as co-counsel at Brookville. But as the state's case progressed, Rob's enthusiasm diminished. When the jury announced its verdict, a pale civil lawyer made the remark of the century.

"I think I'll return to the civil law and the probate practice. The only difference between probate practice and a murder case is that in probate work your client is dead before you are retained."

After this observation Rob has refused to appear in a criminal trial again.

About four o'clock one morning in January of 1948, a senseless murder occurred. A Cincinnati taxi driver was shot twice in the back of the head. His vehicle, with his body still behind the wheel, was sent plunging down an embankment. By nine that morning the crime had been discovered and the cab company had offered a thousand-dollar reward for the arrest and conviction of its perpetrators. Within forty-eight hours three boys were arrested and confessed to the murder and six-dollar robbery of the driver—a married war veteran and father of three children.

The youngest of the confessed trio, being fifteen, was turned over to juvenile authorities; but the two older boys—nineteen and twenty-one—were indicted for first degree murder while in the perpetration of a robbery. Since the pair was penniless the court had to appoint counsel to represent them. Judge Thomas A. Morrow, presiding in criminal court, asked Harry A. Abrams—a former district attorney for southern Ohio—and me to accept an appointment to represent one of the defendants. The judge advised us he would not insist we accept the appointment but that he felt, because of the facts involved, the defendants should be represented by trained criminal lawyers so that no criticism, regardless of results, could arise. It was a difficult decision to make because the case looked hopeless. Up to this time I had never lost a client in Ohio and I wasn't looking for a "burning" case. We could take the easy way out and refuse the appointment but we feared that to do so would establish a bad precedent. Besides, neither Harry nor I has ever had the reputation of running when the going gets tough.

We said we would accept the appointment. The judge named us as attorneys for Asbell "Buster" Adams, aged nineteen, the "trigger" man.

Once we had a jury, the trial didn't take too long. The state presented its evidence with deadly effect. When the state rested there was no question but that the prosecutor had proved our client guilty beyond a reasonable doubt. To save our client's life we offered medical experts, who testified that under the legal definition of insanity Adams was sane but that he should still be classified as subnormal. His mother said he was always "slow to learn." She said that he had been "backward around the house." We established that Adams had been illegally sold and had consumed many drinks of whiskey just before the crime. Lastly, we proved that Adams, with the greatest of ease and a minimum of inquiry, had purchased the murder weapon and bullets from a local merchant a week before Case, the taxicab driver, met his death.

When the prosecutor had completed his opening argument for the state, Harry addressed the jury for the defense. His was an eloquent plea and, as he talked, I studied the jurors' faces for any semblance of compassion. There was none. I knew then we were dead, for, as in the Kuhlman case, the jurors' faces collectively mirrored death. As I arose to make the final defense argument, a feeling of disaster permeated the courtroom. Standing before the jury, face to face with death, I prayed to God that I might somehow pierce the inexorable and merciless shield the prosecutor had wrought. Perhaps I should have told the jurors just what their death verdict would mean to Asbell Adams and, as in the Arwood case, pictured for them the final steps to the death chamber and the barbarous ritual which awaited him there. Instead, I chose to seek their understanding as I pleaded for Asbell Adams's life.

In part I told the jury:

> . . . I am asking you to recommend mercy and by that recommendation to save Asbell Adams's life. Nor am I without legal authority in making this request for mercy, for I say to you that by virtue of man-made laws, as promulgated and spread upon our statute books, this boy's retarded mentality, his lack of guidance, and the intoxicating drinks illegally sold him and their effect upon his judgment and intent are sufficient to warrant a mercy verdict at your hands.
>
> Nor am I without further higher authority in support of my plea for mercy for this boy. Some six thousand years ago Hammurabi, the great Persian king and lawgiver, issued an edict applicable to first degree murder cases. The law he promulgated was "Whoever sheddeth man's blood, his blood shall be shed."
>
> Nineteen centuries later Moses reaffirmed that law when he promulgated the Mosaic law of "An eye for an eye, a tooth for a tooth, an ear for an ear and a life for a life."

These gentlemen of the prosecution are making death in the electric chair a personal matter. They are trying the crime and not the individual. In demanding the death of this boy, they are following the Mosaic law of an eye for an eye and a tooth for a tooth. What they have overlooked is that a New Testament has been written and that Christ has died on the Cross. For it was Christ who some two thousand years ago laid down and incorporated as one of his Commandments our present law "Thou shalt not kill." But Christ, when nailed to the Cross, said of those who had just done him to death: "Father, forgive them, for they know not what they do."

Jesus in his Sermon on the Mount said, "Blessed are the poor in spirit, for theirs is the Kingdom of Heaven. Think not that I have come to destroy the law. I have not come to destroy but to fulfill. Ye have heard that whoever is angry with his brother shall be in danger of the judgment.

"But I say unto you that whoever is angry with his brother shall be in danger of the judgment for, Blessed are the merciful for they shall obtain mercy."

In commenting on mercy Shakespeare wrote: "The quality of mercy is not strain'd; it droppeth as the gentle rain from heaven . . . It blesseth him that gives and him that takes . . . It is an attribute to God himself; and earthly power doth then show likest God's when mercy seasons justice."

I now leave the fate of this boy in your hands. I pray to God you do not make a mistake.

But, as in the Kuhlman case, I knew I had failed. Eight hours later the jury returned a verdict condemning Adams to the electric chair.

After the verdict Prosecutor Carson Hoy came to the defense table, shook my hand, and said, "You deserve a lot of credit even though you lost. You had an unbroken record of victories in this court when you accepted the appointment in this case, a case that was a loser from the start. I want to say publicly that I admire you for not refusing the appointment."

Approximately a year later, after unsuccessful appeals and abortive appearances before the parole board and the Governor of the state, Adams was executed.

CHAPTER 6
until death do us part

Among my souvenirs are a lawnmower handle and the memory of Marie Williams. Her story is not pretty, but neither are the pornographic dreams of some animals that we call men.

That summer morning in 1946 when I first met Mrs. Williams —which is not her name—she could not stop her tears. She was distraught and incoherent. But she was charged with the murder of her husband and two hours hence she was to appear before Judge Alexander to answer that charge. Seated at the table in the corridor of Women's Detention in the catacombs of Cincinnati City Hall, she repeated over and over: "I had to do it. I had to do it."

Now and then she would add other items, such as, "He made me do awful things."

Then she would lapse into tears again.

There was little else she would say.

Her eyes were huge and filled with pain. Her face was hangman white. Her dress was cheap and nondescript. It was worn and frayed but it had been mended and it was clean. She was young and she was slim. Attractive? What beauty she might have possessed was masked by fear.

"He wanted us and a young girl to get in bed together," she said. Her voice was flat and empty.

"Go on," I said.

"He said he wanted to take pictures of the three of us, doing things with each other."

"Go on," I said.

But again the nightmare closed in. She withdrew to some secret place inside herself—a sanctuary of tears—where no one could violate her with their forbidden dreams.

Thus, waiting for court to begin, I sat with her.

Outside, beyond Women's Detention, Cincinnati was waking. Dawn streaked the sky with smudges of gray, then white and pink. The city yawned, turned off its thousands of alarm clocks, and struggled with a thousand groans from a thousand rumpled beds.

But I had been awakened much earlier by a telephone call from the police matron at Women's Detention. She had called my home to tell me, in a sleepy voice, that Marie Williams had asked to see me. The matron told me the charge was murder. And so, while the rest of the city still dreamed, I had hurried through the dark streets, still wet from the sprinkler wagon spray, and finally there in Women's Detention I had sat with Mrs. Williams, listened to her sobs, and waited for dawn and for court to begin.

In silence, I waited. I didn't bother to look around to examine the setting. I knew it by heart. The inside of City Hall and I are old friends. We both arrived on the Cincinnati scene about the same time. In fact, that antique structure is my junior. When it was officially finished, I was already seven years old and making mischief. I like that old-fashioned City Hall of ours. It wears turrets, stained-glass windows, and stonework frosting in the same grand manner that lawyers once wore hats.

"Mrs. Williams," I said.

She looked at me but did not stop crying.

"Perhaps," I said, "you would care for a cup of coffee?"

She looked down at her hands, which could not stop their trembling, and she said nothing.

I let her return to her tears.

"I had to do it," she said. "I had to do it . . ." But she said it more to herself than to me.

Or was she, perhaps, telling her story to God?

"You'd better freshen up," the matron said finally to Mrs. Williams. "It will make you feel better."

Mrs. Williams looked hollowly from the matron to me. I nodded, and so she got up.

I watched the matron lead Mrs. Williams away. My client walked the slumbering walk of a zombie. She allowed herself to be guided mindlessly by the gentle touches of the matron's hand at her elbow. Then they vanished around a corner and I was alone.

Court opened.

The courtroom contained the various participants of bar-room brawls, beery marriage battles, small-fry hoodlums, and, as usual, the odd assortment of unchastened drunks who knew the routine of the court better than brand-new counselors did. Crowded about in the hall just outside the courtroom door, milling and smoking and involved in snatches of conversation, were the lawyers and their clients, holding sad and hurried consultations before the public address system speaker called them before the bar of justice.

When Mrs. Williams was called before the judge, I stepped forward and stood beside her—and thus the wheels of justice began their slow, formal, tedious turning. We both listened as a member of the homicide squad gave a brief statement of the facts as he knew them. Then, just as quickly, Judge Alexander bound my client over to the grand jury; the charge, first degree murder.

"Without bond," the judge said.

Mrs. Williams looked at me; her wide eyes were filled with incomprehension. She was confused. Why had I pleaded her Not Guilty? She had admitted her guilt. She *had* shot and killed her husband. I have seen that same look of confusion many times. I have seen it in the eyes of the public whenever I plead a client Not Guilty. Cold stares say, "Well, Foss Hopkins wants to make another joke of justice." But I've developed armor. The public's angry glances no longer bother me at all. They are those of a jury that tries its cases in the newspapers, where rules of evidence are the headlines and where a man is guilty even after he has been proved innocent. I don't try my cases in the news columns. I am trained to try them where they should be tried: in a court of law.

I know what I'm doing is right. It's too bad other lawyers shy away from the criminal practice, but who wants to be a criminal lawyer these days? Who wants to be the dirty old man of justice?

Clarence Darrow, who wore two-hundred-dollar suits that looked slept in, said it best, and I was there to hear him say it. During the famous Leopold and Loeb trial in Chicago, he took time out in one recess to talk to a handful of us young legal fledglings. He talked about lawyers who avoid the practice of criminal law. "I'm going to tell you boys something," he said, brushing that shock of hair out of his eyes. "If you stay on the sidelines and if you wave the flag when people march by, you're the greatest guy in the world. But if you get out where the action is, if you get behind the horse and carry a shovel, you're a no-good bastard." And what Harry Truman said of politics applies to criminal law: "If you can't stand the heat, stay out of the kitchen."

Anyway, if I had pleaded Mrs. Williams Guilty, her right to trial by jury would have been forfeited. My clients—all who are accused—have a right to jury trials. Trial by jury doesn't mean trial by the evening paper or the eleven o'clock newscast. It doesn't mean a trial with lawyers sitting in judgment. Trial by jury means judgment by your peers.

On my way back to my office from City Hall that morning, I thought again about Clarence Darrow and criminal law. Maybe in fifty or sixty years the legal profession as I know it will be a museum relic, relegated to memory via the television tube, the same as the Old West has been. In Cincinnati I am almost the last of my tribe. The days of the courtroom criminal lawyer are going, going, gone.

Someday, friend, should society by some chance turn its forces against you, you'll dial quickly for a trial lawyer. But the phone will ring and ring.

You will replace the telephone and realize, suddenly, that you are up against all the machinery that society possesses and that you sit there, defenseless. The last trial lawyer will have gone.

"Well," said Ginny, when I finally arrived at my office, "what have you got this time?"

"A rough one," I said. "I'm going to have to tell a jury things they never knew existed."

"What's the case?" Ginny said.

"Hard-core pornography," I said.

She looked at me thoughtfully.

"In books?" she said at last.

"In life," I said. "I've met the lady who lived it."

The next morning Ginny and I met with Mrs. Williams in a cramped and barred conference room atop the Hamilton County Courthouse. Always the setting there is the same; only the cast of characters changes. Those quarters seem like a drab extension of my office. The conference room is in the jail on the top floor of the six-floor limestone courthouse. The building itself, a Johnny-come-lately, was completed in 1919, only one year before I put on my ice-cream suit, picked up my empty briefcase, and boarded a trolley to ride downtown for my first day as a lawyer. A stairway —steep and plain—leads from the fifth floor to the barred door of the county jail. Deputies behind that sturdy door peer out to see who each new arrival is. If your credentials are in order, the door swings open, you are admitted, and clang!, the door swings shut behind you. You are then in an open areaway, with a table and deputies, the walls lined with bars sorting out the cells that are the conference rooms. You wait in one of these little cells for the deputy to bring your client from a cage somewhere beyond.

The room is tiny, suffocating. Bars here, bars there, and four walls that—from one position—you can almost stretch out and touch. The room contains two or three kitchen chairs, a table that has felt the taste of tears, an ashtray, and in the ceiling a brilliant electric light bulb, unadorned by shade or shield. The little conference rooms—actually, cells—easily hold two; three is a crowd. Always, outside in the areaway where the deputies are, muffled conversations, a radio playing, and the ringing of a telephone that you can't see.

When Mrs. Williams entered, I stood, helped her into a chair, and sat again.

"There are some things I must tell you," I said.

She looked at me. Though her features were still strained, she appeared in complete possession of her faculties. Gone, though, was the worn dress. In its place was a blue cotton creation—quite shapeless—which was the height of fashion for all the county jail's female inmates.

I felt like a heel, but nonetheless I plunged into my set speech.

"Mrs. Williams," I said, "you are charged with first degree murder. I want to get something straight with you. A lot of people call on my services and think—because they pay good money—that we can buy their freedom. Well, I'm afraid that's not true. I've been practicing law for a long time and I've been through nearly three hundred murder cases. Some I've won. Some I've lost. And I've had one of my clients go to the chair . . ."

When I said this, she shut her eyes.

But when she opened them again, I was still there. She had not been able to blink away reality.

"Mrs. Williams," I said, "when you buy me, the only thing you're buying is experience. I want you to know that. Just so we start off on the right premise," I added, a little more gently, which surprised me. I like to consider myself detached.

Mrs. Williams, to whom all this was new, only nodded at all I had said.

"Mrs. Williams," I went on, "I demand truth. I've had clients lie to me. One who lied went to the chair. So don't be a sucker, pay my fee, and then try to be your own lawyer. I'll be in there pitching. I may be the only friend you have once the newspapers get hold of this. But I'll be on your side. After all, you are my client. The newspaper readers aren't."

She seemed to gather strength from that thought. At least she seemed to sense that someone—at last—was on her side.

"But," I said, "I don't stand for subterfuge. I don't stand for fixed witnesses. I don't stand for lying and I don't stand for cheating . . ." How many times had I repeated those same words in that little room? "Just so we understand each other," I said.

She nodded.

Ginny, on the other hand, refused to look at me. I could feel what Ginny was thinking. The line of her jaw said, "Hey, boss, quit giving the girl a hard time. For the love of Pete, for once take it easy, will you?"

I shrugged off Ginny's look.

"Mrs. Williams," I said, "I don't want to hear just the parts of the story that will be in your favor. The bad parts are the ones that need dressing up. If you have any bad part to your case, *I* want to be the one who tells it to the jury. I don't want the prosecutor to bring it out. I'll tell it in my opening statement. Then, don't you see, if the prosecutor tries to make a big thing of it later, the jurors will think, 'What's the prosecutor trying to do? Hopkins already told us *that* . . .' "

Silence again in that little room.

"Well," I said to Mrs. Williams, "that's the only way I do business. If you'd rather have another attorney, the courts will appoint one and . . ."

I stopped.

She was shaking her head.

"Then," I said, "we've wasted enough time. Shall we get on with it?"

Ginny flipped open her pad and waited, pencil poised.

The first time through a client's story I only listen. I let my client talk without interruption. Sometimes, as in the case of Mrs. Williams, they ramble. They did not enter the arena as professional storytellers. But I only listen. And Ginny takes notes.

Mrs. Williams sang her song. I was intrigued by her posture and her spirit. I could tell she had always been a meek and retiring soul. Not pushy. But in that room that day she seemed drained of will. She spoke tonelessly. Her accent—faint, hardly there—was that of country women.

She told us that she was twenty-nine years old. "From Owensboro, Kentucky," she added emptily.

When she was seven her parents and older brother had moved to Cincinnati. But a year after that, her mother ran off with another man.

"And my father went berserk," she said, as if describing the weather. "He chased me and my brother around the house, waving an ax at us. But a neighbor stepped in and they ended up taking us to the orphan home. I stayed there till I was of age."

She told of meeting her husband, their marriage, their two little boys, and how her husband had got drafted into the military service.

"Besides the allotment money he sent back home," she said, her voice empty of emotion, "all the time he was away in the army I took in washing from different families. By the time he was discharged we had saved enough—nearly fifteen hundred dollars—which we went and used as down payment on a house."

She stopped, shut her eyes, and waited. Outside, in some jail corridor, I heard a radio play one record all the way through before Mrs. Williams began again.

"Before he went into the army," she said, her eyes still shut, "we got along fine, the both of us. He always gave me money and everything; even the sex we had was normal." Her voice then dropped to a whisper. "But when he came back," she said, "things changed. I guess he was sex crazy . . ."

More silence.

Then, another start. And for the next thirty minutes she detailed her dreaded life with her husband following his release from the service, the episodes running the gamut of obscenity, perversion, and depravity.

"Now what?" said Ginny, as we walked out of the courthouse.

"Well," I said, "I'm convinced of one thing. She doesn't belong in jail. She's got to be with her children."

"Application for a bond?" Ginny said.

"Yes," I said. "She's been through enough."

After a hearing, bond was set at five thousand dollars. Rob and I personally made bond to gain her release.

"But why?" Ginny protested. "The public is strong on this case and—for once—they seem to be on your side. We're flooded with calls offering financial assistance for Mrs. Williams. Why put out your own money? You'll be doing enough. You'll be . . ."

"Tell whoever calls that I appreciate their offers of help," I said, "but I want to go this one alone."

"Why?" Ginny persisted.

"Damned if I know," I said. "Maybe I don't feel right having the public love me."

"That's not the reason and you know it," Ginny muttered.

Wise gal—as well as being the smartest legal secretary in the business.

But there we let the conversation end.

Mrs. Williams was released, awaiting trial. She was released in the company of her two little boys, who needed her as much as she needed them. Those moppets were better tonic for her than any legal small talk or medical pills.

Before the final drama of Mrs. Williams could be played, time —that thief—had robbed our Ohio Valley of summer and had removed every leaf from every tree. Thanksgiving came and swiftly went. Each store window was decorated for Christmas. Then January came—and with it ice and snow. Then when the new year settled into its routine, Mrs. Williams entered the courtroom for her date with destiny. I did not ask how her two little boys were. I did not ask how Christmas had been. I didn't have the courage.

Pick a jury of her peers? Who, I asked myself, among the ladies and gentlemen assembled had endured what she had endured? I looked at Mrs. Williams, seated beside me at the defense table. As she anticipated the stories that had to be told, her big eyes seemed even bigger.

"Relax," I told her.

But she could not relax.

"Are you going to use an all-woman jury on this one, Foss?" a reporter had asked me.

Listen, I told him, it has been five years since I used an all-woman jury and—though that one consisted of charming ladies all —the results were disastrous. My client back then ran a hotel which, though not a house of prostitution, was not the YWCA. My client, it seemed, had not been too observant. When a couple registered as man and wife, fine; but when the female side of the couple registered a few hours later as man and wife with a new husband, my client had not been suspicious. Anyway, I had represented her during World War II when no male jurors were on tap, and I ended up with an all-female jury. Proud ladies. You could see it in their eyes. They were about to try a sister who had sinned. The jurors were

outraged. They didn't want the world—or their next-door neighbors
—to think that they would, by any means, condone such carryings-on.
The accused was to each juror a black mark against the female of
the species. The only verdict these ladies could come up with was
Guilty. After the closing arguments they tromped into the jury room
so fast that the last one in met the first one coming out. That's the
last all-woman jury I'll ever have.

And though Mrs. Williams was not a "fallen woman" as,
perhaps, my earlier client had been, nonetheless Mrs. Williams had
bumped off her old man. How would members of an all-female jury
explain a Not Guilty verdict to their spouses?

When the final jury was seated, plus the one alternate, I had
a mixed jury: seven ladies and five gentlemen.

The judge rapped his gavel; the trial began.

Those of you who have matriculated into the legal profession
via "Judd for the Defense" and "Perry Mason" already know how
trials are conducted. I will therefore not include every twist and
turn of that legal charade that we call courtroom procedure in the
stories this book unfolds. Much that transpires is, to the layman,
tedium. Some of it bores the hell out of lawyers and judges, too.
No matter. Courts of law are not convened to entertain. They are
stylized dances in which the goal is a human truth and human
justice.

That Mrs. Williams had shot her husband was simple for the
state to prove: my client had admitted it.

But the prosecutor didn't relax. He prosecuted to the hilt. His
name was Simon Leis, and he is now a Common Pleas judge.
Frankly, he was one of the toughest prosecutors I've been up against.
He was the outraged prosecutor of the old school. As a defense
counsel, I had to watch myself at every turn. If I made one mistake,
he would be in there, and there I'd be, clobbered.

The prosecution contended that Mrs. Williams had played
around a little while her husband was away in the army. The story
of the shooting, as told by the newspapers, did not help our cause
much, either. One headline said:

MURDER DEFENDANT ADMITS DATING CAFÉMAN
IN COLLEGE HILL WHEN HUSBAND WAS IN ARMY

The state rested its case.

When I called Mrs. Williams to the stand, a murmur ran through the courtroom. As she crossed the room to the chair, her hands were trembling. I was afraid for a moment that she would faint before making the crossing. But somehow she arrived, sat, and waited.

No, she was not the leggy Hollywood beauty one sees in the movie version of trials. But frankly, she had endured too much to play the role of a cutie. She was a lonely woman who had lingered too long in Hell. She wore that same dress she wore when I first met her in Women's Detention. And on her face was the same look of fear.

She sat, looking at me, afraid to look elsewhere, because all around her was the enemy.

Gently I began my questions.

The first thing I asked about was the dress.

She told the jury—in her apologetic country voice—that it had once been a beautiful evening gown.

"An *evening* gown?" I said.

She nodded.

"One that I made over," she said. "It's the only one I have. I cut it down and wore it for my good dress . . ."

Moments later, in answer to my questions, she told of her early life—the father chasing her with an ax, the years as an orphan, meeting her husband, and then her marriage.

"Go on," I said. "Go on, Mrs. Williams."

She twisted her hands, quivering in her lap.

"When my husband came home from the army," she said, staring down at the hands as if they did not belong to her, "he was changed."

"Changed how?" I said.

"He had a horrible look in his eyes," she said. "He would whip the children for nothing at all. I was afraid of him. But he said if I called the police, he would kill me."

A murmur ran abruptly through the spectators. The judge banged his gavel once for silence.

"Go on," I said.

But she had fallen silent. I could see the rebirth of dread in her eyes.

"He tried to choke me four times," she said, her voice lower and with a quaver. "And he gave me beatings. One time that he choked me I had him arrested. But when he got out on bond I was so afraid I took the children and we went and stayed with a neighbor. He said if I didn't withdraw the charges he was going to kill me. So I never could have him arrested after that, you see," she concluded, like a trapped animal.

I walked from my position by the jury box back to the defense table, leafed through papers, and let the awfulness of her testimony sink into the jury.

"Go on," I said at last.

She nodded, but dread filled her voice.

"I went to the Court of Domestic Relations three times," she said, staring at her hands in desperate wonder. She could not bear to look at me. "I told them how crazy he was sexually, that he wanted me to do it any way, shape, or form that I could. He kept saying if I didn't, he would kill me."

You could have heard a pin drop.

"Well, they said they would talk to him," she went on lonesomely. "But he made me write a letter that I had something to do with another man and he went and took that to the court."

I nodded.

"What were some of the sex acts you complained of?" I said.

She took the longest time answering.

"Two, three days after he came back," she said in a low voice, "he called one of our little boys into the bedroom and told me to keep out. I looked in and saw my husband with no clothes on, masturbating. I rushed in and grabbed my little boy . . ."

The jurors were no longer sitting in the jury box. The lady had, with words and trembling hands, transported them against their wills, back into the summer before and into that little cottage where black misery filled each and every room. They were forced to witness, through her words, obscenities that most people never dream of.

They sat, withdrawn and stern-faced, and heard my client recite those dread scenes when on hot and sweaty summer nights she was forced to commit oral sodomy on her grinning husband. They were the legal peeping Toms who watched him, via her testimony, performing cunnilingus on her.

But they had heard only the prologue.

"Go on, Mrs. Williams," I said.

"My husband said he was going to get a Negro man to come in and tear me apart because he was bigger. He said he wanted me to get a young girl, or he would find one, so we could all go into bed together and have all of us do it to each other. He said he wanted to take pictures of us that way. He brought home photos about homosexuality. He also brought cartoon books which he made me read before we went to bed. He told me they would make me more passionate. He had this one story about a mother and her sons which he made me copy so I could know it by heart. The mother had intercourse with her sons every different kind of way and when her daughter came home from college, the sons and daughter also had intercourse. He said, 'When my sons get older we'll have a real good time, all three of us on you . . .' "

The members of the jury refused to look at one another—and I knew why. From that moment on, their lives would be less. They were involved in a drama which, unlike television, they could not shut off. And in a way, so are you. The story of Mrs. Williams is no pornographic novel to be read on the sneak, then set aside in order to get to church on time. The story of Mrs. Williams is real.

To read of these dim-lit orgies in a book such as this or to hear them suggested in stage whispers on a silver screen, of course, is one thing. But to be in that courtroom and to see on that witness stand the benumbed and exhausted participant in such a drama would tear your heart out. I saw this in the eyes of every juror. They were not titillated by the disclosures. They were profoundly shocked. They were not the seekers of sordid headlines. They were the seekers of truth—and the truth had quickly sickened them.

I wanted to stop there, but there was more.

I handed Mrs. Williams half of a lawnmower handle that was a foot long, more than two inches in diameter, and slightly rounded at one end.

"Can you identify this object?" I said.

"Yes," she said. "It's part of a lawnmower handle."

"Have you seen it before?"

"Yes. At my home."

"Under what circumstances?"

The prosecutor was on his feet.

"Objection!" he cried. "Objection!"

The judge overruled him.

Mrs. Williams was permitted to reply.

"My husband," she said, "used it on my body."

Had I heard a juror gasp?

Or had that been my soul?

She described how he used to order her to strip and then, pistol in one hand and lawnmower handle in the other, commit shocking, sadistic, and unprintable indignities upon her naked person.

Some jurors sat with downcast eyes. Others stared straight ahead, their jaws set in anger.

And the public? The public—in Cincinnati and elsewhere—licked its chops as the facts of each episode unfolded. Though many felt compassion for my client, many others hungered only for details of that obscene wedding bed. In the courtroom itself the spectators hung onto every word, crossed their legs, and ached for more. Not all were that way, but enough, I assure you; enough.

"What happened the night you shot your husband?" I said.

She could not bear to look at the lawnmower handle.

"My husband called me into the bedroom," she said. "And he told me to take off my clothes. I had already hid the pistol, but he had that lawnmower handle on the table beside the bed. He had a mean look, too, just like a tiger. I made an excuse to get a drink of water. When I came back I had the gun. He told me to put it down. And I told him he wasn't going to use that lawnmower handle on me again. He said he was going to kill me and he started to jump up . . ."

"And, Mrs. Williams?"

"I pulled the trigger . . ."

"And, Mrs. Williams?"

"And then I called the police."

In addition to her testimony, we introduced evidence: photographs which her husband had collected of men and women and boys and girls in obscene poses; sex cartoons; and obscene stories written in her husband's hand, featuring homosexuality, Lesbianism, and all types of perversion known to man.

At the conclusion of Mrs. Williams's testimony, I offered the lawnmower handle as evidence. Though the prosecutor objected, he was overruled. When this piece of evidence was accepted as an exhibit for the defense, I rested the case.

"Some years ago," I told the jury, "I was reading in *Reader's Digest* Victor Hugo's description of Napoleon's victorious march into Russia and his disastrous return to France. How Napoleon with his army, one hundred thousand strong, made his way to Moscow, where he and his lesser officers were wined, dined, and feted. Although Napoleon was warned repeatedly about the severity of a Russian winter, he refused to issue orders to return to France. Drunk with power and success, he lingered too long before giving orders to march.

"You, ladies and gentlemen of the jury, remember from history how the Russian winter struck and how, through cold and disease and famine, eighty-five thousand soldiers fell by the wayside. Only fifteen thousand emaciated men staggered into the arms of loved ones who had waited for them so long. Because of this disastrous expedition, Napoleon's power and popularity vanished. He was exiled to St. Helena, where he died from heartache and disease. Victor Hugo added a footnote to the page. It read, 'I wonder if God was bored with him?'

"As I sat here and heard the facts unfold in this case, *I wondered if God was bored with Charles Williams?*"

At that point in my summation I had picked up the lawnmower handle and when, in my enthusiasm, it struck the front panel of the jury box a resounding thud, I saw a collective shudder from the jury's seven female members.

The jury was out only thirty minutes.

It's verdict: Not Guilty.

After her trial, Mrs. Williams appeared at my office. The afternoon was gray, wet, and cold, but she wore only a thin summer coat. She entered my office and tendered me her entire wealth: a check for one thousand dollars, plus the deed to her cottage.

"You don't owe me a cent," I said. "Because of the sex angle of your case, I've had thousands of dollars worth of free publicity."

I tore the check in half—and handed it back to her.

Two weeks later, she appeared again. She deposited three packages on my desk.

"Your fee," she said.

She watched as I opened the first package, a quart of preserved pears. The second was preserved cherries. The third was blackberry jelly, the best I ever tasted.

This was one fee which was never recorded, nor did the Internal Revenue Service ever get its cut. It was strictly between Mrs. Williams and myself. It is listed under Psychic Income and it pays big dividends.

CHAPTER 7
mama always makes tens

Fledgling lawyers still toiling over school books and fretting about passing the bar are, of course, taught many things by their instructors. They are taught the proper way to say good morning to a judge, the proper way to write a will, and other items in which their future clients will have need of assistance. On the other hand, fledgling lawyers are not taught how to perform an autopsy, what to do when the public gives them dirty looks, or the finer points of knocking off a bank.

I note the last point here because this will be about the time that I, as the legal representative of my client, did exactly that: knocked off a bank.

Early one morning, before I had time to sneak across the street for breakfast, three visitors appeared in my office. One was a lady, pale and distraught. The other two were gentlemen who looked morose.

"How can I help you?" I said.

One of the men spoke.

"I'm George Lawson," he said.

"Of course," I said. I did not add that he also had the alias Pugnose Whitey Lawson. Some things, at that hour of the morning, are better left unsaid.

"This is Harry Haas," he said.

"Ah," I said.

"And this is Mrs. Rip Farley," he said.

I said nothing. Only the night before, Mr. Rip Farley had been hustled into eternity, in front of the 633 Club in Newport, Kentucky, by a blast from a sawed-off shotgun.

"Rip Farley got hit last night," Mr. Lawson advised me.

"So I understand," I said. "Go on."

"When the coroner searched Rip at the morgue," he said, "he found two keys to a safety deposit box. He went and turned the keys over to the chief of police. He refused to give them to Mrs. Farley here, even though that box is in her name."

Mrs. Farley nodded, as if to say, that's the way things were.

"But what's so important about the box?" I said.

"Twenty G's," he said.

"You're not making sense," I said. "You'll have to do better than that."

Lawson, without hesitation, told me what had happened *before* the shotgun blast. It seemed that the deceased had worked as a "stick man" at a crap table at the Yorkshire Club in Newport. There had been an argument. Rip Farley had been fired.

"So?" I said.

"That's not all," said Lawson.

He went on to say that according to Rip Farley, he was still owed four points of the action, but the management refused to settle or to acknowledge his investment. That's when Rip Farley decided to collect personally. Two nights later he entered the club, headed for the casino, walked up to the dice table, picked up the cash box, and —at a leisurely pace—strolled through the crowd, out the door, and into the night. For some reason no one at the club had challenged him. As one said later, "We thought Rip was just horsing around."

"He wasn't, though?" I said.

"He wasn't," said Lawson. "When he refused to return the money, they got a contract on him."

Then the three stood silent in front of my desk.

"And just what do you want me to do?" I said.

For the first time, Haas spoke.

"We want you to get them keys or figure out some angle so we can get in the box."

"Where is this bank?" I asked.

"The Avondale Branch of the Central Trust Bank," Haas said.

"On Reading Road?" I said.

He nodded.

"Meet me there in fifteen minutes," I said. "We'll see what we can do."

As I pulled up in front of the bank I saw a long black car— just like in the gangster movies—parked directly across the street. Its three occupants, obviously not running an errand to the grocery, were serious gentlemen. They wore dark suits and gray hats. Their eyes never left me as I got out of my car and went into the bank.

"Just made it," I said to the new widow and her friends who waited inside.

They nodded and said nothing.

"Well," I said. "Here we are."

I looked around.

"Ah," I thought, "and there *they* are."

Glaring at us in a manner that led me to believe we were an unwelcome intrusion were two gentlemen, who had deposited themselves in two enormous leather chairs. One was the coroner from across the river in Kentucky. The other was a Newport detective. In their possession, of course, were the keys to my client's safety deposit box.

We chatted a bit.

The officials, however, after conferring by telephone with the Campbell County attorney, refused to release the keys unless they were permitted to view the contents of the box.

"Sorry," I said. "Can't permit that."

I pointed out that the box was registered in my client's name and that neither they nor anyone else had any legal right to interfere with her possessions.

We chatted some more.

And there were more telephone calls. The branch manager called the attorney for the bank. The attorney for the bank said I was absolutely right.

The Campbell County attorney was busy on the telephone, too. He called the Cincinnati chief of police. He called the Hamilton County prosecutor. He called the judge of the probate court.

He was told, each time, that barring a legal injunction, there was nothing he could do.

As I stood there, in the gathering crowd, I realized that the next step on his part would be a legal injunction, so I had to move fast.

Since the coroner and the detective would not give up the keys to my client, the next move was obvious. I put in a call to another client of mine named Sammy, who, I reasoned, would probably know someone who could help me. I had first met Sammy fifteen years before when I had been retained to represent him on a grand larceny charge. The verdict had been Not Guilty. From time to time since then Sammy, when in difficulty with the law, would contact me and request my services. Everyone who knew Sammy swore by him—even, at times, the police, who harbored a secret admiration for the loyalty and devotion as well as poor grammar that he bestowed lavishly upon his friends and cohorts. Pale of face, small of stature, and completely amoral—that was Sammy. But a good man to have in your corner in case of trouble.

However, even Sammy was disturbed by my request.

"Yeah, this here's the club," he grumbled into the telephone.

"Sammy," I said, "I need your help and I need it in a hurry."

"Is that you, Pops?" Sammy had christened me "Pops" because he said I always took care of him. "Anything you want, Pops. You just name it."

"Can you," I said, "get me someone to drill a safety deposit box?"

"Huh? Where is this here box?"

"It's in the vault," I said, "at Central Trust."

There was a long silence.

"Sammy? Are you still there?"

"Yeah, Pops. But did you say this box was in a bank?"

"Yes, I—"

"Is this a rib, Pops?"

I assured Sammy that I was never more serious. Again, a long silence.

"Sammy? Are you there?"

"The boys in Detroit ain't going to believe this," he said. "Hold the phone, Pops, while I discuss the situation with one of my co-patriots."

There followed a muffled conversation. Then Sammy was back on the telephone.

"Pops," he said, "we have decided that you yourself should not be involved in this particular caper. We must therefore decline your kind invitation to participate in this daylight heist. What we mean is, Pops, are you sure you're feeling well?"

"Sammy," I protested, "I feel fine. It's simply that—"

But Sammy interrupted.

"Take a couple of aspirin, Pops. You'll feel better in a few hours."

There was a click—Sammy had returned to the Twilight Zone.

I did what I should have done in the first place: called Mosler Safe Company in Hamilton, Ohio. The company agreed to have a safe expert at the bank within the hour. Upon arrival, the expert, after a quick appraisal of the task, rolled up his sleeves, nodded pleasantly to those assembled, and went to work. Soon the soft hush of the bank was broken by the tooth-hurting whine of the drill, chewing into the safety deposit box.

The bank manager wasn't pleased. Time after time, over the steady hum of the drill, could be heard his shrill and anguished voice vociferously objecting to our deportment and characterizing the entire proceedings as highly irregular.

"There we are," said the lock expert.

He had removed the small steel door and there, nestling snugly in its niche, was Mrs. Farley's safe deposit box. I stepped forward and took immediate possession, much to the gloom of the assembled Kentucky officials. With the widow at my side, we entered one of those little private rooms near the vaults and closed the door.

"Now," I said, "we shall see what we shall see."

We opened the box. Money, money, money! Stacks and stacks of beautiful, beautiful bills!

"Do something with it," Mrs. Farley pleaded.

"Me?" I said.

"Yes," she said.

Without ado, I stuffed every available pocket with currency. I happened, fortunately, to be wearing a topcoat, which concealed the small fortune.

Mrs. Farley and I stepped back out to face the crowd.

As Mrs. Farley, her two associates, and I regrouped by the bank door, I noticed the three characters in the long black car still parked across the street.

"Do you have a feeling," I said to Haas, "that we are bit players in a movie that's too corny even for the Late-Late Show?"

Haas kept his cool. "Don't you worry about a thing, counselor," he said. "You wait a minute before you leave. I'll take those bastards on a ride they'll never forget."

"I suppose," I said—and he was gone.

The eyes of the trio in the black car never wavered as Mrs. Farley and her two escorts crossed Reading Road and climbed into their own car. Without warning, Haas—who was behind the wheel —made a wild and free U-turn in the middle of traffic coming both ways. Cars slammed on brakes. Tires screeched. Honks protested. And away they went—north on Reading Road. The long black car duplicated Haas's maneuver, causing traffic on Reading Road to come to a standstill.

Then, they were gone.

I saw no reason to delay my departure. I strolled in a leisurely manner from the bank to my car, got in, and drove at an equally leisurely pace to my office. I entered, opened my coat, and piled on Ginny's desk the greenbacks my morning's adventure had accumulated.

"What did you do?" said Ginny. "Foss, did you rob a bank?"

"You might say that," I said. "Lock it up. I'm going to a movie."

"But you never go to movies!"

"Believe it or not," I said. "That's where I'm going."

"Which movie?"

"Any old movie will do," I said. "See one, you've seen 'em all."

When Mrs. Farley and her two friends appeared at my office the next morning I did not inquire after—nor did they mention any details of—the Keystone Comedy chase. The three appeared in good physical shape. I assumed they had been successful in outdistancing their pursuers.

"Shall we set about the business of settling your late husband's estate?" I said.

They nodded.

Some estates are settled more quickly than others; this was settled the quickest of any I've ever known. The settlement may not have conformed to the statute of descent and distribution but, at least, it met with the collective approval of all those present. The widow received $13,000, Lawson and Haas each $1,000, and I was paid an attorney's fee of $5,000.

"That," I said, "is that."

It wasn't, though.

That afternoon I received a telephone call from one of the owners of the Yorkshire Club.

"Counselor," the caller said, "this is Eddie. The boys have all asked me to call you and extend our congratulations."

"Thank you," I said, wondering if I meant it. "And convey my best to the boys."

"I trust, counselor," Eddie went on, "you were adequately compensated for your legal efforts on behalf of the widow?"

"Yes," I said—with an empty feeling in my stomach.

"I just called to extend an invitation," he said.

"Oh," I said.

"Yes," he said. "We feel you might like to participate in certain games of chance which the management, from time to time, provides for the entertainment of its patrons."

"An excellent idea," I said—the empty feeling becoming emptier.

After I hung up, I thought the matter out. The least I could do, I decided, was to accept Eddie's invitation and give the club an opportunity to win back the $5,000 whose ownership had been disputed by the club and the deceased.

With the $5,000 tucked in an inner pocket I arrived the next Saturday at the Yorkshire Club. I made my way through the crowd to the casino which, at that hour, was a babble of voices and clickety-clicks and rifflings. With the exception of the door at either end, the perimeter of the casino was lined solidly with one-armed bandits. Men or women sat entranced before each, pulled levers, deposited coins, glared, smiled, stared, prayed, giggled, and muttered —as such participants are wont to do. Close by, at the roulette wheel, a croupier in the traditional green visor raked in stakes with the solemnity of a church usher working a good house. At two blackjack tables dealers mechanically dealt and shuffled and looked bored. Three separate dice tables—positioned longitudinally in the center of the smoky room—were hidden from view, thanks to the wall of flesh attending them. Several young waitresses, wearing more makeup than clothes, flitted through the noise and smoke and people, offering liquid refreshment to those parched by the lure of the game.

As I stared about the casino I had the strangest feeling that people gambled there.

It was as I started to work my way to the center table that I saw Eddie. He was standing a few feet to my left and his face lit up with a big smile as our eyes met. "I told the boys you'd come over, counselor."

"If I remember correctly," I told him, "you invited me to participate in a game of chance. Looks like you're having a depression," I added.

"Oh, we pay our bills," he replied. "What do you want to do, shoot crap?"

When I answered in the affirmative, and with Eddie running interference, we headed for the center table, where, through adroit maneuvering, he squeezed me into a spot directly to the right of the croupier who was covering all wagers at that end of the table.

"What will it be, counselor, cash or credit?" he inquired.

When I indicated cash, Eddie said he would "see me later" as he disappeared into the crowd.

By the time the dice had worked their way around the table

to me, fifteen minutes had elapsed, and I was out $3,600. My efforts were no better than the other players, for $600 was added to my debit during the short interval I held the dice. Barring a miracle I was sunk. Only $800 remained of my original $5,000. With fingers crossed I took four fifty-dollar chips from my diminishing stack and placed them on the line. When the shooter threw a ten I must have groaned out loud because—from directly behind me—a voice said, "Don't worry, mister. Mama always makes tens."

I turned.

A tall, thin lady in her early forties greeted me with a wink. "As I said," she said, "Mama always makes tens."

"Is that really your mother shooting the dice?" I complained.

"None other, mister. And she's the best crapshooter in the whole Commonwealth of Kentucky. Just relax and keep out of the line of fire."

For the first time I glanced at the shooter. She, too, was tall and thin. She bore a remarkable resemblance to her daughter. She wore an ill-fitting dress of some dark material and a small red hat which rested precariously on the top of her head.

I took $200 on the ten at two-to-one odds.

I placed four additional chips in the box marked "come" just as the stickman returned the dice to the lady at the corner of the table. She picked up the dice, touched them to the lone chip on the line in front of her, and then, raising the dice to her lips, blew on them in that age-old rite of the seasoned crapshooter. Her lips —whether in prayer or hocus-pocus lingo—moved incessantly as her closed left hand high above her head shook and rattled the concealed cubes. Suddenly, with her hand extended, she leaned far over the table and catapulted the dice into their crazy zigzag gallop down the expanse of emerald green.

This time she threw a four and when I took $200 in odds, I was out of chips.

As soon as the stickman returned the dice, her lips again began to move. I could not hear what she was advocating, but the dice apparently understood her whispered instructions. She not only made the ten, but with utter abandon she made fours, fives, sixes, eights, and nines—in the wildest and most colorful exhibition of dice shooting I have ever witnessed.

It was twenty minutes later before, either through fatigue or misadventure, she sevened out.

"Ah," I said—and left the table.

With my pockets full of chips I went to the cashier's window. The cashier—behind that small barred opening—made no comment, nor was there any change of expression as his beady eyes evaluated the stacks of chips I presented to him for redemption. With the finesse of a magician he produced currency from somewhere and began to count bills at a speed I could not follow. He handed me the bills. "Ten thousand four hundred and forty," he said. "You'll be wasting your time but you can count it if you want to."

I'll say one thing for Eddie, he was a sportsman through and through, for some thirty minutes later I arrived safe and sound at my home, in the company of a bodyguard he insisted I accept. The mother and daughter I have never seen or heard of again but I often wonder if "Mama" is still making tens.

CHAPTER 8
Mr. Gold comes to Dayton

Murder, as I say, is my business. In the mid fifties, I became involved in the outcroppings of mass murder—the potential death of entire civilizations via a machine of hell called the H-Bomb. I became part and parcel of the fallout that accompanied one of the greatest spy hunts in the world. I speak here of the arrest in England of Dr. Klaus Fuchs, the German-born British nuclear physicist charged with transmitting classified information to the Soviet Union. He described his cohorts in this country. One of them was chemical engineer Harry Gold, who, when arrested, talked a blue streak; his verbal outpourings made him a walking encyclopedia so far as espionage activity in the United States was concerned.

On the surface Gold appeared repentant, wanting to make amends for the sorry business of betraying his adopted land. The people at the Federal Bureau of Investigation—day after day—duly recorded every word that Gold said. They evidently believed him. They must have marveled at his ability to recall dates and details which were at times so remote and insignificant that his recollection bordered on the fantastic. Thus, Gold literally became worth his weight in gold to the F.B.I. and, in turn, to the district attorneys who from time to time would have cause to parade him before a jury sitting in judgment of some man or woman upon whom Gold had bestowed his verbal kiss of death.

I suppose Gold would still be operating today, if we had not tangled head-on. Lest you think that I was operating against the best interests of my own country, let me be quick to point out that I was not. I care less for spies than most. They are, at best, distasteful creatures. And I happen to be fond of my country. Yet, Gold had to be destroyed and I had to destroy him.

Let me approach the matter in its logical order. In one of his many statements to the F.B.I., Gold mentioned a Wright-Patterson Air Force Base engineer, Benjamin Smilg, whom Gold said he had contacted on several occasions between 1938 and 1940 but from whom he maintained he had been unable to obtain any classified information.

The F.B.I. questioned Smilg, who denied any knowledge of Gold's espionage activities. Six weeks later—August 9, 1950— Smilg was officially suspended from duty. A month and a half later the Air Force Central Loyalty-Security Board charged Smilg with associating with an admitted Soviet agent, Stanislaus Anton Shumowsky, in 1933. The board charged Smilg with receiving two thousand dollars between 1936 and 1937 from the Amtorg Corporation, an organ of the Soviet government, via the same Shumowsky. The board charged Smilg with associating with Gold, a known Soviet agent, in 1938 and 1939. The board charged him with failing to report that these two Soviet representatives were the bad guys in the plot.

Smilg denied all charges and requested an administrative hearing before the board.

The hearing was held in Dayton. Eleven days before Christmas in 1950 the board decided—unanimously—that although Smilg had not been disloyal to the United States, there existed "reasonable grounds for the belief that his removal was warranted by the demands of national security."

Smilg filed an appeal but the ruling stood.

A year later a federal grand jury returned a sealed indictment charging Smilg with perjury, suggesting that he lied three times to the Loyalty-Security Board. Smilg was immediately arrested and released on a ten thousand dollar bond.

The next day I sat across from him in the Dayton law office of Paul Ziegler.

We brought to that first meeting the temper and anger of the nation because, in 1950, we were in the spell of McCarthy's witch-hunt in the Senate and the aftermath of the Alger Hiss trial. Communists were hiding under every bed. Blanket accusations were the order of the day. Harry Truman was President, sending troops to Korea. And there I sat, facing one of the alleged witches, and he was seeking my help. He wore no cloak of innocence. Gold's innuendos had cloaked him with guilt.

He was, in the eyes of the public, our enemy. He was our own traitor—just as Julius and Ethel Rosenberg were. Distasteful. That was what the nation thought.

And so I heard him out.

"You believe him?" said Ginny, when I returned to Cincinnati.

I tossed hearing transcripts on my desk. They were from his original hearings before the Loyalty-Security Board.

"Let me read these first," I said.

"If you take this one," Ginny said, "your name will be mud."

"I know," I said.

"Well?"

"Let me read the transcripts this weekend," I said. "I'll tell you Monday."

That weekend I read—and reread—the transcripts of the Smilg hearings. Somehow the tale just didn't ring true. It had been the district attorney's contention that Smilg had told the F.B.I. in the first interview that he had known Gold was an espionage agent. The district attorney contended further that in the loyalty hearing Smilg had reversed his story, denying knowledge of Gold's activities. That a man of Smilg's intelligence would tell the F.B.I. one thing and the Loyalty Board another did not make sense to me. Smilg wasn't an idiot nor was he a congenital liar. He was, instead, a man of high intelligence and superior background.

I tossed the transcripts aside and stared out the window at the night.

"Well," I told myself, "the outcome of this case is going to depend on whom the jury believes: Harry Gold and the F.B.I., or my client."

With that dismal conclusion, I poured myself a hefty nightcap and wondered why I had not gone into civil law.

"You've decided?" said Ginny that Monday morning.

"I'm afraid I have," I said. "We'll take the case."

But I didn't sound happy. I wasn't.

"First," I said, "we have to know everything we can about Smilg *and* Gold."

"When do we start?" Ginny said.

"Right now," I said. "Check the flights to Boston. We have to start somewhere. Might as well start where Smilg was born . . ."

For the next six weeks every minute I could beg, borrow, or steal from my law practice found me in another city. I visited not only Boston but Philadelphia; Washington, D.C.; Baltimore; Dayton; and even Rome, New York. At Boston I talked with four of Smilg's teachers, two former classmates, and a neighbor who had known the Smilg family since Smilg's high-school days. I went over his military record with a fine-tooth comb. At Wright-Patterson Field in Dayton I talked with everyone, even the most casual acquaintances of Smilg's. In Philadelphia and Baltimore I talked with his former employers.

I was one man doing what teams of men from the F.B.I. had already done. I had no vast government bureau behind me. I had only my office force sitting back in my Cincinnati office, making notes like crazy.

Gold was investigated, too, although two years would pass before I confronted him in a courtroom. I spent four days in Philadelphia interviewing his former classmates, teachers, employers, and acquaintances. I read—till I thought my eyes would burn out—the record of the legal proceedings held in the Federal Building there in the case of the United States of America versus Harry Gold. In New York most of my time was spent at the Federal Building on Foley Square, studying trial records and transcripts in the case of the United States of America versus Julius and Ethel Rosenberg and Morton Sobell, as well as our country versus Abraham Brothman. In each case, Harry Gold had testified for the government—and his testimony had been the kiss of death for the defendants.

Meanwhile, back in Cincinnati my office force had been burning the midnight oil at the library. They read and digested several books in which Gold's early life and espionage activities were discussed, together with J. Edgar Hoover's account of Gold's personal life which appeared in *Reader's Digest* in 1951. They uncovered revealing articles in *Life* and *The New York Times*. To top that off, they had borrowed issues of the *Columbia Law Review* which dealt with certain aspects of the Rosenberg, Sobell, and Brothman trials.

Then came the time to gather the pieces of the jigsaw puzzle together.

I sat in my office, after everyone had gone home, and looked at the notes I had accumulated. Gold and Smilg. Smilg and Gold. I could close my eyes and see them moving through time until the present day. I could see, in my mind's eye, where their paths had crossed.

Gold had been born in Switzerland of Russian parents in 1910. Three years later Smilg had been born in Boston. When Gold was four, he arrived with his parents at Ellis Island. When Gold was twelve, his parents were naturalized as citizens of the United States. In 1929, Smilg entered the Massachusetts Institute of Technology. Smilg graduated from the Institute in the same year—1933—in which Gold at twenty-three started to work for a man who introduced him to the Communists. Smilg's first contact with anything of that nature had been when, as a student at the Institute, he tutored Shumowsky, who was later accused of being a Soviet agent. By the mid-thirties, both were settling into the patterns that would shape the rest of ther lives: in 1935, Gold had himself become involved in espionage and Smilg had graduated with his master's from the Institute in Boston, going to Dayton, Ohio, to work with the air force. It was in the late thirties that Smilg and Gold met. But their meetings were not of the stuff from which one can create a James Bond thriller. Smilg had told me of their association.

"It was near Thanksgiving in 1938," Smilg had said to me. "I received a visit at my Dayton home from a man I didn't know. He introduced himself as Harry Gold and said he was a student ·at Xavier University in Cincinnati. He said he was a friend of Shumowsky's, the fellow I had tutored in Boston, and that Shumowsky suggested he visit me. The visit was purely social. Other members of my family were there."

"And that was the end of your association?" I said.

"No," said Smilg. "He visited me several times after that. Always without notice and without invitation. I remember that on one visit he said he had obtained work in another city and was passing through Dayton. I never saw Gold again . . ."

"As for espionage—"

"He asked me for no information which gave me any reason to believe he was an agent or subversive or disloyal to the United States."

"What about Shumowsky in Boston?" I asked.

"We were fellow students," he said. "My tutoring activities with him all took place either in a classroom or at my home, where my parents were at the time. On no occasion during our acquaintanceship did Shumowsky ask for any information on any subject that could be considered suspicious. I knew him only as a fellow student in Boston and later, in Dayton, only as a member of the Russian army."

That was Smilg's story—and it made sense to me. Smilg had, during World War II, become a lieutenant and had quickly risen to lieutenant colonel. He was considered *the* authority on vibration and the fluttering troubles which, from time to time, developed in air force airplanes. When mustered out of the service in 1946, he returned to Wright Field in a civilian status as chief of the dynamics branch, Aircraft Laboratory, with forty subordinates under his direction. Gold had not been in the service of his adopted country. He had been too busy being a spy against it.

What kind of creature was Gold? Said his high-school principal, "He was very mild and quite introverted, but he got top marks." Said Smilg, "He appeared to be unimpressive and innocuous." From 1940 to 1950, Gold worked in New York and Philadelphia as a chemist and, according to his own admission, engaged in espionage activities for the Russians.

"Paul," I said, "there's something fishy about this timetable. When was Gold first arrested?"

"In May, 1950," Paul said.

"And right after that," I said, "David Greenglass was arrested." Greenglass was the machinist at the Los Alamos Atomic Project arrested as an accomplice of Gold's. "Then the Rosenbergs and Brothman were arrested."

"So?" said Paul.

"Well, look," I said. "Gold entered a Guilty plea on July 20, 1950. Greenglass had been arrested then. But before Gold was sentenced, Brothman had been arrested and brought to trial, with Gold testifying against him. Then after that Gold himself was sentenced."

"Maybe the court wanted to see if he would go along as a witness for the prosecution," Paul said.

I looked through my notes from Gold's own trial. There it was, Gold's very words:

> There were conditions which I stipulated for myself. I was the only one that could meet them. Here were the conditions: first, I said the lawyer appointed (for me) must permit me to talk to the F.B.I.; secondly, he must have no Communist or left-wing tinges whatever; and in conducting whatever mitigating circumstances there are for my defense, he must not put on a circus or a show. The third point was that I must be permitted to plead Guilty . . .

As attorney for Gold, the court had appointed John D. M. Hamilton, former chairman of the Republican National Committee. Hamilton had agreed to go along with Gold's stipulations. In his statement to the judge in Gold's behalf, Hamilton said at the outset: "I would be perfectly willing to accept any statement of the crime that District Attorney Gleeson might make without supporting evidence. I come here to explain a crime and not to excuse one. I come here to state a case and not to plead one." It took three hours to state that case.

The judge, as reported in the press, gazed at Gold and his counsel in "shocked amazement and incredulity."

At the conclusion of Hamilton's plea, the court asked Gold if he had anything to say before sentence was passed. Observed *Time* magazine:

> There was something oddly inanimate about jail-pallid, soft-eyed little chemist Harry Gold as he rose and addressed the court. In a low but distinct voice, he began, "I shall be very brief. There are four points, and, with one exception, all of them have been adequately set forth in this court on the 7th of December. I am making note of them now because they represent matters which have been uppermost in my mind for the past few months. First, nothing has served to bring me to a realization of the terrible mistake that I have made as this one fact, the appointment by this court of Mr. Hamilton and Mr. Ballard as my counsel. These men have worked incredibly hard and faithfully in my behalf. . . . Second, I am fully aware that I have received the most scrupulously fair trial and treatment that could be desired. . . . Most certainly this could never have happened in the Soviet Union or any of the countries dominated by it. Third, the most tormenting of all thoughts concerns the fact that those who meant so much to me have been the worst besmirched by my deeds. . . . Fourth and very last, I have tried to make the greatest possible amends by disclosing every phase of my espionage activities, by identifying all of the persons involved, and by revealing every last scrap, shred, and particle of evidence. Your Honor, I have finished.

The judge, unlike Gold's attorneys and the F.B.I., sensed something amiss. He didn't buy the district attorney's suggestion that Gold be sentenced only to twenty-five years; the judge gave Gold the limit: thirty years. Gold, testifying in the Brothman trial, admitted he was a liar. "I had become so tangled up in this web of lies that it was easier to continue telling an occasional one than to try to straighten the whole hideous business out." He admitted, as I say, that he was a liar. The F.B.I. did not—and thereby hung our defense for Smilg.

But before we could defend our client, two others—partly as the result of Gold's testimony—went to their deaths. They were Julius and Ethel Rosenberg, who were electrocuted in June, 1953.

I knew nothing about the guilt or innocence of the Rosenbergs; but I *do* know, based on my study of Gold, that if I had had anything to do with the prosecution and sentencing, I would have spent many sleepless and tormented nights after their conviction and execution.

Executions are so final.

The Rosenbergs could have been—and probably were—guilty of espionage; but for the prosecutor to tell the jury that Gold, a confessed perjurer and spy and cheat, "furnished the absolute corroboration of the testimony of the Greenglasses" is beyond my comprehension.

Gold, without question, was an introvert who craved recognition and a status of importance and affluence. My investigation disclosed he had an ambition to become a famous scientist in his chosen field of chemistry and had worked diligently in a futile attempt to achieve that goal. The recognition he could not, through personal accomplishment, acquire was attained by Gold immediately after his apprehension as a cohort of Dr. Klaus Fuchs. In two short weeks, he jumped from oblivion to international fame. There, on equal footing, he stood on the world stage with a famed nuclear physicist by his side. At last he was important. He no longer was Harry Gold working for a pittance as an unknown and unrecognized chemist but, by his own admission, the American partner of Dr. Fuchs. Although he fancied himself the greatest spy in all history, he was in fact no more than an errand boy for the Soviet Union.

Substituting perfidy for repentance, machination for remorsefulness, and augmenting his statements with subterfuge, deceit, and cunning, Gold led his listeners down a long and tortuous path of intrigue, treason, betrayal of country, and espionage activities in which he claimed to have played a leading and important role. His account rivaled the best of spy fiction.

Gold had everything to gain and nothing to lose by talking to the authorities. He had delivered the goods to Russia. His mission was completed. Caught redhanded by the F.B.I., he faced death. His only chance of survival was to cooperate and to testify as a government witness in the Brothman and Rosenberg-Sobell trials.

The Rosenbergs, Sobell, Brothman, and Greenglass were all expendable, for they too had successfully played and completed their individual parts in the conspiracy to betray the United States.

I came to the inescapable conclusion that Gold was an egomaniac and pathological liar, skilled for years in perfidy, who had no real conscience or regard for the truth, lying so easily and so much by habit (frequently unnecessarily), that I had grave doubts as to his ability to differentiate between truth and falsehood. Gold, in his almost childlike attempts, had been unsuccessful in obtaining any information, classified or otherwise, from Smilg. This, according to Gold, was his one failure in the espionage field. "He was the only nut I couldn't crack," Gold had told the F.B.I. in a statement shortly after his arrest. "This guy just wouldn't give." It was my opinion that Gold, resentful and infuriated, interpreted Smilg's lack of cooperation as a personal affront to his proved ability as a spy for the Soviet Union.

Because of this fancied grievance against Smilg, Gold welcomed the opportunity afforded by his apprehension, to relate to the F.B.I. and later testify to the circumstances surrounding fourteen alleged trips he made to Dayton, Ohio, to visit Smilg and try to obtain classified information for the Russian government. So Gold sowed the seeds of suspicion and distrust which, through a chain of unpredictable events, culminated in Smilg's indictment and trial on a charge of perjury.

When in August, 1950, he learned that as a direct result of the information he had given the F.B.I., Smilg had been dismissed as chief of the dynamics branch, Aircraft Laboratory, I am sure Gold felt he had settled his score of some twelve years' standing with Smilg. But in 1952 when the news of Smilg's indictment at Dayton, Ohio, filtered through to Gold in the penitentiary, his cup ran over; for here was an unanticipated development which placed him in a position not only to help himself further by cooperating with the federal authorities but, at the same time, to render one last invaluable service to the Soviet Union.

Gold, without question, knew of Smilg's rapid advancement in the field of dynamics and his worldwide recognition as a leading expert and authority on surface fluttering problems at transonic speeds. His conviction would be a blow to the United States and would simultaneously remove a potential threat to the Soviet Union.

Gold had appeared twice as a witness for the government. Once in the Brothman trial, and again when the Rosenbergs and Sobell were convicted. Both juries had believed him, and it is a matter of record in the Rosenberg-Sobell trial that counsel for the defense did not challenge his testimony by any cross-examination whatsoever.

In fact, the prosecutor stated: "It was so obvious to everyone in the courtroom that Gold was telling the truth." There was no reason to believe the Smilg jury would not extend to him the same credence, and with the Attorney General of the United States, the F.B.I., and the district attorney putting their collective stamp of approval upon his veracity, the case appeared foolproof. Smilg didn't have a chance. Gold had never been defeated. He was batting a thousand.

Because the F.B.I. believed Gold, I knew the jury would too. In this country, or at least in the eyes of the juries, the F.B.I. is infallible. And, for that matter, so are Treasury Department agents and postal inspectors. Generally this is so. But they are also human. They investigate in a thorough and efficient manner. I seldom quarrel with their results. I quarrel only with the fact that sometimes they don't investigate five minutes more—and uncover additional facts which could, at times, change the complexion of the trials.

"How do you plan to tackle this one?" Ginny said, perplexed.

"By destroying Gold," I said.

"That's a large order, Foss."

"I know," I said. "And I'm afraid. Is it too *large* an order?"

June 13, 1955. The case of the United States of America versus Benjamin Smilg was called to trial in the federal courthouse at Dayton, Ohio. Presiding was Judge Lester L. Cecil, who had been appointed by our new President, Dwight D. Eisenhower. For the prosecution, there were James E. Rambo and George Heitzler; for the defense, Ben Shaman, Paul Ziegler, and me.

It took seven hours to impanel the jury.

Rambo's opening statement was brief. He said the evidence would be in two categories. The first concerned Smilg's "lie" to the loyalty boards about not having known Gold was a spy. The second was evidence to show that Gold had visited Smilg fourteen times while he (Gold) was in the Ohio vicinity.

My opening statement was, of necessity, longer. I told of Smilg from his birth to that June day in the Dayton courtroom, establishing the sort of person he was. I emphasized that evidence would prove that Gold at no time received information from my client. I also pointed out that in those yesterdays of 1938 and 1939, Russian officers and other Soviet officials as well as Soviet engineers and scientists had not only been welcomed by the city of Dayton but had, in addition, been furnished by the government with detailed information concerning developments in military planes. I cautioned the jury that they would "have to interpret the evidence employing the yardstick of the atmosphere and conditions of the late thirties and not those prevailing in 1955."

I paused, crossed my fingers, and announced:

"The evidence will demonstrate that Harry Gold is an unmitigated liar and perjurer. He will testify for the government for two selfish reasons: to help himself, and to be of service to the Soviet Union by causing the destruction and ruin of Benjamin Smilg . . ."

As I returned to the defense table, I thought, well, if the government can play the patriot, so can the defense.

And the action began.

Witnesses for the prosecution followed one another in logical manner. Stenographers testified that the transcript of the loyalty hearings was, indeed, the transcript of the loyalty hearings. F.B.I. agents testified to their interviews with Smilg. On cross-examination, though, we discovered that the agents had not been exactly sure of all that Smilg had told them, and it was my contention that the F.B.I. had then placed the wrong interpretation on what these agents had heard. If I accomplished anything during that questioning, it was to establish the possibility that, by chance, the F.B.I. *had* misinterpreted Smilg's answers. More witnesses for the prosecution—and then: "The Government will call Harry Gold," the district attorney said.

As if on cue—was it on cue?—the witness-room door swung open and there, with a United States marshal at his side, stood Harry Gold himself.

It was the first time I had ever set eyes on him.

He was even shorter than I had imagined, no more than two or three inches over five feet. He was slightly stooped, which made him appear that much smaller. He looked much older than his stated age of forty-three. The double-breasted suit he wore was pin-striped and in need of pressing.

He took the oath and immediately got on the witness stand.

He testified to the usual items: that he was in prison at Lewisburg, Pennsylvania; and that he was serving that thirty-year sentence for espionage. He then told of the fourteen visits he said he made to Smilg in Dayton—the heart of the prosecution's case, really, when you get right down to it. He described Smilg's attitude toward him as "cold, distant, and cool."

"On one occasion," Gold testified, "I came right out and asked for particular data. I explained to Smilg that engine performance information would save the Russians hours of research and much money. I told him I would arrange for him to be paid for any information he might give the Soviet Union and I told him further I could get his brother's college expenses paid in return for classified information. Smilg became tense and hostile and said to me, 'You don't know what you're fooling with.' "

The prosecution's point: Smilg should have reported this, and other such contacts, to security. That was the reason for Gold's testimony. The defense's point: such conversations and contacts were fiction created by Gold.

"You may cross-examine," said the prosecution.

The moment of truth had arrived. For three years I had been waiting to confront Gold. He, too, had been waiting with impatience for another courtroom scene in which he could star—for since his last appearance in the limelight of the Rosenberg-Sobell trial five years had gone by. And to be a numbered inmate in the federal prison system is not to be the stuff that newspaper headlines feast on. Here again—in Dayton—Gold had the chance to enlarge his own image and feeling of importance.

I knew him well—though I had only just now set eyes on him.

He was the greatest con man of them all.

For the prosecution, he had been the ideal witness. His testimony had been delivered in a soft—almost gentle—but audible voice. He had chosen his words with great care, actor that he was, using them for their greatest—and most telling—effect. He seemed logical, sincere, and believable. A great witness for the prosecution, but a deadly one for the defense.

And he knew it.

And so did the jury.

I knew that an ordinary cross-examination would never do for him. He was too wise. As suggested by John Wexley in his book *The Judgment of Julius and Ethel Rosenberg:*

With such a witness [as Gold] there need never be the slightest concern about "going over the story." Not only were his powers of retention almost photographic, but with his fertile imagination he could be relied upon to meet any contingency arising in cross-examination. Not only could he resist successfully any attempt to shake him, but he could even confound his questioner with an unexpected outpouring of phantasied detail. Last and most important, Gold believed or seemed to believe his own phantasies almost as promptly as he invented them . . . and not merely during the time he was describing them, but in a permanent sense. Hence, he could be depended on with each additional court appearance to achieve with more and more assurance the appearance of veracity.

I looked at Gold with care—and he studied me the same way.

My theory, which I was about to test, was this: if I gave Gold ample opportunity to exploit himself he might reach the point of absurdity—then, perhaps, his case against Smilg would come tumbling down about him. But my theory was easier to concoct than to make work. Gold was that efficient an adversary.

Smilg sat at the defense table, watching. So did my two fellow defense attorneys. But as I approached the witness stand I had the same feeling that I have now as I write this: I wasn't defending Smilg at all. I was defending you, whoever you are, against the yet untold lies of a yet undiscovered Gold. If Gold could destroy Smilg with lies, you are also vulnerable.

For the first hour, I fed Gold questions, and Gold in turn fed the jurors a running account of his life, accomplishments, and exploits up to his graduation from Xavier in 1940. My inquiries stressed his early life and education, focusing mainly on his days as a college student and his graduation with honors. He told in detail of his family's struggle against poverty.

I discussed with Gold the statement he had made to Hamilton in the earlier trial concerning his propensity for lending money to friends and strangers—and his embarrassment when the loans were paid back. Gold admitted these items.

He testified that at Xavier he was the lone Jew among six hundred Catholics at that Jesuit institution, but that he had always been treated with respect. "Not once," he told the jury, "during the years I had attended Xavier was there any manifestation of anti-Semitism."

"Did you feel you had betrayed their confidence by your espionage activities?" I said.

"That is true."

"I believe," I said, "you expressed your feeling of remorse at the time you were sentenced in 1950, didn't you?"

"That is true."

"At that time, did you state, 'The most tormenting of all thoughts concerns the fact that those who meant so much to me have been the worst besmirched by my deeds. I refer here to this country, to my family and friends, to my former classmates at Xavier University, and to the Jesuits there, and to the people at the Heart Station at the Philadelphia General Hospital. There is a puny inadequacy about any words telling how deep and horrible is my remorse'?"

"Yes," he said. "I did."

"And you still feel the same way today?"

"Yes, I do. Only more so."

I nodded.

Was he relaxing—just a little? I couldn't tell.

He was going great guns and enjoying every minute of it. I did not try to gain his confidence for fear that move would be too obvious. But I had to allay any apprehension he might have harbored about my ability to expose him.

His voice had become a little stronger and was assuming a ring of confidence that had not been there before.

I questioned him about his earlier life.

"Why did you become an espionage agent for the Communists?"

"I was sorry for the Soviet people," he said, "and I felt a debt of gratitude to Tom Black for getting me a job during the Depression. Black was trying to pressure me into joining the Communist Party and I wanted to get him off my neck."

"Do I understand that by becoming an espionage agent, you would get Black off your neck?"

"That's right," he said. "I didn't want to join the Communist Party. I didn't like them."

"And these are your reasons for becoming a Russian spy?"

Gold simply nodded his head.

I shot a glance at the jury. For the first time since he had taken the stand, I noted perplexed expressions on several of the jurors' faces.

I had Gold trace his meetings with Dr. Fuchs in New York in 1944 and their rendezvous later, in New Mexico, where Gold said he received certain documents from Fuchs which he delivered to a Soviet Consulate employee in New York.*

Gold testified that he had been arrested in 1950 by the F.B.I. and that he gave them a complete account of his spying activities.

I reviewed the fourteen visits he said he made to Smilg's home in Dayton. He admitted that he never received any information, but he insisted that he had told Smilg he was employed by the Russians.

"If you received no information from Smilg," I said, "why did you tell the F.B.I. about the visits you made to his home?"

Gold hesitated.

"I didn't want to hurt Smilg," he said finally. "But I realized what I had done and I wanted to make a clean breast of the whole thing."

"In other words," I said, "you were only trying to protect Smilg, is that it?"

"I didn't think he had anything to worry about. He didn't give me any information."

"You told the F.B.I., didn't you, that Smilg was 'the only nut I couldn't crack.'?"

"That is correct," he said.

"Isn't it true," I accused him, "that the real reason you named Smilg was, that by cooperating, you hoped to get a lighter sentence, but also to attempt to aid the Soviet Union by depriving this government of the services of Smilg as an expert and world authority on fluttering problems at transonic speeds?"

His eyes suddenly narrowed. But his face registered hurt. For the first time, he realized that I was after him. But Gold had gone

* While writing this account of the Smilg trial, my briefcase containing seven pages of original trial notes was stolen. Although the account that follows is reasonably accurate I have had to rely upon my memory for many of the details.

too far in his repentant role to retreat; he had to maintain his remorseful position come hell or high water.

"You mean," he said, his voice soft and sad, "that you don't believe me?"

In some way, I admired the guy. He was smart as a whip. But I said only: "That's exactly what I mean."

He stared at me.

"And all you have testified," I went on, "in this trial is the truth, so help you God?"

His eyes never wavered.

"I have told the truth," he said.

"Do you recall testifying before a grand jury in New York in 1947 concerning your association with a man by the name of Abraham Brothman?"

"I do," he said.

"You lied, did you not, to that grand jury?"

"I did."

"Why?" I said.

"Brothman persuaded me to conceal our espionage relationship."

"Did he threaten you?" I said.

Gold shook his head.

"You just did him a *favor?*" I said.

"You might call it that," Gold said.

"But you were under oath there to tell the truth, weren't you?"

"I was."

"And you nonetheless committed perjury?"

"Yes," he said. "I did."

"Of course, you're telling the truth *now?*"

"To the best of my ability."

"From 1938 to 1950 you followed the orders of your Russian superiors, did you not?"

"I did."

"Did you always tell *them* the truth?"

"No," he said.

"You actually lied to them about trips you didn't take and you furnished them with fictitious names of people you said you were trying to recruit as spies, didn't you?"

"Yes," he said. "I did."

"You lied to them over a period of twelve years, but you're telling this jury the truth?"

Was it my imagination—or was Gold less positive than he had been before? I glanced at the jurors but their faces were impossible to read.

"As I said before," he said, "to the best of my ability."

"You're telling the truth now?"

"To the best of my ability."

"Mr. Gold, have you ever been married?"

"No. I'm single."

"Then who was Sarah?"

"I have no idea," he said.

"Perhaps I can refresh your memory," I said. "You surely remember a Philadelphia girl named Sarah who was a young, gawky, long-legged girl? She worked for Gimbels. She's the one you told people you had married because some underworld character was attempting to recruit her for a house of prostitution. You surely remember your honeymoon in Atlantic City, don't you?"

"I told my employers, my Russian superiors, and others that I was married," he said. "But it wasn't the truth."

"And about a year later you told people that your wife had twins—a boy named David and a girl named Essie, didn't you?"

"Yes," he said.

"Then Essie broke her leg and David had polio."

"Yes," he said.

"And I believe that you told how your wife Sarah had fallen in love with an elderly real estate broker and had obtained a divorce, didn't you?"

"Yes," he said.

"You also told people that your brother had been killed in the service and died fighting for his country, didn't you?"

"I did."

"*Was* your brother killed in the military service?"

"No."

"In other words all these things—your romance, your marriage, your wife, your children, your divorce, and your brother's death—were figments of your imagination and represented lies?"

"That is correct," he said.

"But you're telling the truth now?"

"I am."

"Following your arrest in 1950, for a period of ten days, you lied to the F.B.I., didn't you?"

"Yes," he said. "I did."

I looked at the jury. Their eyes were no longer fixed on Gold. They had been leaning forward; now they were relaxed.

"Did you ever make this statement," I said. " 'It is a wonder that steam doesn't come out of my ears at times'?"

"It is really remarkable that it didn't occur," he said.

"Because of the lies you told?"

"I had gotten into one of the doggonedest tangles that I—"

"And you lied for a period of six years?" I cut in.

"I lied for sixteen years," he said. "Not six."

"As I understand it, you were working as a chemist and every now and then your Russian superiors would call upon you to go on some mission. Is that correct?"

"That is correct."

"In other words, you were a part-time chemist and a part-time spy?"

"You might put it that way."

"Well," I said, "how could you change over from one occupation to the other so quickly?"

"You see," he said, "I've got a switch."

"You've got a *what?*"

"I've got a switch in my mind. When I went on a mission for the Russians, I turned a switch in my mind. I focused my eyes, like radar on an objective, dismissing all else from my mind. I went ahead and got the job done and then returned to my job as a chemist."

The jurors had come to attention, trying to absorb this last statement of the government's star witness.

"Have you any other switches?" I asked gently.

"Yes. I have another switch. When I return from a mission, I turn that switch and become *Harry Gold, the loyal American* . . ."

He half rose from the witness chair—and brought up his hand in a smart salute.

"That goddamned phoney son of a bitch!" whispered a male juror. A woman juror, near him, nodded agreement.

"Mr. Gold," I said, "have you ever, to your own knowledge, suffered from schizophrenia?"

"As far as I know, I have not," he said.

"That's all, Mr. Gold. Thank you."

"But—"

"That's all . . ."

I left him on the stand. I turned my back on him and walked back to the defense table. Later Walter and Miriam Schneir would write in their book *Invitation to an Inquest:*

> In June 1955, four years after the Rosenberg-Sobell trial, Gold was brought . . . to Dayton, Ohio, for the prosecution in the perjury trial of one Benjamin Smilg. Searching cross-examination was conducted by defense counsel, William F. Hopkins, who had obviously studied Gold's testimony at the Brothman-Moskowitz trial. Unlike the Rosenberg-Sobell jury, the Ohio jury was made aware of Gold's ability to perpetuate fantastic deceptions . . .

Had I won? Yes—and I had destroyed a man.

I wondered—with deepening melancholy—as I resumed my place at the defense table what the Rosenberg-Sobell jury verdict might have been had Gold been put through the questions he had faced in Dayton. Well, no matter. The Rosenbergs are dead. They cannot be recalled. One year after Smilg's acquittal Gold, together with Greenglass, would be taken to Washington to testify before the Senate Internal Security Sub-Committee. For three hours on April 26, 1956, Harry Gold would be involved mostly in rambling and introspective mutterings. The Associated Press would label his testimony as testimony that rivaled fiction. A reporter from the *Washington Star,* noting the committee's failure to probe the real motivation of Harry Gold, would recall a Russian proverb: "The heart of another is a dark forest . . ."

Gold would be returned to his cell in Pennsylvania and to obscurity.

CHAPTER 9
the children's hour
—today

Not all my clients are adults; some have been children. Because to have children as clients is to indict a world populated by urchins of a larger growth, this chapter will of necessity be a melancholy one. I have met children of every color, attitude, and ignorance. To sit in my office and see a father—successful, expensively dressed, community pillar, country club *bon vivant*—virtually get on his hands and knees and with tears in his eyes beg me to help his child causes me to question maturity's validity. I am, because I am a defense attorney, expected by such men to pull from the fire coals which they themselves have caused society and its laws to light.

The present-day Children's Hour is a sad and lonely exercise in parental stupidity.

Half the major crimes are committed by children between the

ages of eleven and seventeen. I'm talking about rape and murder and burglary.

"But we gave him everything," some distressed parents murmur, expecting pats on their empty heads. Since they raised their child by the book, they can't figure where he—not they—went astray. They gave him everything. But freedom from prison is something that can't be bought. There is no way to *un*burglarize a store, *un*murder an old man, or *un*rape a twelve-year-old girl. Yet these parents murmur, "We gave him everything . . ."

I have heard that song so often I no longer answer. What's the use? A peculiar psychology is going around. Pundits say give children their heads and the children will turn out all right. Pundits say, "Down with discipline!" That's the song they sing. Well, if that is your song, too, listen carefully. Just the other day I talked with a gentleman from one of the largest private detective agencies in the Midwest. He read me some confessions that teen-age shoplifters had written. Frightening! We've got children walking the streets—*dangerous children who don't know the difference between right and wrong.*

The father on his knees? His teen-age kid was accused of murder. He blubbered nonsense. Then, he sniffed, blew his nose, and condemned himself for not supervising his son. Too late, pal. That's what I wanted to tell him but I didn't. He is only one of the thousands of parents who bring children into the world, then sit back and say that legally and socially they are not assuming responsibility for the children. Let servants raise them. Or let a Boy Scout leader listen to their pennywhistle tales of woe. Listen, in Cincinnati every night at 11 P.M. there's a slide that goes on television reading, *"Where are your children?"* It should read, *"Children, where are your parents?"* I've defended too many children accused of rape and murder for me to send love letters to Dr. Spock.

Worse are the imaginations these children of ours possess. Their imaginations are angry. I never put any credence in anything a child between eight and fifteen tells from the witness stand. Their stories can be deadly. Once I defended a father who had been charged with taking indecent liberties with his own daughter. The public cried for justice, but where was the justice in that case? I *knew* the fifteen-year-old daughter was lying through her teeth but I had no way to prove it. Then a most peculiar thing happened. When the case was carried over to the next day, the girl went home and secretly wrote a confession, telling that she was lying, and for some farfetched reason she put the confession that night between the pages of the family Bible. Don't ask me why kids do twisted things like that. All I know is that later that same evening the teen-ager's mother, who admitted she seldom looked at the Bible, went to it for solace—and found the daughter's written words. Luckily for the father, the case ended in his favor as the result of that "confession." But that fifteen-year-old girl was trying to send her own father to jail. And why? She burst into tears and sniveled that he had refused to let her run wild and that she had wanted to get even.

Some teen-age girls are fresh and beautiful and full of genuine wonder. But some can be dynamite. John Henry Wigmore, one of our greatest legal writers, once wrote that girls in their teens are the most dangerous witnesses the court can hear. Psychiatrists who have studied the inner storms and errant behavior of misbehaving teenyboppers suggest that no sex charge brought by one of these kids should ever go to a jury without first having the teen-ager's social and mental history examined and testified to by a qualified physician.

If you think some teen-age girls are tramps, consider the parents a few of them have. I'll never forget the mother whose daughter I was defending; the daughter had been accused of a theft. There I was, sitting in the office that hot summer afternoon, trying with words to rehabilitate the child, but there sat the mother—proud as a peacock— saying in a whiny nasal voice: "Do you know, Mr. Hopkins, that my daughter has a good job at ——————" (she named a house of prostitution). "The first night my daughter was there last week, everyone wanted her. She was high girl," her mother added with pride.

"Good Lord," I muttered. "And you're *proud* of that?"

The daughter, a sensual and attractive bit of fluff, stopped chewing gum, looked at me thoughtfully, and said in a manner far beyond her years, "What's wrong, Mr. Hopkins? Don't you ever play?"

She never changed. She went on, using her charms on whoever had the price of admission. A few months after our meeting I heard she had been wrapped in cellophane and carried naked to a visiting celebrity's hotel room. I'll not name the visiting celebrity because his name is a household word you'd never again allow in your house. When I heard of that sorry adventure I felt sadder than ever. I knew that somewhere—right then—her mother was probably proud as a peacock at her daughter's rapid rise in the world of—well, shall we say "finance"? A few years after that I saw the daughter again, or at least I think I did. They age fast in that business. I saw her in police court one morning. She looked as old as her mother had looked in my office that day. Whatever youth she had, had been sold forever.

Are we in an age of moral bankruptcy in which the things my parents taught me are foreign and impractical? All I know is, if we don't regain control of our children we shall soon reach a point of outright anarchy.

Too many small-fry losers assemble in my office these days for me to be cheerful about the subject. One lad, only eleven when he first sat across from me, is now an old prison hand. When I first worked with him he could, I suppose, have been saved from that dreary existence, but his mother was too busy smothering him with love. She was smothering him with the wrong kind of love, though. She was afraid if ever she put her foot down and made him walk the straight and narrow, he would stop loving her. Well, I wonder what she thinks now? She loved him right into prison. Each time his crime got bigger. Now a confirmed criminal, he has been to the penitentiary several times. He has no spirit left. See him walk. The shuffle of old cons. The youth that should be bubbling in him has bubbled away. Once, at the start, I had him sent to a psychiatrist—at my expense. But when the report came back it wasn't about him, it was about his mother. She loved him, but she lived in a soap-opera world. Her kind of love wasn't enough. Now he's beyond redemption. How close are *your own kids* to that point?

So goes the Children's Hour in criminal law. Never a charming interlude. But listen carefully. For your children, the Children's Hour ends the minute they take their first step toward prison gates, however insignificant that step might seem to you, no matter how petty the offense, and no matter the ease with which you can gloss the affair over. At that point, the Children's Hour has—for your children—ended. Unless corrected by you, the parents, the trip of your child from your front porch to the prison gates will be swift. I had a boy like yours, perhaps, in here only the other day. As he sat—smugly—beside his parents, I could sense the moods that filled the office. He figured they'd buy him freedom; and they figured the same.

But that day I was tired. I suppose I shouldn't have, but I let them have both barrels.

"Let me tell you something about yourself, son, a few years from now," I said, "when your record finally catches up with you. No matter which way you turn, you're going to do nothing but lose. Your parents won't be able to buy a key to the prison and no lawyer, even if he wanted to, could talk fast enough to keep you from prison. So there you will be: sentenced and . . ."

He scrooched deeper into the leather chair, but his cool gaze told me I was wasting my breath. Well, I've wasted it before, so I kept going. Hope springs eternal, as the saying goes.

"Son," I said, "I'll spell it out for you. You'll get a free ride to Columbus, so as you ride up there, enjoy the view. For years, except on television, that will be the last time you see a drugstore or a pizza place or a car you'd ache to own. Once you're behind those walls, everything is over, even the smells of the outside world. Prison has its own smell. When you first get there, you'll spend thirty days in isolation, where . . ."

"What has this to do with borrowing a car?" his father said. "Listen, I told you we could square things. I . . ."

"You'll meet other first-timers in isolation, much like yourself," I went on, ignoring the father. "And after thirty days, if you're given a clean bill of health, you'll be turned loose in the general population. Now, I figure because you're a bright guy, they might give you some kind of office work. No matter. There are no soft touches anywhere. Look around the prison yard for a preview of how you will become. Check the eyes of lads no older than yourself and see what prison has done for them. They're there, looking at things, but their eyes are dead. And watch the prisoners move about the yard. Slow. The old prison shuffle. All they're doing is going through the motions of living. They do the same things we do: eat, see stars, commune with friends, but they do it with a difference. After a while they do these things mechanically. And so will you. And, in your cell block or in the yard, maybe you'll be lucky. Maybe you won't be sexually molested too much. Maybe you won't be forced to be the 'wife' of a tougher con in return for protection. Those things happen behind the walls, son. Don't kid yourself they don't. I mean that."

For the first time I detected fear in the eyes of the lad.

But too late.

"Let's get out of here," his father said, angry. "There are other lawyers."

And they were gone—as if justice were a commodity one shopped for and bought only because the price was right or the package was pretty. Well, I have news for fathers who think that. Defense attorneys have no potions to sell and we can't weave magic spells. If we were capable of either, I wouldn't stay in this profession ten seconds.

What kids don't reckon with is this: the moment anyone—be he son or daughter or mother or father—is convicted of a felony, that person is marked for life as surely as if you'd cut off his ear or nose. Once you have been convicted, the world never lets you forget it. Your fingerprints— and your record—are on file everywhere. The Federal Bureau of Investigation makes sure of that. Any time you apply for a job you will be asked on the application, "Have you ever been arrested or convicted?" Lie about your past if you like, but sooner or later, your past will catch up with you because as a convicted felon you are marked—for life. Thousands of years ago when people held up their hands to swear the truth of what they were about to say, the judge peered carefully at the palm. He could tell—instantly —if you had ever been convicted. If you had, your palm would have been branded with a red-hot iron, marking you. Today we do with fingerprints and modern technology what the ancients did with branding irons, but both scars are permanent.

Once a young lady who had been convicted of prostitution came to my office, seeking legal help. Hers was a sad tale. She had been convicted only once of selling her body; the incident had occurred several years earlier, but she had been unable to escape her record. She told me—and I have no reason to doubt—the sordid details of her first misadventure. The moment had been so sordid, she said, that she never again violated the law, but had gone straight, found a good job, and thought the past was behind her.

"After they convicted me of prostitution," she said, haunted by the memory, "I was taken to the city workhouse with others who had been convicted for the same thing. I was a scared kid, but they were old hands. It was awful. Once we got to the workhouse and to the women's section, we all had to line up in the corridor with others, standing around or in their cells, making fun and jeering. And they made us strip, right there in front of everybody, and stand still while a doctor came along the line and examined our private parts to see if we were clean . . ." She shut her eyes. The memory was too searing. "As if we were in an eastern slave market or something," she added with a lonely whisper. She opened her eyes, wiped away a tear, and said, "Can you see why I went straight once I got out? I could never go through that again. I got a job, met a nice guy, only he didn't know about what had happened. And . . . and . . ."

And her past caught up with her. That is what happened. You see, there is a law in Cincinnati to the effect that if ever a woman has been convicted of prostitution, she can be arrested at any time thereafter, taken to the workhouse, and examined to see that she is not diseased. This had happened to the girl sitting across from me. She was in a downtown bar with her boyfriend, when a plainclothesman remembered her face from the mug file and arrested her—there on the spot. He was doing his duty as law provides. But the romance ended. The poor girl again went through the shame of that line and that examination. And her guy? Vanished back into the world of respectability.

"Why should he marry me?" she said emptily. "It's all over with us. I could see the look in his eyes when the officer came over. I mean, really. Why should he have to buy with a wedding ring something he thinks other guys bought with a few bucks?"

I asked her what she expected of me.

She wanted to know if something could be done about her record so she would not be picked up again the same way.

I told her there was nothing I could do; she had made the record, the law was the law. And thus ends another Children's Hour. And your daughter? If, perhaps, she embarks on what she considers a lark and gets caught in a raid? Will she endure what this unfortunate young lady must endure? Or have you, perhaps, passed along to her a few old-fashioned values? I'll never know—unless I see her someday in court, charged with prostitution—or worse. I would rather see her picture in the paper, announcing her wedding, than her picture in a district police station, announcing her availability for arrest. What happens, though, is up to you.

Crime on the streets, too, is part of the Children's Hour, and the thousands of tax dollars wasted on studying crime in the streets could be put to better use. If any city wanted to stop this business of crime on the streets, the solution is simple. You don't need year-long studies. All you need to do is apply common sense.

I have made the suggestion—or complaint, call it what you will— so often that every time I turn around I find myself on this or that television talk show making a fool of myself all over again. Everyone listens, agrees, and then goes home, doing nothing about it.

"I take my premise," I said once on one such talk show broadcast, "from Baker, Oregon. According to an official F.B.I. report, several years ago that town had an epidemic of juvenile delinquency. So the town fathers got together and went back to that old Confucian law which says that if a child does something, the parent is responsible. An ordinance—a curfew—was passed. I think that everyone under seventeen had to be home at eight-thirty on weekday evenings unless out with an adult. In the summer this was probably extended to nine or nine-fifteen, you understand. The ordinance went even further. It said that the first time a child was caught on the street after curfew, he would be held at the police station and his parents would be sent for. And the parents would be told—in no uncertain language—that this was a warning. Any reoccurrence meant prosecution, vigorous prosecution."

"What happened?" said the TV moderator.

"It's a very peculiar thing," I said, "but after a few parents went to jail for a few days, the F.B.I. report showed a 98 per cent drop in juvenile delinquency in Baker, Oregon, for the next year. So you might as well say 100 per cent! So I say this, then. That I am absolutely positive that here in Cincinnati—or any community—if we had such a curfew, worked out properly, of course, we could get rid of at least 50 per cent of our crime. But if we don't we will have lost control of our children. We will harvest the bad seeds sown in the fifties . . ."

From the studio audience, murmurs of agreement.

"And that," said the moderator, "is how you would reduce crime?"

"There's more," I said. "The next thing I would advocate is this. When I was a young man on Lexington Avenue in Newport and McMillan Street in Cincinnati, there was one policeman who walked the beat. He carried a mace. I've been whacked across the fanny numerous times with it and so were all the other kids. *Cheese it, here comes the cop!*—that's what we kids would yell. But you know something wonderful? This fellow was the first to help you when you were trying to do something in those neighborhoods. He knew everyone who was getting married, he knew every resident by his name, which family was having a baby, which needed bread, who was going out on her first date—everything! Whenever a stranger appeared in our neighborhood—our world of only three city blocks—the cop knew it first. And, in his own way, he would spy a little to make sure no crime was being planned or committed. I feel that if Cincinnati, which has around eight hundred fifty policemen now, would hire another three hundred, put each one on his feet on a beat, and have the beat small enough—a couple of blocks at the most—so that he could get to know the people there, no crimes would be committed because the officer would always be just around the corner. I'm sure that crimes are not committed in the presence of policemen. Now, I think if we added these three hundred policemen, we could eliminate another 25 per cent of our crime. Add that to the 50 per cent we'd cut crime by having a curfew and already, you can see, my plan would reduce 75 per cent of the crime."

"What about the other 25 per cent?"

"I'll get to that," I said. "At least, I'll get to another 10 per cent. Consider, if you will, that crime is a thing of stealth, committed usually in the dark. That's when most are raped or murdered. I advocate, then, that we spend a million or two on street lighting. Simple as that! Well-lighted streets combined with a cop on the beat—now, there's a real combination for you. I am sure that crime doesn't operate where it can be so easily—and quickly—detected. It would be hard to break into a neighborhood store if the street were as well lighted as the downtown streets are. So I think lighting would take care of another 10 per cent of the crime. That means that with curfew, cops, and lighting we could reduce the crime in the street by 85 per cent. Which, sadly enough, brings us to the remaining 15 per cent."

"What can be done about that?"

"Nothing," I said. "Nothing whatsoever. Because we are always going to have people who have criminal proclivities that we cannot do anything about. These will be the psychopathic characters, some insane, some with compulsions, some oversexed. We shall always have these. Some will be shoplifters, the kleptomaniacs who can't quit. But I think that if we stop 85 per cent of the crime on the streets, ladies could stroll about safely again after dark."

"That sounds fine, but how do you go about financing these extra policemen and all that lighting?"

"I figured it out once," I said. "The whole thing would cost between four and five million dollars. I estimated policemen at ten thousand dollars a year, more than most make now, but they should make it, so that comes to around three million dollars right there. And the lights? Well, maybe a million or a million and a half added to the ones we have now. That should do it. In the city of Cincinnati, it comes to about eight dollars per year per person—sixty-five cents a month! Now I would call that pretty good insurance to have a decent place to raise kids and to stroll on warm summer evenings. At least we wouldn't have happen here what just happened upstate. A sixteen-year-old girl went out early in the evening to the drugstore for her parents. The next time her mother and father saw her they saw only her body—raped, torn to pieces, strangled. Sixty-five cents a month per person? Is it worth it?"

Oh yes—so said the audience.

But, as I say, I have sung that song many times. All agree with the lyrics. Only there the matter ends. And so we have with us, each and every night, the Children's Hour of the damned.

CHAPTER 10
and yesterday...

The children of today, how do they get that way? The young felons I have defended and tried to reform, what have they had or not had that makes them so different from us? Or, what did we have that makes us so different from them? When all is said, I can answer only for myself and my brother.

Since we are all the end products of the kitchens of our childhoods, may I invite you into the wonderful kitchen of mine? This was the turn of the century when the country had only forty-five states, the average worker earned twenty-two cents an hour, only eighteen out of every thousand homes had telephones, and Mississippi had more people in it than California did. Men wore derbies, steam-powered threshing machines shrieked steam-whistle love songs at fields, kids swam in the Cincinnati canals, and Teddy Roosevelt was

162 ::

considered the American colossus. My brother and I lived in the age of Booth Tarkington's *Penrod and Sam,* but we read books like *Pluck & Luck, The Bowery Boys,* and *Might and Main*—listed as "stories of boys who succeed." That was us, all right! When Rob wasn't pretending to be Frank Merriwell, I was. An ice cream soda—rare luxury —cost a dime and so did arnica salve. Turkey was ten cents a pound, goose was five cents a pound, coffee was fifteen cents a pound; fifty cents bought a pretty shawl, and a tailor-made ladies' suit—advertised as fancy—was ten dollars. Men's suits? Nine dollars.

And our childhood kitchen? Beautiful. A cathedral of food scents and mother's magic. Our kitchen had a wood-burning stove. On it, bubbling even on the hottest summer day, stood an enameled coffeepot. On the kitchen cabinet of brown wood stood the coffee grinder we used to turn by hand, pretending we were streetcar motormen. Rope portieres hung in the door that led into the dining room. This was the era of hair-waving irons and hatpins. And Alice Roosevelt—from the top of her pompadoured head to the tips of her button shoes—was everybody's "wonderful Gibson girl." This was the loud and brassy era of Eva Tanguay, Harry Lauder, Adgie and her Lion, Maxine Elliott, Maude Adams, and Anna Held, who was accused of "causing sexual unrest with her lovely legs and eighteen-inch waist."

Perhaps I was a slow learner, but *my* first recollection of life was in Newport, Kentucky, across the river from Cincinnati, when I was four or five years old. We lived at 560 Lexington Avenue. My mother, nineteen years younger than my father, had had my brother Rob and me before she was twenty-one years old. She had met my father when he was a conductor on the Norfolk and Western train that chugged by her Adams County, Ohio, farm. Just a teen-ager then, she would occasionally ride his train, and my father, handsome in his blue conductor's uniform with the gold trim, was to her everything a girl should want. Straight as an arrow, he stood well over six feet tall, and was the soul of charm and dignity. As for my mother, she always had her say and she was strong-willed. She wasn't a quiet person; if she loved someone, she made certain he knew it. And she loved my father. She was a good-looking girl all the days of her life. She worshipped the ground my father walked on. They both fell in love—and stayed there forever. A boy couldn't want better parents. Their love filled every room of the house. I feel sorry for today's children whose modern parents consider that kind of love square and old-fashioned. That kind of love should never go out of style.

The Newport of that era is not the Newport of today. Switch-engine smoke, bacon frying, bread baking, kerosene, and a wet wash whipping in the wind—these things flavored its air. And the smell of the adjacent Ohio River and the dark hills beyond added to the flavor.

The old Newport neighborhood contained assorted ancients, us assorted children, and—in between—characters by the score. Our next-door neighbor, for instance, had an Uncle Harry who, whenever he attended vaudeville, always bought two seats because he wanted someplace to put his overcoat and derby. And these neighbors them-selves were the first in the block to own a steam automobile, which they seldom took out on the streets. They were afraid the gadget would blow them to smithereens.

Religious upbringing? Well, since my father was a Methodist and my mother was a Presbyterian, as a family we fluctuated between the two. I favored the Methodists for a sound reason: I liked to play tennis, the Methodist Church had two tennis courts, and you can draw your own conclusions. I have since read everything about religion I could put my hands on and I now see why some people do not believe in the Immaculate Conception or that Christ rose from the dead. But I have evolved a way of thinking that satisfies my needs. Sure, I have made many mistakes and I'm ashamed of most of them. On the other hand, if I *hadn't* made those mistakes I would not be where I am today. We learn from our mistakes. My personal religion anyway is such that I can learn from my mistakes. I have never intentionally done a dirty trick to anyone. Does that help?

Mother didn't approve of alcohol, but it was there. My father, although not a drunkard, liked his nip now and then. I can still see him, sitting in that rocking chair and saying to my mother, "You know, by George, I feel a cold coming on . . ." My mother would give him a look and, when she turned to face me, she would give me a secret wink. Then, without a word, she'd get the jug and pour my father a shot. "She always pours with a stingy elbow," my father told me many years later. "But, by George, she's a sweetheart . . ."

Beautiful moods. That's what my childhood home brimmed with. Perhaps *all* childhood memories are that way, but in my case, the memories ring true. It wasn't till I was eleven that I learned that mothers and fathers fussed. And then I learned it only by accident. With my parents I had gone to see a movie in which a husband and wife on the silver screen got into a fight to end all fights. I watched, slack-jawed with wonderment. Unable to contain myself I blurted out, too loud: "Why do married people fight?"

Everyone in the movie house was convulsed. And all the way home on the streetcar, my father kept looking at me with love and gentleness, muttering now and then, "By George . . . by George . . ." He loved me—and I loved him. Moments like that, remembered from the fragile moods of all our yesterdays, glisten with the warmth of polished gold.

I remember my father well. I can close my eyes right now and *there* he stands!

He was, as I said, a tall man; my brother and I called him "the Governor" because he had the dignity of that title. Was he lonely? All men are. Not lonely for wife and family—he had those—but lonely for the dreams that men dream and never see bear fruit. I suppose, now that I think about it, he was probably the loneliest man God ever put on the face of this earth. His dreams remained just that: dreams—and nothing more. He had wanted to go to Harvard Law School and become a lawyer, but that dream fell apart fast. As I mentioned earlier, his father, William Hopkins, came upon bad times in his Morrow, Ohio, mercantile business. Before he could bail himself out, he died. The burden of supporting the family fell upon the shoulders of my father. So the Governor put away the dream of Harvard and went, instead, to work on the railroad for a dollar a day. He did many things: he was a telegrapher, fireman, and finally passenger conductor. Once, during our childhood, he was offered a managerial position with the railroad. This would have meant that we would move to Norfolk, Virginia. I'll never forget that evening as we sat around the kitchen table after dinner. My father, the proud Governor, looked around at us and then abruptly said: "No. By George, no. We'll stay here where our friends and relatives are."

My mother only smiled with relief.

"There are things more important in life than a raise," he said, settling the matter once and for all.

That is the way—in those sweet days—fathers were.

Rob and I could hardly wait to be excused from the table so that we could dash out into the neighborhood and spread the wonderful word that our world had not come to an end after all. I remember later that night catching lightning bugs and seeing, for the very first time, the Big Dipper. Our world back then, you see, was rich with wonder and love and adventure.

Other days I remember? One that played a large part in my decision to become a lawyer was the Saturday the Governor came in, hot and sweaty, from his run and said, "Boys, I've been thinking about it all the way from the train yard. Get ready. As soon as I've had a bath, we're going to take the trolley to Fort Thomas. There's something there I've been meaning to show you . . ."

Off to Fort Thomas on the little green streetcar we went: me, Rob, and the Governor. At the end of the line we got off. He led Rob and me straight into a dark and dusty but cool little store that sold just about everything. He fed pennies into the kaleidoscope for us, told us to look in, and there—flickering before our very eyes—unfolded quick segments of the Pearl Bryant drama. She was the country girl who had come to visit two college students in Cincinnati, the last trip she would ever make on the face of the earth. Her body, minus its head, had been discovered later in the vicinity of the store in which we stood. The two students later accused of doing her in were convicted, and subsequently hanged in the courtyard of the Newport courthouse. After looking at the pictures, we went out back to where they had found her body. Later, on another day, the Governor took us to the courthouse basement, where was displayed the noose which had yanked her two convicted murderers from this world straight into the next. And, several times after that, Rob and I rode bikes to the end of the trolley line where, with shovels, we dug, looking for the lady's head. We never found it.

There was nothing ghoulish about the Governor's motive for taking us there. He was passing the bits and pieces of his dream of the law along to his sons. I never forgot it.

The Governor, born August 2, 1858, died on January 3, 1938—just before reaching his eightieth birthday. My grandfather, William G. Hopkins, born February 6, 1823, had died in 1885. My great-grandfather, Colonel John Hopkins, who knew Sam Houston, was born November 5, 1786, and died in 1874. Bits and pieces of all these ancestors were passed along, via the Governor, to Rob and me. I can remember sitting in the living room, watching the Governor rock in the rocking chair and launch into real history that concerned real ancestors.

"Now you consider your grandfather," he would say. "By George, there was a man for you . . ."

And history would unfold before our very eyes. All we needed was imagination and the slow, steady words of the Governor.

Because of the Governor, Abraham Lincoln was real. To other kids struggling through Newport's Park Avenue Grade School, Lincoln was a bearded face that peered mournfully at them from the wall, his next-door neighbor being George Washington in an identical frame. But the Governor had actually *touched* Lincoln. When Lincoln visited the area on his early travels—before he was elected President—he had spent one night with Colonel John Hopkins in Hopkinsville. Later, and even more important to me, when Lincoln came through Ohio as President of the United States, the Colonel put my father (then only four or five years old) on his shoulders, leaned forward in the crowd, and Abraham Lincoln shook my father's hand.

"By George, I'll never forget that!" the Governor used to tell us.

This Colonel Hopkins was a tall and courtly man. He had a great farm that had many tenants. Once, when one of his tenants was being kidded because his bride of six weeks had given birth, the tenant—not the brightest—came bewildered to Colonel Hopkins and asked what went wrong. "Now don't you worry none," Colonel Hopkins told him. "I can promise you that will never happen again."

A beautiful story about this wonderful Colonel Hopkins: because his wife was sick he took his hired girl to the county festival to let her ooh and aah over the sights. Now, it seems that the festival had a contest. Each time you purchased something you were given tickets to be used as votes for the festival queen. As the Colonel and the hired girl wandered about the festival grounds, the other young belles made fun of her country ways. "Oh," one teased, "are *you* going to enter the beauty contest?" The poor hired girl—all starched out in fresh but country clothes—turned beet red. Tears sprang to her eyes. But the Colonel said only, "Well, ladies, I wouldn't be surprised . . ." And do you know what that wonderful gentleman did? He went about, buying everything. He ended up with the most votes, and as a result she ended up as the festival queen. I can still hear my father telling Rob and me: "Boys, it was a beautiful scene. By George, there was the Colonel, six feet four, wearing a high silk hat and a frock coat, presenting the trophy to his hired girl. They say that when he took off that high silk hat and made a low sweeping bow, nothing more beautiful had ever happened in the county . . ."

With a father like that and ancestors like that, who needed television? Consider the time, on a railroad pass, the Governor took us to see the sights of Washington. We walked about the capital that hot summer day till my tongue was hanging out, but I'll never forget entering the one cool rotunda where, scattered about larger than life, were statues of the nation's great. In front of one, my father stopped, becalmed.

"By George," he said. "There's Sam!"

We stared—and with good reason. Sam Houston was our link with American history. We were of the same family. As we stood before that statue, all the stories of Sam Houston that my father had told flooded back—and the very statue seemed alive, looking down on us in stony contemplation and seeming to say, "That's the way history did me, lads. It was the way your father learned from his father: the real Sam Houston story . . ."

A piece of the real Sam Houston story is missing from the histories they wrote about this man, but I know what the piece is because it has been passed down, father to son, like a verbal family heirloom. Sam Houston went through life fast. He was, I guess, what we'd call a "red-blooded American," but he was also devil-may-care. He was a lawyer at high speed. Some lawyers take a long time to develop, they move slow-motion into the future, but not Sam Houston. I don't think Sam Houston knew exactly where he was going; he only knew he was going somewhere lickety-split. Before he was forty he had become Governor of Tennessee.

Sam Houston and my great-grandfather Colonel John Hopkins were first cousins back in the sweet days when a first cousin meant "family." When Houston was Tennessee Governor, Colonel John Hopkins settled on a great farm in Hopkinsville. Well, to make a long story short, when Sam Houston decided to get married—he was quite a ladies' man—he picked a Tennessee society belle from a little village called Gallatin. The wedding was a silk-hat and frock-coat ceremony well lubricated by jugs of Tennessee dew. My great-grandfather was among the guests. Sam Houston and Eliza Allen, his eighteen-year-old bride, went off in their buggy to start the honeymoon, and the rest of the kin gathered in farmhouses scattered throughout the wild and lonely countryside to finish the jugs. What happened next is history that has never been told—except by father to son before fireplaces, the last telling by my father to Rob and me in Newport, Kentucky, on a long-ago icy winter night. I can still hear the wind moan through the Ohio River Valley and, above the noise of that wind, the Governor's slow and easy voice talking history at us.

"By George," the Governor said, "there sat your great-grandfather in that crowded farmhouse living room filled with relatives from as far as three states away. There was singing and shouting and general whoop-de-doing, only all of a sudden, the front door opened, and there stood the bridegroom, Sam Houston. He was alone. They say he had a glassy stare in his eyes and they say they figured he was drunk, but it wasn't that way at all. The room was quiet as a mouse, nobody knowing what to do, whether to josh the bridegroom as was the custom, or what. The meeting was that strange. Well, Sam Houston didn't say a greeting to anyone. He just walked by the fire they had roaring in the fireplace. He went to where your great-grandfather sat, he sat beside him, and in a strange voice, all he said was, 'Gimme a drink.' So there he sat, drinking one right down after the other. Nobody said anything because what was there to say? They started talking amongst themselves and pretty soon the place was loud as ever. Only there sat Sam Houston, drinking, and there sat Colonel John next to him, both silent and both serious as tombs. Finally, though, Sam Houston turned to his cousin and in a lonesome voice that was lonelier than man was ever meant to be, he said, 'Cousin John, she wouldn't have me. She wouldn't have me . . .' And he passed out.

"Boys, you'll read in your history books how Sam Houston resigned as Governor and went west to Texas, met this Indian woman, wanted to marry her, but she was wise and said no. You'll read how he was President of Texas and later on went to Washington as the Texas senator. He even wanted his Indian woman to come with him, but she was wise. She said no to that, too. What I'm saying, boys, is that you'll read these things in the history books, but they will always gloss over why he left Tennessee for Texas. Well, now

you know why. He married a woman who did him that way on his
wedding night. Their wedding was later annulled. But that's the real
story of Sam Houston—and why he did what he did. I heard it from
my father the same way as I told it to you. And he heard it the same
from his father, who was there . . ."

As a lawyer, aware how legends are enlarged with each telling,
I say only this: I heard my father tell this story many times; I heard
it as a child and I heard it as a mature man; and not once did that
story change in the telling. Each time, till the day the Governor died,
he told the story the same way. Nothing added. Nothing enlarged.
Nothing tinkered with. My father had a sense of history; this sense of
history refused to allow him to change history. So that, as far as I'm
concerned, is the way things were and Sam Houston was.

And that is the way our childhoods were: filled with love and
history and winter winds.

My brother Rob? He feels the same, which, when you consider
the way we both are, surprises me a little. We are as different as
night and day—in just about everything but the love we loved our
parents with. In high school, Rob studied. I didn't; I played football
and coasted—uneasily—through academic matters. Because I didn't
study I had to go to summer school two years straight. My folks,
looking from Rob to me, thought I was awful; yet the Governor said,
"He'll come around. By George, I'm sure of it . . ." Nonetheless,
my relationship with my brother Rob is interesting. We are within
two years of each other. He eats fish; I hate fish. He reads Shakespeare; I hate Shakespeare. I like criminal law; he doesn't. Everything
he likes, I don't, and everything I like, he doesn't. This wasn't always
so. As children we formed the "Lexington Avenue Athletic Club" in
Newport. At the University of Cincinnati, we both played football.
But on the other hand, he doesn't gamble—and I love to. Frankly, I
don't understand how two such diametrically opposite people can
come from the same beautiful parents! Today we practice law as law
partners who respect each other as professionals, like each other as
men, and love each other as the brothers we are.

And, of course, there was Uncle Oscar! Now, *there* was a
childhood influence to end all childhood influences. He was the
brother of my mother's father—or, to put it another way, he was my
grandfather's brother on my mother's side. Although Uncle Oscar

owned five hundred acres in Adams County and was reasonably well off, he was too tight ever to marry. Each fall, as soon as the Ohio Valley became crisp with the hint of winter, Uncle Oscar would appear at our Newport home for his annual autumnal visit. I can still see him now, coming up the walk: ramrod straight, carpetbag in hand, a black broad-brimmed hat on his head, and on the lower half of his craggy face, a neatly trimmed gray beard which made him the spitting image of General Ulysses S. Grant.

He would cough once, knock, and there he'd be in our living room, occupying the Governor's favorite chair and spinning tales of the Civil War. Uncle Oscar, it seemed, had participated in every battle the Civil War had, even the ones that had occurred simultaneously several states apart. Geography wasn't his strong point; but making up history was. Once I asked my brother Rob how Uncle Oscar could have got about so quickly to so many different battles, and Rob had a simple explanation: "Uncle Oscar rode a fast horse."

In those bygone days of childhood we had a player piano. I'll never forget the magic autumn when Uncle Oscar walked in and saw it. He was beside himself. During that visit, history was set aside for the world of music because Uncle Oscar was, of himself, a center of the performing arts. He soon mastered the gadget. He refused, though, to diversify. He played only three numbers: *William Tell, The Wedding of the Winds,* and *Poet and Peasant.* While he pumped the player rolls through, he pretended that he himself was playing. He would wave his arms grandly, attack the keyboard with fervor, and would be in a musical frenzy that was, for Rob and me, too beautiful to keep to ourselves. So we sold tickets for one of his concerts.

For the occasion we persuaded Uncle Oscar to dress up extra special—comb his beard, that is, and put on his wide-brimmed hat, which he placed beside him on the piano bench while playing—but we didn't tell him what he was dressing up for. People gathered and Uncle Oscar—prompted by us—went to the piano and began to play. Unfortunately, one of the paying customers had once been to Carnegie Hall. When Uncle Oscar was going well, arms waving, scowling, swaying, this little girl was unable to contain herself. She jumped up, right in the middle of *Poet and Peasant,* and shouted: "Bravo! Bravo!"

In an instant, Uncle Oscar stopped pumping the piano, silence filled the room, he stood up, glared at her, pointed to the door, and bellowed: "Out!"

The girl, unaccustomed to such temperament or artistry, burst into tears.

"Out!" bellowed Uncle Oscar. "I'll not play as long as whippersnappers shout funny words at me! Out! Out!"

The matter was resolved without our refunding her admission. We let her sit in the kitchen. Placated, Uncle Oscar continued the virtuoso performance, continuing it so long that he played *Wedding of the Winds* several times more than the audience could stand; but so awed were they by his artistry, anger, and beard that they sat quietly through every repeat rendition. That was Uncle Oscar's first and last professional performance.

Of all the childhood moments in which Uncle Oscar figured, none compared to the Great War Game. One chilly Saturday afternoon Uncle Oscar called Rob and me aside and asked if we would like to play war. He didn't play war the easy way. He had us round up every kid within what seemed two miles. We chose up armies, spent the early part of the afternoon drilling, and long before mothers called everyone in for dinner, off we all marched, led by Uncle Oscar in full Union Army regalia—with two six-shooters, real and loaded, strapped to his side.

The battlefield was the mill bottom in Newport, about a block from where we lived. Uncle Oscar directed the battle. A horde of kids lined up on one side and another horde lined up on the other. In the center stood Uncle Oscar—and the battle started. While we ran around, waving sticks at one another and shouting "bang, bang" with great enthusiasm, Uncle Oscar added to the din by calling for cannon he didn't have and by shooting his two six-shooters in the air. The din was so beautiful and frightening that a neighbor called the police. Down through the weeds charged the Newport gendarmes —dressed in those days the way Mack Sennett dressed his Keystone Cops—and there stood Uncle Oscar, oblivious of the officers, banging away at the sky and braying for troops to charge here and charge there. And just at that moment—this is hard to believe but true—I dashed through the weeds and stumbled over a dead lady. She was right beside Uncle Oscar, who was still banging at the sky with real bullets. Up came the cops—and into the bushes I dived.

One of the officers pulled me out by the seat of my pants and demanded: "Who are you?"

I looked at the officer, then at the dead woman, and then at Uncle Oscar, who had, by then, been relieved of his artillery by the law.

"I," I said, "am the murderer's nephew."

Poor Uncle Oscar.

As they led him off to the horse-drawn paddy wagon he gave me the funniest look. So I ran home and hid under the kitchen table. For the second time that day I got pulled back into circulation by the seat of my pants, this time, though, by my mother, demanding where Uncle Oscar had vanished to. After I stopped bawling, she and my father learned where.

"By George," the Governor muttered. "Well, by George . . ."

He muttered it all the way to the police station, where he got Uncle Oscar released. The cops had quickly found that the woman, having died of exposure, had been there several days. And besides, they pointed out, the corpse had no bullet holes in it.

But that was childhood and that was Uncle Oscar, who invariably ate his dessert first, his reason being, "Well, I like dessert better than anything else, so I want to make sure I have room for it . . ."

Parenthetically, others have dropped in and out of my life to shape both me and my career. Once, as a fledgling lawyer, I thought it would be nice to be a judge, so off I went to see Nicholas Longworth—who had married Alice Roosevelt—and his associate Rudolph Hynicka, then chairman of the Hamilton County Republican Central Committee. The interview lasted even less time than it takes me to write about it here. The men impressed me tremendously, especially Mr. Longworth with his high, stiff collar and glistening bald dome, not a strand of hair on it. Here, I told myself, was a man who had shaken hands with the President and who had married the President's daughter—in the White House, no less! Heady associations for a fresh young squirt like myself. But the meeting was brief. In three minutes my dreams of a judgeship went flying out the window. "Much too young," they murmured politely, and there I was, back out on the street. I have since been offered certain political offices, but no. My association with politics was over. Still, I was impressed. If Mr. Longworth had not sent me on my way, who knows? I might never have practiced criminal law.

I also met—several times—Clarence Darrow. I suppose I must have sat in, adding little or nothing, on nearly two dozen conversations between that great man and Judge Stanley Struble. I still believe that Darrow deserves a better description than the one Adela Rogers St. John gave him in her *Final Verdict*.

And, also early in my law career, there was another important influence: George Remus, Chicago trial lawyer turned bootleg king. He ran his operation in Cincinnati. I met him first when I cross-examined his wife, Imogene, in a divorce proceeding the day before he shot her to death in Eden Park. He was found Not Guilty of the shooting by reason of insanity, sent to Lima, and subsequently released. Since I had met the "great mouthpiece" only briefly I was surprised when, upon his release, he appeared in my office. He was a jovial sort of man, to the point of being roly-poly, and there he sat, calling *me* "Counselor." He told me about some of the cases he himself had tried in Chicago. He told me of his associations with Clarence Darrow. I listened, awed. Before I knew what was happening, this lawyer was making a strange request. He said he had watched me try several cases and was impressed with my potential, but added amiably that as a criminal lawyer I had a lot to learn.

"Maybe," he said, "I can be of assistance to you, help you acquire a little more polish . . ."

His idea was to keep in the background, sitting perhaps in the third or fourth row in court, and—should he have any thoughts or suggestions on my conduct of a defense—to pass them along privately. And for the next half-dozen years that happened. It was the same as having a personal tutor. Some of his ideas I still use today. For one thing he believed—fantastic as it sounds legally—that the only two times a lawyer himself gets to "testify" are in the opening statement and the final argument.

"So," he told me time and again, "you'd better take full advantage of your two opportunities."

Also, he said that if a defense attorney discovered anything damaging about his client, he should tell the worst of it in the opening statement because, as he said, "It will come out in the trial anyway.

Of course, you'll have no right to mention your client's criminal past, for instance; but if the prosecutor objects and later brings the same facts out himself, the jury will think he's not playing fair. They'll say to each other, the defense tried to tell us that already and the prosecution wouldn't let him."

Yes, George Remus taught me many things.

My early days of playing the role of the great criminal attorney were not all that great. In those sweet days, fortunately, one didn't need a degree to go to law school; one needed only one year of pre-law. So I attended law school at the University of Cincinnati, and while attending classes, I took one of those quick "cram" courses on passing the bar, went up to Columbus, did same, and never did go back to graduate from the law school itself. While attending law school I played the banjo I had won in the army. I studied law and at the same time traveled about, playing banjo at club dates, sometimes earning as much as two hundred dollars a week, which was big money in those days and isn't hay now. Also, for a while on Saturdays my brother Rob and I worked ten hours at the Richmond Clothing Company, wrapping clothing, earning two bucks for the full day. Life wasn't all roses back then. But neither was it all thorns. We had love, opportunity, discipline, hope, ambition. Now all is memory. My parents sleep peacefully, and so do Uncle Oscar and Sam Houston and the thousands of aunts and uncles and great-grandparents, extending back through the ages, who had made of their lives a bridge that I, myself, today might know of loneliness, law, and love. For me, the Children's Hour of yesterday is done. The Children's Hour of today is far different.

Not an Uncle Oscar in the lot.

And no Governor.

And no Governor's lady.

CHAPTER 11
miracle on
miracle lane

Sammy—the character who refused to help me rob a bank in an earlier chapter—broke one of my afternoon reveries with a telephone call from Dayton, Ohio. He mentioned that he was in jail.

Sammy's conversation is filled with words like *dese, dem, doze,* plus *dat* for *that* and *de* for *the.* Had a Hollywood casting office sought a Damon Runyon character, it would have disqualified Sammy as too good to be true. I note that here because throughout the narrative I will refrain from trying to commit Sammy's beautiful speech patterns and dialect to the printed page. The words sound natural coming from his mouth, but on the printed page they seem affected and lose much of their charm.

"What's the charge?" I asked Sammy on the telephone.

"At the moment," he said, "due to eavesdroppers, it becomes

impossible for me to discuss my present predicament. This is, however, a bum rap and, Pops, I am in need of your assistance."

That afternoon found me in Dayton, Ohio, closeted with Sammy in the antiquated Montgomery County Jail. Sammy was filled with melancholy. A slight but wiry gentleman with slicked-back hair and an angular face in which were set reproachful and wary eyes, Sammy looked as if the slightest breeze might blow him off his feet. But he was made of strong stuff.

"What a basket of noodles I'm throwing in your lap this time," he said. "The joke is, I'm innocent. Pop, how's that for a twist?"

"Suppose you tell me from the beginning," I said.

"Over the Labor Day weekend," he said, "some characters kicked in the Albers Miracle Lane Supermarket, cracked the box, and made a twenty-five-G score. But yours truly is at home, with the frau and bambino, minding my own P's and Q's, and the doorbell rings, which is at four in the morning. There stands an acquaintance carrying a large grip. He asks me to keep the grip and I ask no questions. 'For your trouble,' he told me, 'here is a gift for the kid.' He hands me some bills, which I stick in my bathrobe pocket, I carry the grip to the living room, I put it behind the sofa, and then I go back to bed . . ."

He paused and seemed sadder than ever.

"Go on," I said.

"Well," he said, "about a week later and early in the morning when all law-abiding citizens should be in bed, somebody is pounding on the door. When I answered, I perceived they were the cops, maybe ten of them, rushing to and fro, waving artillery, and there I stood, barefoot in my nightie. I inquired of the lieutenant why they were honoring me with the nocturnal visit. 'Keep your goddam mouth shut,' he said, 'or I will bust you over your noggin.' Then they found the grip behind the sofa. When the lieutenant asked me what was in it I said I didn't know because it belonged to an acquaintance of mine. They opened the bag—and you never saw a more beautiful set of burglary tools.

"Then they found the bills in the pocket of my robe. So they invited me to dress and go with them to the pokey, which I did. And I've been here ever since. Two days ago the grand jury indicts me and three other guys—John Doe, Richard Roe, and James Doe—

for the burglary of the supermarket. I never heard of these Doe and Roe characters and I asked around the pokey here; nobody else has heard of them either. Whether they is or isn't guilty, Pops, I don't know, but I *do* know I had nothing to do with this heist." Sammy subsided. He had a hunted look in his eyes and he slumped forward in complete resignation to the blow fate had dealt him.

"Are you sure, Sammy, that you've told me everything?"

He shrugged.

"Well," he said, "there are a few slight details which I unfortunately may have glossed over. You know, Pops, I am not without funds and, because of my generosity to certain individuals, many people tell me things I would not otherwise have knowledge of.

"In the last few days it has come to my attention that the money the police found in my bathrobe was part of the loot from the heist. They had a record of the serial numbers on the bills— and the numbers matched."

"Oh," I said.

There was a long pause.

"Is there anything else you might have glossed over?" I said.

"Well," he said, "among the tools in the grip they found part of a metal pin that just happens to match perfectly with the other part, which is the hinge on the supermarket safe door. Why any character would choose to collect such worthless pins I do not know," he concluded, his voice filled with sadness, "but that pin has got me pinned real good. Pops, I'm a dead duck."

He carefully combed his chair.

"I hate to give you a sure loser," he said, "but I feel better to have you among those present at the wake. Maybe—" he added with a sick grin—"I'll be saved by an earthquake or something."

"Sammy," I protested, "you could always—"

But he was way ahead of me.

"No, Pops," he said. "I don't rat, and besides, the boys in Detroit frown severely on such things. I ain't going to cop out to something I didn't do, so they are just going to have to try me in court. I wouldn't blame you, Pops, if you took a powder, but I need you, and I'd like to deal you in."

Would you, who are an honest citizen and who look upon bad guys with distaste, have gotten up and left Sammy to his fate?

Are the services of lawyers only for those who get straight A's in walking the straight and narrow? Should we, perhaps, dispense with defending everyone and toss the whole kit and kaboodle into prison without benefit of a trial? Why have courts if only the good guys get justice? Isn't justice for all? What would you have done? I know, I know. You would have washed your hands of him and thus washed your hands of a system of justice which you yourself might someday need. Every Sammy I defend makes it more certain that if you shoot someone (by chance, of course) you will get a fair hearing, too.

That's why I said: "All right, Sammy. I'll go along for the ride."

A look of relief spread over his face.

"That's my Pops," he said.

"I'm going to see Paul Ziegler," I said, "and retain him as co-counsel. You'll need him."

"Anything you say, Pops. The more the merrier. We'll need six pallbearers."

Paul Ziegler, who had been my co-counsel in the Harry Gold affair, wasn't enthusiastic after I had outlined the case.

"Your client doesn't need a lawyer," Paul said. "Foss, he needs an undertaker. He's dead."

"You sound just like Sammy," I said.

"We're going to look foolish," he said, "when the jury hears the evidence."

"It won't be the first time we've looked foolish," I stated. "Remember the Roy Gambrel robbery case.* We came out smelling like roses. I know one thing for sure, Sammy has never lied to me. If he says he's innocent you can bet the family jewels that he is. But since he won't name the person who brought the burglary tools and since he won't plead Guilty, that leaves only one thing, a trial. Sammy said maybe an earthquake would come along and save him."

"Why not?" said Paul. "Count me in. With our luck, maybe a tidal wave will come along and wash all this trouble away."

I regret to report that no tidal wave appeared in Ohio that year—and so, there we were, in the courtroom of Common Pleas

---

* Tried in Dayton, Ohio, in 1953. Gambrel was acquitted.

Judge Calvin Crawford, impaneling the jury, which only took the morning to do. Opening statements were scheduled for the afternoon.

The state was represented by the county prosecutor, augmented by a former hard-hitting United States district attorney who was billed as "special trial counsel" for the prosecutor's office. His opening statement on behalf of the State of Ohio lasted over an hour and was a detailed outline of the evidence and testimony which would be offered by the state for the consideration of the jury.

I actually believe that if Paul and I had really known the extent of the prosecutor's case against Sammy, as outlined by the former district attorney, we would have been tempted to head for the hills.

He first told the jurors that the grand jury had returned an indictment charging Sammy—in conjunction with three other individuals whose names and identities were unknown to the State of Ohio—with maliciously and forcibly breaking and entering the Albers Supermarket, located on Miracle Lane, Dayton, Montgomery County, Ohio, on the fifth of September, 1955, with intent to steal property of value. He next described to the jurors how entrance was gained to the supermarket and the method employed to open the safe. He stated that for some time prior to the burglary, the owners of the supermarket had, as a precautionary measure, kept ten twenty-dollar bills in the safe and that a record of the serial numbers had been retained. This money, said the former district attorney, had, several days subsequent to the burglary, been recovered at the defendant's home in Cincinnati together with a bag of burglary tools and a part of a broken hinge pin to a safe door which matched the other half at the scene of the crime. And then came the bombshell.

"We will introduce the testimony of four eyewitnesses who will positively identify the defendant and place him at the scene of the crime two days prior to the commission and two other witnesses who will identify the defendant's red Buick convertible, which was parked near the store at the time." He hesitated for a moment and looked toward the defense table, and then, turning back to the jury, in a cold and deadly monotone continued.

"We not only will prove the defendant guilty beyond a reasonable doubt but beyond any faint or imaginary possibility that he could be innocent. At the conclusion of the case we will expect and we will demand a guilty verdict at your hands."

With that devastating declaration, the former district attorney sat down. Without question he had made a deep and, I was afraid, lasting impression upon the jury, and I personally had a feeling he meant every word he said. In any event, he had knocked my opening statement into a cocked hat. Paul asked for, and was granted, a short recess and as soon as the jurors filed out of the courtroom, I turned to Sammy. "Well," I inquired "what about it?"

It was a shaken and ashen Sammy who answered me. "Pops, I ain't been in this town for over five years, and those characters who say I was are either half-blind or they have been conned into putting the finger on yours truly, which is me. About my car, I don't know. I did loan it to a guy about that time but if he had it in Dayton, I don't know nothing about it and that's the truth!"

"Paul," I said, "we're in so damn much trouble in this rat race already that I can't possibly hurt Sammy, so I'm going to pull a Dalton."

"What the hell does that mean?"

"When I came to the bar in the twenties," I said, "there was a lawyer by the name of Abraham Lincoln Dalton practicing law in Cincinnati. Dalton was a good trial lawyer and practiced criminal law exclusively. He must have been over seventy and was one of the three Negro members of the Cincinnati bar. He stood well over six feet tall, weighed over 250 pounds and was completely bald. Whenever he appeared in court he wore a gray Prince Albert coat with velvet collar and cuffs and as he stood towering over a jury he was a sight to behold. In every criminal case, regardless of the facts, he made the same opening statement. It was brief and to the point, and I've decided, under the circumstances, to copy his technique. He would stand and bow formally to the judge. 'If your Honor pleases,' he would say, 'gentlemen of the prosecution and gentlemen of the jury. The defense will develop as the state's case progresses. I thank you.' And with that, he would sit down. As I see it, the prosecutor holds all the cards and the only thing we can do is sit back and pray he overplays his hand."

"I see what you mean," Paul commented, "and I agree with

your strategy, but I wish that earthquake Sammy talks about would hurry up and come along."

A moment later Judge Crawford said to the defense table: "Gentlemen, you may proceed."

At the prosecutor's table, the two lawyers were ready with pencils poised over yellow legal pads. They were set to record the highlights of Sammy's defense—and to reduce that defense to smithereens. I hesitated as long as I dared, then stood and bowed to the court.

"If your Honor pleases," I said, "gentlemen of the prosecution and ladies and gentlemen of the jury. The prosecution, in its opening statement, has claimed that it will establish that the defendant, on September 5, 1955, in the company of others, burglarized the Albers Supermarket on Miracle Lane here in Dayton." I paused, looked at the jury, and said, "I say to you that he can't prove it."

I sat again at the defense table before the prosecutor and the former district attorney realized I had completed my opening statement.

Slam! The former district attorney, his face a study of what we might generously describe as pique, slammed his legal pad the length of the table.

"If that guy ain't more careful," interposed Sammy, "he's going to have a heart attack or something."

The judge rapped for order. Then, in a stern voice, he asked if the prosecutor wished to address the court, his tone implying that courtrooms are not for slamming legal pads in.

"At this time," the former district attorney said, "we would like to move, your Honor, for a recess."

"But we just *had* a recess," said the judge.

"That," said the former district attorney, "was before the defense's opening statement—if it can be called that."

The judge rubbed his chin. "The court," he said, "is at a loss to understand what the defense's opening statement has to do with your request for a recess."

"It is," said the former district attorney, "because of the brevity of Mr. Hopkins's erudite remarks. We had anticipated that the opening statement of the defense would be of some length and we therefore will need time to check the availability of our witnesses."

The judge was irritated. "The court," he said, "will expect you gentlemen to be ready to proceed in exactly five minutes."

He left the bench. Exactly five minutes later, there he was, back on the bench again.

"You may call your first witness," the judge said.

For the next two days, we were inundated with witnesses whose collective testimony established beyond doubt that a burglary had taken place and that the money found in Sammy's robe as well as the pin from the hinge were part of the event. Identification witnesses admitted, on cross-examination, that they had originally picked Sammy's photograph from the police files as the man resembling the one they had seen near the store two days before the unhappy deed. Two other witnesses said they had seen Sammy's red car there.

In all my trial experience over the years I have never participated in or heard of a case prepared and presented with the thoroughness, know-how, and deadly intensity exhibited by the prosecutor and, in particular, by the former district attorney. No detail was overlooked or neglected. When the state rested its case, the former district attorney had kept his word (given to the jury in his opening statement) that the prosecution would not only prove the defendant guilty beyond a reasonable doubt but beyond any faint or imaginary possibility that he could be innocent.

The prosecution had Sammy almost convinced.

"You know, Pops," he said, "I think they proved I took part in this heist. I wasn't there but I'm beginning to think I was. You don't think I got a wheel loose or something, do you?"

It wasn't until after the state rested its case that I learned that the former district attorney and a police sergeant had, upon reviewing Sammy's record, become so incensed that they had stated publicly that if Sammy was found Not Guilty they would immediately resign their positions.

"You may proceed with your defense," Judge Crawford directed.

"We will call the defendant," I said.

The former district attorney's eyes never left Sammy's back as he marched to the witness stand, and although he made a supreme effort to conceal his delight at the prospect of crucifying Sammy on cross-examination, it was evident to all that he was more than elated at the opportunity our gamble would afford him.

Sammy was a good witness. He spoke in a clear, audible voice which had a ring of sincerity to it that might, under less unfortunate circumstances, have impressed the jury. In answer to my preliminary questions, Sammy stated his name, address, age, and marital status.

"Have you any children?" I said.

An expression of tenderness filled Sammy's face.

"I got a daughter," he said. "She's ninety-three days old today. Her name is Bobby Lou—and she's a doll."

Sammy's subjective evaluation of his daughter's attractiveness roused a mixed reaction from the jury and the former district attorney. For the first time in the trial, the jurors smiled. The former district attorney, his face set in a fixed frown, started to object but for some reason remained silent.

For the next fifteen minutes Sammy, in answer to my questions, described how the burglary tools and the money had found their way into his apartment. He denied any complicity in or knowledge of the burglary itself.

I had just about completed my direct examination—when it happened.

Without warning, Sammy turned to the jury and—over the agonized howl of the former district attorney—delivered the most amazing statement I have ever heard a witness offer in a criminal trial.

"Ladies and gentlemen," Sammy said, "yours truly, which is me, is what is known as a rogue. But I ain't no box man. In fact, I wouldn't know how to open a can of sardines if you gave me the key . . ."

The former district attorney pounded the table—blow after blow. Oblivious, Sammy continued.

"I use bustout dice at American Legion conventions," he offered.

"I object!" brayed the former district attorney.

"I cheat at church bingo games—"

"Object! Object!"

"And I beat handbooks by past the post information."

The judge in a futile attempt to restore order brought his gavel down with a resounding thud.

Bedlam.

The former district attorney, screaming "Object! Object!" moved toward Sammy in a menacing manner.

But Sammy, ignoring the commotion, shouted his oration at the jury.

"If you think," Sammy shouted, "for one minute that I am dumb enough to case a joint for a couple of hours before a heist so witnesses can identify me later when I know my picture is in every rogues' gallery, then please do not send me to the penitentiary, send me to the nuthouse for that is where yours truly, which is me, belongs. I thank you."

Serenity enveloped Sammy. He relaxed in the witness stand and looked about with tranquillity.

"I move," brayed the former district attorney, "for a mistrial and that the defendant be held in contempt of this court!"

Whack!

Again the judge's gavel.

The judge, his voice low but brimming with authority, said: "I see no necessity to declare a mistrial. That motion will therefore be overruled. Secondly, this court needs no assistance in determining who is or who is not in contempt. That motion is likewise overruled. Thirdly, the court on its own motion is striking the defendant's statement from the record and I am instructing the jury to disregard said statement in its entirety. And lastly, I am warning and cautioning the defendant that if there is any recurrence of this type of conduct, he will be held in contempt of court. Mr. Hopkins, you may proceed with your direct examination."

It was a red-faced and disgruntled former district attorney who finally resumed his seat beside the prosecuting attorney. I had to agree with Sammy's prognosis for I, too, had become convinced that if the man didn't quiet down he surely would suffer a heart attack or "something," as Sammy had predicted earlier in the trial.

As Judge Darby would have said, the time had come to desist and desist I did. I told the court, "We have no further questions, your Honor. You may cross-examine, gentlemen."

A scowling and indignant former district attorney rose—and submitted Sammy to a blistering verbal attack which became so heated that the judge at times was forced to admonish both. The battle lasted two hours—and then a moment of calm.

"Gentlemen," said the judge, "it is four o'clock. Due to the lateness of the hour, final arguments will not commence until nine tomorrow morning. Mr. Bailiff, you may adjourn court . . ."

Paul and I headed straight to his office, where each offered the other the honor of making the final defense argument. Paul finally foisted the chore off on me.

"You need the experience," he said generously—and poured me a Scotch.

I didn't sleep much that night. The more I thought about the case, the more hopeless it became for there wasn't anything to say in Sammy's behalf. This was the second time in my law practice that I had experienced the frustration and incompetence I now felt. Usually a lawyer, in final argument, can subjectively review the evidence and testimony presented at the trial, drawing inferences therefrom, and complete his address by a discourse on the presumption of innocence and proof beyond a reasonable doubt. But here the evidence was so damning and the exhibits so deadly that such an argument would not only be futile in its conception but devastating in the result obtained.

The prosecutor, the next morning, opened for the state. He hit hard and what he had to say made sense. He had been talking for some time and was approaching the conclusion of his argument, when he mentioned something about the jury's deliberation, which, for some reason, gave me an overpowering idea that immediately began to ferment in my mind. It was wild and unorthodox and, I am sure, unprecedented in law, but I had decided to become a member of the jury. I had no hope of crashing the revered and inviolable sanctity of the jury room but there was no reason I could think of which would prevent me from deliberating with my "fellow jurors" in the open courtroom.

"I think I have the answer," I told Paul.

"Swell," Paul said, but his voice was glum. "I was holding out for that earthquake."

There was only one chance in a million that my strategy would succeed but I had to take the gamble. As I stood to address the jury I realized this was going to be my toughest assignment.

"If your Honor pleases," I began, "gentlemen of the prosecution, and ladies and gentlemen of this jury. For years one of my secret ambitions has been to sit on a jury in a criminal case and objectively weigh the evidence and testimony presented by both the state and the defense, and to deliberate with my fellow jurors in order that a just, fair, and legal verdict might be returned. My calling as a trial lawyer has thus far and I fear will always prevent the fulfillment of that dream. But as I listened to the prosecutor in his opening argument, I could not help but wonder just how I would perform my sworn duties if I were a member of this jury. So I have decided to take a novel approach in this, my final argument, and for the first time in my life become a juror sitting in judgment of a fellow man. I fully appreciate that I may be severely criticized and censured for what I am about to do, and it may well be that by so doing I will render a disservice to my client. But I am willing to accept full responsibility for this hazardous undertaking and departure from recognized standards of procedure and gamble that, by doing so, we all may somehow see the light and justice will prevail.

"The first question I would ask myself, if I were a juror on this panel, would be: Has the State of Ohio proved beyond a reasonable doubt that the Albers Supermarket on Miracle Lane in Dayton, Montgomery County, Ohio, was broken into on the fifth of September, 1955?"

After spending a few minutes reviewing the testimony of state witnesses and the exhibits offered, I told the jury, "When I consider the unimpeachable evidence produced and the exhibits introduced, I must come to the inescapable conclusion—and I am sure you must agree—that the state has proved beyond a reasonable doubt the breaking and entering of the Albers Supermarket on the date set forth in the indictment and it therefore must follow that the answer to the first question must be an unqualified yes.

"If I were a juror the second question I would ask myself would be: Has the State of Ohio established beyond a reasonable doubt that money or other valuables were stolen from the supermarket following the breaking and entry? Here again the proof is clear and concise, for after only a cursory review of the testimony of the state's witnesses and the exhibits offered it must be accepted that the store's safe was forced open and some twenty-five thousand dollars in checks and cash were missing. It therefore must be evident—I am sure you will agree—that the state has proved beyond a reasonable doubt the theft of something of value during the burglary on the date set forth in the indictment.

And again it must surely follow that the answer to the second question is an unqualified yes.

"If I were a juror in this case the last—and by far the most important—question I would ask myself would be: Has the State of Ohio proved beyond a reasonable doubt that the defendant, in conjunction with others, burglarized the Albers Supermarket on Miracle Lane on September 5, 1955, with the intent to steal something of value?"

The jury listened as, step by step, I first reviewed the testimony of the officers who had found the money in Sammy's robe pocket, then the testimony of the other state witnesses—identifying Sammy's car plus this and that. Lastly, I reviewed the testimony of the four witnesses who had identified Sammy himself as the man they had seen at and around the store two days before the burglary. Each had positively put the finger on Sammy, and I pointed out that their testimony could not be ignored.

"The only defense," I said, "was the testimony of the defendant, who denied he had taken part in the burglary and who testified further that a man he knew only slightly had asked him to keep the grip for him. The defendant testified he asked no questions of the man and that the man handed him some money as a present for his child.

"That, then, is the testimony offered by the state and the defense in support of the involvement or noninvolvement of this defendant in the crime set forth in the indictment. As a juror in this case, after a fair and impartial consideration of the evidence and testimony presented, under my oath and because of my oath, it is my opinion the State of Ohio has proved beyond a reasonable doubt that the defendant did burglarize that store and therefore it must follow—and I am sure you must agree—*that the correct verdict in this case is one which finds the defendant Guilty as charged . . ."*

My Judas-like condemning of my client shocked everyone in that courtroom. Contemptuous jurors glared at me. Muffled cries of protest came from the spectators—and were quickly silenced by the bailiff. As I walked back to the defense table—never more hated—the former district attorney and the prosecutor stared in disbelief.

For I had committed the unpardonable sin: I had sent my client to prison.

The room burned with the heat of the hate concentrated upon me.

With the exception of the judge, Paul, and Sammy, I am sure everyone in the courtroom hated my guts.

The judge—a perplexed expression on his face—had watched as I turned from the jury and started back to the defense table. He knew, because of the many times that we had faced each other in federal court, that I didn't sell clients down the river; but he was bewildered.

This was also true of Paul.

I had just arrived at the defense table when Sammy in a hurt but solicitous voice whispered: "Anything wrong, Pops?"

Had I played my part too well? I didn't know. I was, right then, the loneliest man on earth.

"Mr. Hopkins?" said the judge.

I turned.

"Have you finished your . . . ah . . . argument?" said the judge.

I hesitated before answering.

The timing—thanks to the judge—had been perfect!

"I was sure I had, your Honor," I said. "But I have just thought of something else. And with your permission, I would like to continue."

"Certainly."

I turned and walked slowly back to the jury. Now I had to obliterate the havoc I had wrought.

For a long, long moment I stared at the jurors who—their faces filled with loathing and disgust—stared back at me.

"A terrible and frightening thought just occurred to me," I said. "Is this case too perfect? Is the evidence too pat? Could the defendant be telling the truth? Could he be innocent? Is he a victim of circumstances and mistaken identity? It is true that just a moment ago I told you that if I were a member of this jury I believed the proper verdict was one that found the defendant Guilty as charged. But perhaps I was too hasty in that decision. And therefore, I now say to you, if I were a member of this jury, to be absolutely sure and satisfied, I would want to explore the facts further and to reexamine the fair inferences to be drawn therefrom before returning my final verdict in this case.

"At first glance here is a perfect case for the State of Ohio. The Albers Supermarket has been burglarized and a week later this defendant is arrested. Found in his apartment at the time is two hundred dollars in identifiable twenty-dollar bills stolen from the store safe, together with a bag of burglary tools containing a portion of a steel pin hinge which is subsequently identified as the missing part of the original hinge pin of the safe door. In addition, four disinterested witnesses have identified this defendant as being in the vicinity of the store two days prior to the burglary. What more could the state prove to establish a perfect case against the defendant and what, in additional proof, could a juror demand of the state before returning a Guilty verdict? With all of this I agree and yet, as a juror, I would be worried. A sixth sense—call it what you may—would urge me to reexamine the evidence and surrounding circumstances before committing myself to a final determination of the guilt or innocence of the defendant—because as a juror, I would have to be sure.

"If I were a juror, the first question I would ask on reexamination of the evidence would be: Where is the balance of the twenty-five thousand dollars stolen in the burglary? As proved, two hundred dollars were found in the pocket of the defendant's robe; but I have not heard one word concerning the balance of twenty-four thousand eight hundred dollars. If I were a juror it would seem logical to me if the defendant kept two hundred dollars of stolen property in his apartment, but I fail to see why the balance—or at least his share —was not also found by the police in their thorough search of the premises.

"The defendant to me seemed to possess more than average intelligence and if I were a juror I would question that he would keep in his home such incriminating evidence as burglary tools used recently in a burglary, together with a broken hinge that could be readily identified as coming from the scene of the crime. The defendant testified that a casual acquaintance, identified by him only as Jim, brought the burglary tools to his home and gave him the two hundred dollars as a present for his child. If I were a member of this jury, I would have to come to the conclusion the defendant knew the man who left the bag at his home and probably knew the tools had been used in a burglary and that the money given to him was stolen property. It might follow that the defendant is guilty of receiving stolen goods, and although I might despise him and condemn his way of life, if I were a member of this jury I could not bring myself to convict him merely because he may have knowledge of the identity of the perpetrator of this crime, or because—under his code —he refused to disclose his name.

"Four witnesses have identified the defendant as being at or near the store two days prior to the burglary. In reexamining these identifications, if I were a juror, I would first consider that the witnesses originally identified the defendant through photographs from the police files and that prior to seeing the defendant in person they had been advised by a police sergeant that burglary tools and money from the store had been found in the defendant's apartment.

"Lastly, if I were a member of this jury, I would ask myself one final question: Would a man of the defendant's intelligence, knowing his photograph was in the rogues' gallery of the Dayton and Cincinnati police departments, exhibit himself in broad daylight for two hours at or near a store he intended to burglarize within the next two days? I am sure you must agree with me that such an individual would have to be bereft of all reason.

"Where before as a member of this jury I was sure and satisfied, I am now highly disturbed—for a doubt has begun to haunt me. Where before I was sure and satisfied, I am now hesitant and uncertain—for I cannot say that I feel an abiding conviction amounting to a moral certainty of the truth of the charge. If I were a member of this jury, I would have come close to making a horrible mistake. But now I can leave this courtroom with freedom of mind, knowing I have not convicted an innocent man, or a man who may be innocent, for I have a reasonable doubt as to the defendant's guilt."

I turned to the judge.

"I have," I said, "now completed my argument, your Honor."

Judge Crawford leaned forward.

"The jury," he said, "will take a ten-minute recess before the state's final argument and the court's charge."

As the jury filed from the jury box, Sammy leaned over the defense table and said: "Thanks, Pops, for the terrific effort. The only trouble is, I don't think the jury will buy it. There's too much evidence against yours truly, which is me. But thanks anyway for trying."

Court reconvened. An outraged former district attorney—his face red—rose to address the jury. He wasted no time on the accepted legal niceties. He started right off.

"I knew it!" he bawled. "I knew it! I knew it!"

He pointed straight at me.

"This latter-day Pied Piper tells you nothing in his opening statement—and then has the audacity to become an unqualified and unsworn member of this jury and attempt to persuade you that black is white and white is black. He takes you by the hand. He leads you down the primrose path of make-believe and childish fantasy . . ."

For a full hour he roasted Sammy and he roasted me.

The judge's well-modulated voice charging the jury upon the law applicable to the case was a relief to my ears. As the jurors filed out to begin deliberations, I glanced at my wristwatch. It was exactly five o'clock.

Time dragged on.

After one hour of deliberation, the jury was taken to a local hotel for its evening meal.

The jurors came back and began deliberations again.

At eight o'clock, I bid fond farewell to Paul and the courtroom. There was nothing more I could do for Sammy and since I had a murder case starting in Cincinnati the next day, I decided to head down the highway for home. Paul could handle anything that would arise in Dayton.

I awakened with a start. The telephone was ringing.

"Foss, this is Paul. How are the seismographs registering down there?"

"What the hell are you talking about?" I complained.

"We've had shocks and tremors up here for the last fifteen minutes," he said. "Damn near leveled the courthouse. Looks and feels like we got our earthquake."

"Paul," I said, "you're drunk. Go to bed."

"The jury came in with a Not Guilty," he said. "Do you understand? *Not* Guilty!"

"It must have been one hell of an earthquake," I said.

"Four of the survivors asked me to give you messages," Paul said. "Sammy said to tell Pops thanks. The prosecutor told me to tell you it was the last time he was going to permit you to sit on one of his juries. Judge Crawford said to tell you it was the first time in his judicial experience he had a panel of thirteen jurors decide a case, and although it was highly irregular, he said he didn't know what he could do about it. The foreman of the jury asked me to tell you that it was a pleasure to have you on the jury."

"I knew he was smart," I said, "when we accepted him as a juror. You know, Paul, I had no idea my comments as a juror would—" but he interrupted me. "The hell you didn't. You knew exactly what you were doing and it came out just the way you hoped it would."

"One more thing, Foss," Paul continued.

"Yes?"

"I've changed my mind about miracles. Do you remember the show *Miracle on 34th Street?* Well, I'm going to name this one *Miracle on Miracle Lane.* You've made a believer out of me."

I heard a click and the phone went dead.

Sleep finally came to yours truly, which is me.

CHAPTER 12

State versus Robert Vernon Lyons murder one

I

May 27, 1956, was, for the Ohio Valley, a wild and wet day. Rain fell without letup, flash flooding was everywhere, a viaduct-retaining wall collapsed, and in one section of the city—Saylor Park—two homes were damaged by landslides which the downpour had caused. Thunder crackled and boomed through the man-made canyons of downtown Cincinnati. As I looked out my twelfth-floor window at the storm I could see that though it was morning, the street lights were on. The day was dark, forbidding; and always there was the wind's moan, twelve stories up.

"What can you expect?" I told myself. "This is also the year of Elvis Presley, the '$64,000 Question' and 'Peyton Place.'"

I was, in fact, feeling as gloomy as the day—and I had good reason. Robert Lyons's brother was coming to see me at three that stormy afternoon. I had almost refused to see him. I mean, what was the use of anything? Robert Lyons, so said the Cincinnati police, had not only confessed to murder but had actually reenacted his alleged crime before the motion-picture cameras of the police.

The case had broken April 11, 1956, about five in the afternoon, when the Cincinnati police dispatcher received a telephone call. "This is William Worthington Pugh speaking," the caller said. "Send the life squad to 2752 Hill and Hollow Lane. I just got home, my wife passed out. I don't know what's the matter." And later that chilly spring twilight, when the police arrived, they found thirty-four-year-old Audrey Pugh—slim, solemn, attractive, given to gentle silences— sprawled dead in the Pugh home. She wore only a pajama top and a robe. She had been stabbed many, many times.

The city was horrified. Death is always a melancholy adventure but for death to arrive so abruptly—well, the newspapers were filled with reports of the investigation that followed. To make matters worse, the dead woman and her husband were both from Cincinnati's society. Pugh was president of a printing company founded by Achilles Pugh years before. They had been a quiet couple, not given to the social affairs that delight other society dwellers. But since they were among the first families of the city, the city fathers were doubly enraged. And the police were never more helpless. The police chief personally handled the initial investigation, but nothing came of it.

Nearly two months had passed. Again black headlines filled the papers.

THE METER READER DID IT! wrote Harry Mayo, and Ralph Brady in the Cincinnati *Post* said:

> Robert Lyons, 43, a water works employee, admitted with a smile at dawn Saturday that he stabbed Mrs. Audrey Pugh to death April 11th in her home. . . . He said he did it because of a "bawling out" she gave him for entering her house through a basement door instead of the service entrance, as she had asked. "She got pretty nasty with me down there (in the basement). I just ain't used to that," he told police. Lyons said the murder weapon was a paring knife . . .

On each page of the newspaper, it seemed, Robert Lyons stared back out at the public.

"Slayer Enters Jail," one caption read. "Slayer in Court—Tension Gone, He Smokes," another read.

And there I sat, waiting for the brother of the "confessed slayer" to come in.

I thought at first of not seeing the brother. What could I do? The murder had been confessed and reenacted, hadn't it? But instead I had said, "Come in at three and we'll talk it over."

Thunder boomed again over the city. It seemed to shake the building. A bad summer, I thought. The windows were streaked with the driving rain. The office was dry, serene, a sanctuary. The rain continued deep into the afternoon—and there, across from me, sat the brother of the meter reader. He was saying: "I didn't think you would see me but Bob Cates told me you would. We ain't got much money to hire a lawyer like you but Bob Cates told me to talk to you anyway."

I nodded. I told him that Bob Cates was a friend of mine, that our office had represented his son in a civil case, and that any friend of Cates's must be all right.

Bill Lyons relaxed a little. He said that he had just talked to his brother in the county jail. He said that his brother wanted to see me the next morning.

"What exactly did your brother tell you?" I said.

"He told me he didn't do it."

"Didn't do what?"

"Bob said he didn't kill Audrey Pugh," he said.

Without a word, I pointed to the headlines in the newspapers.

"Has your brother ever been in a mental institution?" I said finally.

My visitor shook his head.

"If he didn't kill Audrey Pugh," I said, irritated, "why did he confess?"

His brother's gaze didn't waver.

"Bob said he was conned into it," he said.

"You're kidding," I said, getting up. This was too much for me. I was through. I'm not the most patient man in the world, and I lost patience there—fast. I sat back down again, though. The brother of the accused appeared to be a decent citizen. He spoke in a sincere manner. Regardless of whether his brother had stabbed Audrey Pugh or closed the Suez Canal or married Margaret Truman, Bill Lyons seemed to be an honest man who was not deliberately misleading me in an attempt to aid his brother. "Bill," I said, "*who* conned your brother into confessing?"

"Bob said it was two detectives and the prosecutor."

"But why in hell did your brother act out the murder before their movie cameras?" I demanded.

"Bob said it was part of the act."

"Bill?"

"Yes?"

"Do you actually believe your brother?"

"Of course I do," his brother said. "I would know if he was lying."

Wind rattled the office windows and drenched them in the squall.

"So what do we do now?" I said.

"Well," said Bill Lyons, "he said if you'd come over to the jail tomorrow, he'd tell you all about it."

"Swell," I said.

"You'll be there?"

"Sure," I said, looking at the weather. "Even if I have to charter a boat . . ."

The next morning I drove by the office, picked up Ginny Heuser and a young assistant, Harvey Woods, and proceeded to the courthouse, where we three planned to interview Robert Lyons. The windshield wipers maintained the easy rhythm of the song on the radio, which Harvey, not cheering us in the least, sang. The song was "Mack the Knife." I wonder about young assistants sometimes.

"Harvey," I complained, "do you have to sing?"

"We can't all play the banjo," he said.

Finally we entered the jail atop the courthouse. The warden beamed at the sight of us.

"And what brings you three?" he said.

"Robert Lyons," I said.

He looked sad.

"You going to represent *him,* counselor?"

"His brother asked me to talk with him," I said.

"Well," said the warden, "I wouldn't want to be in your shoes when you plead him Not Guilty. They'll run you out of town."

Before I could comment, the warden sent for Lyons and our amiable chat was over.

Moments later, the three of us crowded into the little conference room, and there stood Robert Lyons, gazing at us with the same steady look as his brother, but I could detect fear in his eyes. I said nothing to Ginny or Harvey, but I had seen Robert Lyons a thousand times before—and I'm certain that you have, too. He was taller than I had imagined. He seemed more rawboned. He was rangy physically. But there emanated from him a universal meekness, a lifetime of unsaid but implied pardon-me's, and the sense that the moment your gaze was averted, he would fade into the scenery. He was the sort who would forever be at the end of every line that ever formed. He was the face in the faceless crowd, blending until lost among the other faces.

There was about him a kind of gentleness, too. The meek, they say, shall inherit the earth, but he was proof that before one receives one's inheritance, one must first go through a lot of shoving around.

We shook hands. I introduced Ginny and Harvey.

"Your brother Bill was in yesterday," I said. "He said you wanted to see me. Have you any objections to telling me what happened?"

"No," said Lyons.

His gaze never left my face.

"First things first," I said. "I'm only interested in the truth. I deal in facts and facts alone. As you know, you're charged with first degree murder and your life is at stake. I have had two clients burn and I don't want you to be the third . . .

"You've already lied to somebody," I went on. "You told the police you killed Audrey Pugh. You backed that up by doing it again before movie cameras. You also signed a confession saying you stabbed her to death. Then, a few days later you tell your brother that you didn't kill Audrey Pugh. What are you, Lyons? Some kind of goddamned fool? First you put yourself in the electric chair and now you tell us you were only kidding and didn't mean it. The trouble is, the public doesn't know you were playing a game. They believed you. So if you're going to get out of that chair, you're going to have to be loud and clear . . ."

Not once while I delivered my tirade did the man's eyes leave my face. He faced me quietly, seeming to digest all that I offered.

"Well," I said, "let's have it. And it had better be good."

Silence for a moment, then Lyons spoke.

"Let's get one thing straight, please," he said. "I didn't kill Audrey Pugh."

"If you didn't," I challenged, "why in the name of God did you—"

"I know it sounds crazy," he said. "I don't blame you for not believing me. But I didn't kill Audrey Pugh."

"But you *did* sign a confession? And you *did* reenact the murder before a movie camera, didn't you?"

He nodded.

"Lyons," I said, "have you ever been in a mental institution?"

He shook his head.

"Then why did you confess to a murder you didn't commit?"

"I got conned into it," he said.

"By whom?" I said.

"Two detectives—and the prosecutor."

"What the hell do you mean?"

"They conned me into signing a confession," he said simply.

"And what about the movie bit?"

"That was part of the act," he said.

"To hell with it," I said. I shoved my chair back from the table, and stood. I had just reached for the doorknob when I happened to glance at Ginny. Her head was slightly cocked as if straining to hear something she had missed. Her eyes were focused on Lyons's face. Della Street of "Perry Mason" fame is a rank amateur compared to Ginny. Ginny possesses a sixth sense. Call it telepathy, intuition, or extrasensory perception, but when Ginny puts her stamp of approval on a client you can bet the old family homestead that the odds are one hundred to one that he is telling the truth.

Ginny glanced at me. Her look of disapproval was sufficient to cause me to resume my seat.

"Foss," she suggested, "what do you say we listen to the whole story?"

Ginny seemed pleased when I said to Lyons, "All right, let's have it from the beginning and don't leave out anything."

"I think," said Lyons, "that it was May 25 that I was working the Cheviot route. It's a short one and I got through early, around noon. Well, when I came out of the last house a car was parked behind mine. There were three men. Detectives Moore and Stagenhorst and Prosecutor Roney. Roney told me that they would like for me to take some more lie-detector tests and asked me if I would. This was the fourth time I had been questioned.

"The first time was a day or two after Mrs. Pugh's body had been found, when Captain Martin sent for me. I've known him for years. We used to play baseball against each other. I told him that I had read the Pugh meter about noon on the day Mrs. Pugh was killed and that she had bawled me out for making too much noise. Then, the following Monday when I got home from work the police were waiting for me. They took me over to the Ramey house, next door to the Pughs', to see if the maid could identify me. Only she wasn't home so they took me to City Hall and put me in jail. I asked them what the charge was and they told me 'suspicion.'

"The next morning they took me out of jail to detective head-quarters, and the Ramey maid—I don't know her last name—came in. She said I had been to the Rameys' house at one or one-thirty on the day Mrs. Pugh was killed. She said I looked wild-eyed and that I changed my jacket. I didn't say anything. After the maid left, Martin asked me if he let me go would I come back the next morning and take some lie-detector tests. I told him I would and he released me. The next day I went back to City Hall and they gave me lie-detector tests for about three hours. I never did find out how they came out," he added, almost apologetically, "but after they finished, they told me to go home."

Pardon me for living, he seemed to be saying.

"Go on," I said.

"Well, then about two weeks later the police came to where I lived, at my father's home on Setchell. It was real early in the morning. I was still in bed. They told me to dress and while I was dressing, they searched the house. They drove me to the new police building on Lincoln Park Drive. They questioned me for over twelve hours. They never let up. I don't know how many detectives and police took part.

They accused me of killing Mrs. Pugh. They told me they knew I murdered her. Finally, I said, well, that if they thought I killed her, why didn't they charge me? After I said that, they stopped asking me anything and they drove me home.

"For the next six weeks I worked at my job reading meters until Roney and the rest picked me up in Cheviot. I told Roney I would go along with him and Roney got in my car with me. Moore and Stagenhorst, the detectives, were in another car and I followed them. We drove to a restaurant. I think it was the Wigwam. We had something to eat and I had a soft drink. We stayed there about two or three hours. Not once did anybody mention the Audrey Pugh murder. We just talked about sporting events but mostly about baseball. They knew that I used to pitch on a softball team. I guess Charlie Martin had told them. We discussed softball for a long time. Roney was always talking about women and waitresses. How they were stacked and built, but I didn't pay much attention to him.

"It was about four when Moore said, 'Let's go.' I drove my car with Roney and we followed the other car. We finally stopped on Galbraith Road, where Roney told me Dr. Lyle had his office. We all went inside and I was introduced to Dr. Lyle. He asked me to come into another room and the rest stayed outside. For over two hours he gave me lie-detector tests. As soon as he would finish one, he would start another. The questions were always the same and I gave the same answers over and over again . . ."

In the corridor outside I heard a deputy say, "Well, I guess the rain has stopped."

"We sure been having a mess of weather," another agreed.

Then, silence.

Bob Lyons went on with his story.

"It got to be about six-thirty," Lyons said, "and Dr. Lyle told me we would take a break. We went out and had a sandwich and some coffee and then they took me back to Lyle's office. Dr. Lyle again took me into the same room and for three more hours he gave me tests. About ten, Dr. Lyle said he was finished. Moore said we were going down to City Hall. So I drove my car with Roney and the other two were in their car. Roney told me going down that Dr. Lyle had told him that I was lying and that I did not pass the tests. He told me this three or four times.

"They took me to the same room in the basement where I had been before and started questioning me. I told them I was tired; that I had been up since four-thirty that morning. I told them I didn't kill Mrs. Pugh. They told me I was lying. Well, this went on and on. They said I killed her. I said I didn't. Moore showed me a picture of a fingerprint and he said it was mine. He told me it had been taken from furniture in the upper hall where Mrs. Pugh was found. I told them it couldn't be my fingerprint because I had never been upstairs. Moore told me that fingerprints don't lie and that it was my print. They kept hammering at me that I was going to the chair if I didn't cooperate. They said they had me cold and that I was a cinch for the hotseat if I didn't play ball. They were getting me all mixed up. I was so tired I couldn't even think. They kept on and on.

"I kept telling them I didn't kill Mrs. Pugh but they just wouldn't listen. I got so punch-drunk and groggy I believe I would have confessed that I killed my own mother to get them off my back. Roney took me over to the side of the room and put his arm around my shoulders. He told me he was the homicide investigator for the prosecuting attorney. He told me he had enough evidence to put me in the electric chair. He told me they knew I was a decent person. He told me that he worked for the county and that Moore, Stagenhorst, and I all worked for the city. That we were all one big team. He told me he had helped others who had been in the fix I was and that he wanted to help me. He told me that he wrote the ticket in murder cases in the prosecutor's office. He said that my fingerprint would put me in the chair. He told me I didn't have a chance unless I cooperated and played ball. He told me if I played ball he would see that I only spent a year or two in a veterans' hospital. He told me I must have blacked out or that it had to be self-defense. He said he could tell me exactly how it happened. I told Roney I hadn't been upstairs and that the fingerprint couldn't be mine. He said that fingerprints don't lie and unless I cooperated it was my funeral. It looked like I was a dead pigeon and didn't have a chance.

"Roney told me he could tell me exactly how it happened. He said I went to the Pugh home to read the meter and that Mrs. Pugh was slow to answer the door. That she called me a fool and told me to stop yelling. Roney told me I got mad and went upstairs to the kitchen and that Mrs. Pugh was at the sink, peeling potatoes, and had a paring knife in her hand. Roney said that I asked Mrs. Pugh why she had bawled me out and that Mrs. Pugh told me I was making a fool of myself again and that she started chasing me with the knife all the way to the front door. He told me Mrs. Pugh slapped me a couple of times and that I could not get out the front door. He said I had to take the knife away from her and stab her. Roney told me that he knew that was the way it happened and that I had better play ball.

"I was scared, tired, and sick. As I look back now, it's hard to believe, but that morning it looked like the only way I could save myself. So like a damn fool, I told them I did it."

Ginny's hand—which had been skittering across page after page of her notebook—recorded his every muted and apologetic word. My eyes had never left the face of the accused. The "sweatbox," as the interrogation room at City Hall is called, is no misnomer for that chamber. A small room, no bigger than a three-room apartment's dining area, it is soundproof, contains the charming appointments of a junior executive, and exudes a sense of calm which is deceptive. The room is bugged. Detectives in the next room can hear every word. They can also look through a one-way mirror into the room itself. Sometimes, it has been said, the police leave a pair of suspects alone in the room and eavesdrop from the next room, in the hope that the suspects will incriminate themselves. The City Hall interrogation room has, since time immemorial, been the scene where time stood still for suspects, under the unwavering gaze of watchers and listeners.

"They called in a girl," Lyons went on. "She took down what they said to me and what I said to them. Almost all the confession is in their words. You'll find this out when you read it. Then they took me to General Hospital, where they examined me. From there they drove me to the Pugh home, where they told me they wanted me to show them exactly what had happened. There was a little guy running around, directing things. I think it was Hover, the prosecutor. The first part was easy, about knocking and Mrs. Pugh letting me in, getting bawled out, and reading the meter. But when it came to going upstairs that was a different story. Roney said, 'You went upstairs next,' and so I started up the steps. When I got to the top, I turned left. They were taking movies all the time. There was a detective at the top of the stairs where I turned left. I don't know his name but he looked like a guy that plays detective in a play on television every week. Anyway, this guy at the top of the stairs grabbed me and turned me around so I would go into the kitchen. The way I had turned they told me went into the garage. I don't know whether this shows in the movies but it happened just as I am telling you. I stood there in the kitchen and then Roney said, 'You went to the hall next,' so I followed him through another room into the front hall where they said Mrs. Pugh had been killed. They asked how many times I had stabbed her and I said, 'A couple of times, I guess,' and that I couldn't remember. They asked me where I got the knife. I told them, 'In the kitchen, I guess.' So they took me to the kitchen and showed me a lot of knives in a drawer and I finally picked one out and told them it looked like that one.

"They drove me back to City Hall and had me sign the confession and then took me to court. That's the last I saw of Roney and the rest but two days later after I was up here they came and took me back to Dr. Lyle's office where they gave me lie-detector tests for a couple of hours. Why, I don't know. The next thing that happened I saw my brother," he concluded, "and sent for you."

Harvey, my assistant, slipped me a piece of paper, folded. I opened it and read: "I think he's telling the truth."

But young assistants, for all their charm and lack of singing ability, are not realists. As I sat across from Lyons the cold hard facts of the everyday were drowning me. That self-defense could not be employed was obvious. Where the defendant admits to being on the premises and later confesses and reenacts the crime, the legitimate defenses of mistaken identity and alibi are also useless. I wadded Harvey's note, stuffed it into my pocket, and thought gloomily that the situation seemed hopeless. The public knew Lyons was guilty. So did the prosecutor. So did the newspapers. That left only Harvey believing in his innocence. Ginny? I couldn't tell. I couldn't read her eyes. I didn't know what she felt. As for me, I wasn't sure.

But I had to say something, so I said, "What actually did happen that day at the Pugh residence?"

"Well," he said, "I got to the Pugh home about noon. I went to the basement door and pounded on it and hollered, 'Water man.' It wasn't long before she came to the door. I don't remember how she was dressed. She said, 'Don't come down here hollering, "water man"; come up to the door next to the garage and ring the bell.' She opened the door and I went through another room in the cellar to get to the meter. I read it. It looked like the consumption was low. Only after she bawled me out I didn't want to stay around and take a test of the meter and get more bawling out, so I marked it 'Sweaty.' She had told me to pull the basement door shut so I pulled it shut and left . . ."

At those words, Ginny's pencil came to an abrupt halt. For the first time, she seemed relaxed. I was certain that she had made up her mind about Lyons, but she gave no indication of her conclusion.

I was still in the dark.

"And that is the full truth, Bob?" I said.

"I told you I didn't kill the woman," he said. "I lied once and I'm not going to lie again."

"I have to go on what you tell me," I said carefully. "But don't get the idea that I'm not for you, because I am. I'm going to defend you. I don't want you to say you killed her if you didn't. All I want is the truth. But if I should ever find out you lied to me, we part company. I'll step right out of the case."

"I'm not lying to you," he said. "What I told you is the truth. I didn't kill Mrs. Pugh."

From that point on, we covered many subjects: the Ramey maid, the sweaty dial, the clothing and jacket he had worn that day, his early life, schooling, his boyhood, his twenty-one years as a meter reader, his marriage, his daughter, his divorce—in fact, every intimate detail that could help us in our appraisal of the man.

When at last we finished, I was exhausted. The interview had lasted six hours, and not once had anyone mentioned a break or food. As I shook hands with Lyons, I said, "Is there anything else you want to say?"

"Just that every word I told you is the truth," he said. "Whoever killed Mrs. Pugh is still at large. I did not do it."

He headed for the prisoners' quarters and we for the portals of the jail. Moments later we were out on the sidewalk—and the fresh air felt beautiful. I was wringing wet. I had developed a splitting headache. As we walked to the car, Ginny said, "I suppose you want to know what I think?"

I nodded and she continued with a bombshell. "I think your client is already in the electric chair!"

Harvey and I stared at her in amazement.

"Now wait a minute," she said. "Don't jump on me until you hear me out. The way I figure it, if you win this case you're going to have to lift Lyons bodily out of the chair. He's strapped in the electric chair right this minute and they're just waiting to turn on the juice. This is one murder case where the rules are all going to be chucked out the window. There won't be any presumption of innocence or proving Lyons guilty beyond a reasonable doubt. He's already proved himself guilty beyond a reasonable doubt by his confession and this movie bit showing how he killed this woman. You know and I know he's not crazy, so you can't plead insanity. Whether you like it or not, you're going to have to follow the French law that he's presumed guilty until proven innocent. I don't know how you're going to explain his fingerprint or his confession or the movie but if you expect any jury to vote Not Guilty you're going to have to prove him innocent beyond any peradventure of a doubt."

What she said made sense but she still hadn't answered the all-important question of what she thought of Lyons's guilt or innocence. I had mixed feelings about her opinion. I think I wanted her to believe him and yet, at the same time, I was concerned about Lyons's future if we erred in our evaluation of his credibility. If his story was pure fabrication it could not by any stretch of the imagination hold up in court—and Lyons's fate was sealed.

She didn't keep us in suspense. "You'll probably think I'm a damn-fool female," she said, "but in spite of all the evidence against him I have a feeling he's telling the truth."

I told Ginny that I didn't think she was a damn-fool female. I also felt that Lyons could be telling the truth. But what worried me was the confession, the movie, and, most of all, the fingerprint. As Roney had said, "Fingerprints don't lie."

"If they can establish he confessed, and they will," I said, "and if they can prove that they found his fingerprint on a piece of furniture in the hall where her body was found, and they told him they did, and if they can show the movie of Lyons reenacting the murder of Audrey Pugh, and they will, I'll be damned lucky if I get out of the courtroom alive."

Harvey and Ginny both nodded assent.

When neither commented further, I continued. "We have an impossible case on our hands, but if I am going to defend Lyons we will have to go ahead on the assumption that the case is not impossible. Do you remember what the scientists said about the bumblebee? After studying the bee they decided the bumblebee couldn't possibly fly because its body was too heavy for its wings to support. The only trouble was, the bumblebee didn't know this and flew anyway. Well, we're going to have to adopt a page from the bumblebee's book. This case is impossible and we haven't a chance, but we don't actually know that and so we're going ahead and, come hell or high water, we'll plead Lyons Not Guilty. This case will probably be the most unpopular one I handle in Cincinnati. The public is not going to approve of my defense of Lyons. Every man, woman, and child knows Lyons is guilty. You watch what happens when I try to upset their applecart. They'll try to bury me in rotten apples."

I was just getting warmed up when Ginny interrupted me.

"Before you drown yourself in glee," she said, "this morning at the office reporters have been ringing the telephone off the wall. I promised them I would call after our conference with Lyons. What do you two great brains want me to tell them?"

I pulled the car into the garage and, as we climbed out, I thought that one over. As I saw it there was no way to soften the blow to the public. They were going to have to accept the fact that Lyons had repudiated his confession. They wouldn't be pleased, but then, the public had already voted my client Guilty. They wanted only the real court of law and the real jury to reaffirm their decision. I realized that the refutation of the confession would be a bombshell, and that the reverberations would be overwhelming. But why delay a bomb?

"Read to me," I said to Ginny, "the last thing Lyons said to me."

Notebook pages flapping in the wind and rain, Ginny read as she trotted along between Harvey and me.

"Whoever killed Mrs. Pugh," Ginny read, "is still at large. I did not kill her."

"When you return the calls," I told her, "tell them just that and no more. That should do it."

With those words, the die was cast—and we three were in the Lyons case for keeps.

II

While Bob Lyons remained in his county jail—eight feet long, five feet wide—the city fumed because he had recanted. He did not catch the brunt of the city's anger. Our office did. One headline proclaimed: METER MAN CHANGES STORY. Another announced: LYONS DENIES PUGH MURDER. The quote "Whoever killed Mrs. Pugh is still at large. I did not kill her" parlayed a satisfied city into one that did a slow burn at first, then pulled out every vindictive stop in its verbal arsenal.

The day after our interview with Lyons, I was tied up in court all morning on another matter and did not arrive at the office itself until noon. I was greeted by Ginny, who actually seemed pale as she gave me a handful of telephone messages.

"Where," she muttered, "have you been?"

Without giving me a chance to answer, she said. "I got here early to catch up on my work and I ran into a buzz saw. For the last three hours that switchboard has been lit up like a Christmas tree. Look at Jan."

Jan's hand was trembling as she completed a call.

"That young woman," Ginny continued, "has absorbed intolerable abuse from the people who think you are to blame for Lyons's changing his story. I know how rough the calls were; I took a lot of them myself. It's a crying outrage."

Before I could comment, a coatless Harvey came out of his office, his face livid.

"You'll never get me out of this goddam case unless you fire me!" he raged. "I'll bet I've talked to fifty people this morning. I tried to be polite but it was impossible. Not one would leave his name. Everyone has been nasty but this last bastard called you a no-good crooked son of a bitch and said you ought to be tarred and feathered and ridden out of town on a fence rail."

Harvey stopped—"Say, was the courthouse ever burned down?" he inquired.

I told him that shortly before the turn of the century the courthouse had indeed been burned down by a mob enraged and dissatisfied with the verdict in a murder case and that a pitched battle between the mob and the state militia raged for two days before order was restored.

"So that's what he was talking about!" continued Harvey. "He said if Lyons is acquitted they're going to burn the courthouse again and this time they hope you'll be inside when it happens."

I finally got Harvey quieted down but it wasn't easy. He wanted to slug somebody but didn't know where to start.

When I told Ginny I was going to the federal law library to do research for a brief we were preparing for the Court of Appeals, she suggested that Harvey go with me. Before we left I directed her to let no one in the office conduct any phone conversation concerning the Lyons case unless the caller would give his or her name and address. When Harvey and I returned to the office, Ginny said we had received fifty-three more calls but not one caller would give his name. The mail didn't start arriving until the following morning, but when it did it was an avalanche. It was fortunate for us that it had not arrived simultaneously with the original telephone calls, for I doubt that my office force could have withstood such a two-barreled barrage.

The letters arrived by the score and were from a tri-state area. Harvey, staring at the pile, had recovered his sense of humor.

"Not a Christmas card in the lot." He grinned and looked out my office window to the street twelve floors below. "Somebody down there hates us," he said, "and I think it's all of them."

All the letter writers believed in Robert Lyons's guilt, and they all thought I had shown inadequate professional ethics in convincing Lyons that he should repudiate his confession.

An attack of this sort had never disturbed me to any great extent before. I had been through such vilification in the "Bingo wars," the police towing "racket," the Abbott murder case in Hamilton, the Harry Gold affair at Dayton, the road scandal case in Indianapolis, the True murder case in Kentucky, the Nichols robbery case in Columbus, and a host of other cases here and there in which I had been counsel. I was not concerned with the personal attack. Over the years I had acquired a suit of armor which stood me in good stead. What worried and frightened me was the intensity and magnitude of the attack voiced by the unnamed army of justice-loving individuals, some of whom might be potential jurors at the trial. I was appalled that so-called nice people, particularly in complacent conservative Cincinnati, could so far forget their heritage and sense of fair play as to participate in a vicious attack of this nature.

On June 15, 1956—a hot day on which the temperature climbed into the mid-eighties—the Hamilton County Grand Jury indicted Robert Lyons on the charge of first degree murder. He was immediately served with a copy of the indictment and his arraignment was set for two days later.

The Cincinnati Civil Service Commission fired Lyons from his $80.81-a-week job as meter reader. The reason? "Discourtesy to the public and failure of good behavior."

On June 17, 1956—a clear and bright day of the sort that now and then catches our city by surprise—I walked the several blocks from my office to the courthouse, arriving there just before ten and the scheduled arraignment. The sun was hot and promised to be hotter. As I passed people on the street, this one or that one would stare at me. My picture had been in the newspapers enough. At first there would be doubt, then recognition. Then they would look away.

The third floor of the courthouse, where criminal courtroom Number 2 is located, presented a scene that dismayed me—and I will be the first to admit that little the people of the city do can ever surprise me. I am, I suppose, the coroner of polite society, the trafficker with the sordid that society pretends doesn't exist. I have seen the greats and the near-greats snivel like babies in my office, trying to protect their precious little names from all-too-true charges of shoplifting or indecent exposure or other more distasteful sexual escapades. I have seen the evil in most men exposed, laid open raw, and I have, as a surgeon does, bathed the wound and mended it via that system we call courts of law and advocacy. But so long as the wound belongs to another, polite society takes nourishment from the despair of others. And so it was that morning on the third floor of the courthouse. I shouldn't have been surprised, but I was. I should have expected the mob to be there, but somehow I didn't. I turned the corner from the elevator to walk straight into it. The corridor before me—between me and the courtroom—was a solid mass of humanity, tightly packed, women outnumbering men ten to one, a bargain sale of human justice, bathed in the smell of sweat, the scent of a hundred perfumes, the babble of voices. And there they stood, backs to me, blocking my path. I decided to find another route.

Hurrying along another corridor I headed for the county clerk's office, which provided me with a circuitous approach, through back doors, to the rear of the courtroom. As I entered the courtroom I came face to face with Criminal Bailiff Bill Wiggeringloh, who looked bewildered.

"Did you ever see anything like this?" he said. "Counselor, it's been this way for two hours and it's getting worse. Some fool locked the courtroom door. Wait till they open it and this mob finds the room is already half-filled. All hell is going to break loose."

I looked about the courtroom. Bill was right. Occupying the seats normally allotted to the public were courthouse attachés and employees, together with a few citizens who through some connection had gained admission.

When the courtroom door itself was at last opened, the public swarmed in. Pandemonium. To clear the courtroom of the angry overflow unable to get seats took many deputies and considerable time. Two tables, instead of one, had been allotted newsmen. I recognized reporters from the three local newspapers and the local broadcasting facilities. But there were several at the press table I did not know, which was reasonable. They represented distant papers and the wire services. The case had reached the big time. I stepped back into an anteroom, where I waited with Bill Wiggeringloh and Bob Lyons, whom Bill had brought down from the jail upstairs. Then the three of us entered the courtroom. Instant blindness! Flash bulb after flash bulb exploded before us, creating hundreds of swarming blue dots and white blurs. The movie camera sun-guns beamed constantly. Poor Lyons. He recoiled from the explosion of light, but there was no turning back. We marched into the whiteness and found our place at the defense table.

At ten-fifteen when Judge Charles E. Weber ascended the bench, Frank Kispert, criminal clerk, called the case.

After the preliminaries Kispert turned to Lyons and read him the indictment, which charged my client with the murder of Audrey Pugh. "Are you Guilty or Not Guilty?" said the clerk, when he had finished reading the indictment.

"Not Guilty."

And again, although the plea had been expected, the city exploded in anger. Late that night clouds gathered and a thunderstorm drenched the city. But the clouds lacked the vehemence of the citizens at whom they dumped water and hurled lightning bolts.

On August 3, 1956, I went home early—exhausted. When I arrived home, hot and sweating, I saw the yardman operating the power mower. I stopped him and told him I would take over the mower for a short time. It would relax me to do so, I thought. I gunned the motor, continued the pattern he had started, and—well, that is all I remember of that day.

"How are you feeling, Mr. Hopkins?" a disembodied voice said.

I opened my eyes.

"What the hell am I doing in a hospital?" I complained sleepily. Then it came back. I had been pitched from the mower. Had tried to get up . . . Couldn't . . . End of recollection.

The nurse said I had been in the hospital since the afternoon before. She told me not to move because I was in traction. When the doctor appeared, he said I had a slipped disc. "It can only be repaired by bed rest and inactivity," he said.

"Great," I grumbled. "Hand me the goddam phone."

Ginny answered. "Aren't you kind of late?" she said. "Harvey and I have been waiting two hours for you."

"I am in the goddam hospital," I said. I wasn't feeling cheerful, I assure you. I explained my difficulty.

"So where do we go from here?" she said.

"You and Harvey check Lyons's route as we'd planned," I said.

"OK, Foss," she said.

Harvey, who had been listening on the extension, said only: "I guess this means you're not going to teach me to shimmy, huh?"

I could have got more sympathy from Ma Barker.

Three days later, Ginny appeared at the hospital. She plunked herself down exhausted in one of the chairs, kicked off her shoes, and said:

"Do you realize that Harvey and I have spent twelve hours a day talking to chauffeurs, upstairs maids, downstairs maids, yardmen, gardeners, nurses, housewives, not to mention dozens of lords of dozens of manors?" She wiggled her toes and sighed. "We must have covered at least fifty miles. But the point is, Foss, my feet hurt and nothing makes sense."

"Certainly *you* don't," I said. "Explain yourself."

"Look," she said. She and Harvey had prepared a map showing

the 138 homes the meter reader had visited on the fatal day. She had placed a red circle around the Pugh residence and—where possible —noted the times on the individual lots which had been indicated to them by witnesses who, for one reason or another, remembered my client's visit on the day in question.

As I studied the map, a pattern emerged. I saw what Ginny saw. The thing was crazy. I just couldn't believe that many witnesses had been that wrong about their estimate of time.

Then it came to me.

"Do you suppose that on that particular day," I said, "Lyons worked his route in reverse?"

Ginny brightened.

"Grab a cab, go to jail, and ask him," I said. "Find out if we're right. And if we are, find out why he didn't tell us this before."

It wasn't long before Ginny called. She was excited.

"You're right," she chortled. "He said in the excitement he just plain forgot it."

Suddenly I was tired. I scarcely heard Ginny's "I'll be seeing you" as she hung up.

The following days and weeks moved along at a snail's pace.

I had just about come to the conclusion I would have to file a habeas corpus proceeding to "spring" me when my doctor entered my room at the hospital and without any preliminaries unwrapped a package disclosing a contraption that could easily have been mistaken for a seventeenth-century instrument of torture.

"This," he said, "is a chair brace. Let's try it on for size."

The nurse handed me a pair of my shorts and assisted me with my hospital gown. She removed the gown before I could say "Jack Robinson" and I, in turn, donned the shorts in nothing flat.

I executed this maneuver with great finesse for I had become highly proficient in such fundamental "striptease" techiques as a matter of self-defense during my somewhat lengthy sojourn in the hospital.

With the doctor pulling and nurse tugging, it wasn't too long before they had me tightly encased from my hips to my armpits in a framework of steel and leather. I could hardly breathe but they both assured me how fortunate I was that the brace fitted so well. At least

I could stand upright, and when the doctor ordered me to walk I was able to negotiate a few solo steps.

Over my protests they made me ride in an invalid's chair to the hospital entrance where my wife, Anne, waited in her car. I sat rigid as Anne drove me home. Each turn the car made was a constant reminder that my back was far from healed. That night, I slept for twelve hours.

I awakened the following morning stiff but rested and immediately put in a call for Ginny. She came out to the house that afternoon and brought with her the completed report of her investigation. And what a report it was. It listed in chronological order fifty homes, twenty-five on each side of the Pugh residence, and contained affidavits and verbatim statements by witnesses establishing the time that Lyons had been to their individual residences on the day of the murder.

The report, supported by unimpeachable evidence, covered every minute of Lyons's time from 10:30 A.M. to 2:30 P.M. and established beyond any doubt that he could not have been at or near the Pugh residence at the time claimed by the state.

Convincing the jury of that was one thing, but how do you go about *un*making a movie in which your client shows how he did the killing? Or *un*make a confession? And always, looming like a nightmare about to unfold, was the specter of that fingerprint.

By agreement of all counsel and with the approval of the court, the Lyons trial was set for November 1, 1956, at 10 A.M. before Judge Carson Hoy. Some three weeks earlier, in the presence of Robert Lyons, Prosecutor C. Watson Hover, Judge Carson Hoy, and myself, the sheriff drew from the jury wheel seventy-five candidates for the jury. That was only the beginning. The list of names of the jurors was served upon Lyons and me the next day, a gloomy day. The sun didn't shine once. The newspapers were filled with election stories: Eisenhower versus Stevenson. The radios were littered with election advertising.

Now the real work of jury selection began. I tossed the list to Ginny.

"The same detective agency?" she said.

I nodded.

This business of hiring a detective agency to investigate the background and reputation of each possible juror is standard practice.

That both sides, prosecution as well as defense, retain detective agencies to explore the background of the candidates is a fact in cases of such magnitude. This is done to assure each attorney of the information he needs to make the subjective judgment as to whether this juror stays or that juror goes.

Ginny, Harvey, and I spent the last few days before the trial planning strategy and studying the jury list and the confidential information on each potential juror which had been furnished us by our investigators.

"The question is," I said, "what kind of jury should try Lyons?"

"Yeah," said Harvey. "His peers, but who are his peers?"

When we thought of the sad little street along the Ohio River where Lyons had been born and raised, we knew that his peers were not people of wealth and social position.

"Certainly no one who has inherited money," Ginny offered.

"Maybe the crowd from the H & H Café," said Harvey, "around the corner from the Lyons house."

"The jury wheel didn't empty out that neighborhood bar," I said, "but you're on the right track. And we're going to need people like that if we're going to walk Lyons out of that courtroom."

That the majority of the jury had to be composed of men and women who occupied a rung on the economic ladder comparable to Lyons's was, of course, a foregone conclusion. They had to know what it meant to work for someone else—and the hazards involved. They had to have accumulated little worldly wealth and to have acquired the melancholy knowledge that life is no bed of roses. They had to be people who understood regimentation—and the pressures that had caused Lyons to sign that stupid confession. They had to be, simply put, part and parcel of the hardworking, freedom-loving, and law-abiding citizens who form the core of American justice, ride buses to work, and drink beer at the corner pub.

So, at long last the Lyons case was actually going to trial. As far as I was concerned, the sooner the better. A lot of work had gone into our preparation, and we were as ready as we were ever going to be.

And then it happened. I received a phone call. The party on the line refused to give his name but, under Ginny's urgings, advised her that his call concerned the Lyons case. Why she permitted him to talk to me I don't know except that I have always felt that Ginny has a gift of clairvoyance which from time to time manifests itself in the decisions she makes.

"Mr. Hopkins?" inquired a voice. I acknowledged my identity and the voice continued: "I am sure you will understand my reluctance in disclosing my name when you hear what I have to say."

"Go ahead," I said.

"I want you to understand," the voice said, "that I believe in law and order but I also believe in fair play. I don't like what is going on. I think as Lyons's attorney you should be advised of a certain malfeasance upon the part of the coroner in his autopsy report."

"What's wrong with the report?" I asked.

"There's nothing wrong with the report," the voice continued, "but it does not contain one item which the coroner found."

"And what is that?" I asked.

"He found a piece of metal in Mrs. Pugh's shoulder," the caller said, "which has been identified as the broken-off point of a knife blade."

"Well, what has all this got to do with Lyons?" I asked.

"I don't know whether you know it or not," the voice said, "but the prosecution has a knife with one blade missing which came from Lyons's home and the composition of the metal in the remaining blades matches 100 per cent with the piece taken from Mrs. Pugh's shoulder. They intend to introduce the knife as the murder weapon and then surprise you with the matching piece."

I heard a click. The voice had severed the connection. To say that the news which I had heard demoralized me would be the understatement of the century.

"How do you like that?" I muttered. This cry brought Ginny and Harvey on the double. God! I was furious. Furious at the coroner for his concealment of this evidence. Furious at Lyons for playing me for a sucker and furious at myself, Ginny, and Harvey for being taken in by his story.

"I'm going to jail," I said, "and when I get through with that meter reader there's not going to be enough left to go to trial!"

Ginny had, at my direction, heard and recorded the telephone conversation. While her face was drawn, she did not seem to share my opinion as to the hopelessness of our position.

"Now wait a minute, Foss," she said. "Don't you think we'd better talk this thing over?"

"Talk it over, hell," I said. I grabbed my hat and headed for the door.

We were at the jail in five minutes. A moment later Lyons shuffled into the consultation room.

"What the hell's the idea of your lying to me?" I began. Lyons's face registered bewilderment.

I didn't give him a chance to answer.

"I told you before and I'm telling you again that a man can't represent himself, for if he tries he has a goddam fool for a client. I begged you to tell me the truth but you lied to me."

Lyons opened his mouth to answer but I continued my harangue.

"We have spent time and money in the preparation of your case. I have a lot at stake but you have much more. You could lose your life. I don't want to see you get hurt and I don't want to get up before a jury and make a fool of myself. Now listen to me. They found a knife at your home. One blade is missing. It's a pocketknife. In Mrs. Pugh's shoulder there is a piece of metal. That knife has been sent to the laboratory to be tested and the metal taken from Mrs. Pugh's body matches the metal in that knife one hundred per cent. Why in the name of God won't you level with me?"

"But I am leveling with you," he said.

I stood up to leave. I wasn't about to walk out on Lyons but I wanted him to think I was. Ginny stopped me.

"Why don't you hear what he's got to say, Foss?" she said. "We haven't anything else to do."

I resumed my seat.

"I am leveling with you," Lyons said. "Everything I've told you is the truth. I did not kill Mrs. Pugh. I can tell you how the knife got broken but I don't know nothing about a piece of metal in her shoulder. I broke the blade right after I got out of the army. I broke it about halfway off. I kept the knife but I don't know what I did with the part of the blade that broke off. It happened about 1945. Out in Deer Park or Rossmoyne. I think Redmont or Rosemont Avenue.

There is a letter down at the Water Works from a man that said I was hammering on his meter and broke it. I had to write a statement. Nick Tierney would know about this. The Ford box was stuck and I was trying to open it with my knife. I think the blade broke half or a little more off. That was the last time I carried a knife. I guess I put it in the dish on the buffet. The fellow that read it after me had the same trouble. It got stuck. They do that a lot."

I couldn't believe what I was hearing. This case had been crazy since its inception, but Lyons's explanation was too good to be true. It was too much to expect that the records of the Water Works would corroborate him. But on examination I found that the records corroborated Lyons one hundred per cent. There was the letter from the disgruntled citizen and a statement over Lyons's signature setting forth that he had broken a blade of his pocketknife trying to force open the meter box in question.

I next consulted a metallurgist, who advised me that because of the universal ingredients of the metal employed to make the millions of knife blades that are manufactured, it would be impossible to identify one piece with another unless the two pieces of a broken blade could be physically joined.

Once again Lyons' credibility had withstood a severe test and the state's alleged murder weapon, if offered, could easily become a boomerang of considerable consequence.

I was not naïve enough, however, to believe or hope that the prosecutor would fail to hear of our visit to the Water Works Department. I am sure that he was tipped off, for not once during the trial did the coroner testify as to the piece of metal he had found in Mrs. Pugh's shoulder—nor did the prosecutor mention Lyons's broken knife.

One week before the trial the ballyhoo began. The presses rolled in an awesome display of news coverage, unheard of normally in this community. News stories of international import were crowded off the front page to make room for articles covering some facet of the approaching murder trial. Important bulletins on national affairs became secondary to the Lyons case as radio and television stations, not to be outdone by the press, went all out in their coverage of the pre-trial activities. Let it be said that by the time November 1 rolled around, thanks to the news media, every man, woman, and child in the tri-state area and even beyond had been made aware that Robert Lyons was going to trial and that he had confessed to murdering Audrey Pugh.

At long last it was November 1. I arrived at the courthouse at nine forty-five and immediately took the elevator to the third floor. The hallway leading to courtroom Number 2 was again packed solidly and again it was necessary for me to take the route through the clerk's office to reach it.

To provide additional spectator space, two rows of folding chairs extending the width of the courtroom had been placed in front of the permanent seats. Running parallel to the folding chairs—and an arm's length away—were four tables for the press. At each table were two chairs facing the bench and on the table before each chair was a place card naming the newspaper, radio, or television station allotted that space. It was almost as if someone were giving an enormous dinner party. Approximately ten feet in front of the news media were two long tables forming a large L. The defense portion of the tables faced the jury, twenty-five feet distant; the prosecution portion faced the judge. Every seat was filled. Outside in the corridors, the babble of malcontents who had not got seats for the circus could be heard.

Bailiff Cecil Gray rapped the marble with his gavel and announced, "This separate session of the Court of Common Pleas, his Honor Carson Hoy presiding, is now in session." Again the gavel struck.

"Are you gentlemen ready to proceed?" the judge said.

"The State of Ohio is ready," said C. Watson Hover.

"The defense is also ready," I said, "but there is a matter I want to take up with the court prior to the impaneling of the jury. I wish to move that the jury herein be sequestered during the trial of this case. I feel that any juror might and probably will be impressed and influenced by others if this jury is not sequestered . . ."

I went on, noting that no other case since the Anna Marie Hahn murder trial had had so much publicity as ours. I noted that after the murder itself, the community was—"rightfully so," I suggested—up in arms. I noted that the public had a high interest in the outcome and that thousands—"including headline writers," I wanted to add but didn't—had voiced their opinion as to the guilt or innocence of my client, mainly the former. I told the judge we would have had to have been deaf, dumb, and blind not to be aware of the Pugh killing and not to have formed such an opinion.

"This motion," I said, "if granted will probably not be a popular one with the jury. I may well be criticized, but I must take that chance. I believe that I would be derelict in my duty if I did not make this request, for we are here trying a man for his life . . ."

Those in the audience murmured, then the murmur of its own volition died.

I mentioned the Sheppard murder case in Cleveland, noting that the jury, not sequestered, had listened to Walter Winchell broadcasting his opinion of the doctor's guilt.

"Although," I concluded, "you admonish the jury not to read newspapers or listen to radio broadcasts or view telecasts, you know and I know that it will be impossible to shield each of them from outside influence and potential contamination. We don't want the news media or the public at large to decide this case. We want and have the right to demand that the duly impaneled jury decides Lyons's guilt or innocence upon the evidence and testimony it hears in this courtroom and not upon diverse opinions based upon conjecture and half-truths unchallenged by recognized legal tests."

The prosecutor opposed my motion, saying he did not "feel it necessary to impede the progress of this case by adding an additional burden to this jury."

That put the matter squarely up to the judge. He did not hesitate. His reply was swift.

"While it is true," he said, "that this case has attracted an unusual amount of public attention, I have full confidence in the integrity and sense of fairness of the people of this community generally and of this jury panel. I intend to instruct the jury fully upon its duty to try the case solely upon the law and upon the evidence introduced in open court and to exclude from its mind any impressions gained from any other source. I feel certain that the jury finally selected in this case will realize the importance of following these instructions implicitly. The motion to sequester the jury is therefore overruled. Should a situation arise later during the trial of this case which in the opinion of counsel requires a reconsideration of the matter by this court, counsel may feel free to renew his motion."

And that was that.

"Call the first juror," the judge ordered the clerk.

I returned to my table and began to earn my money.

In the absence of extrasensory perception, telepathy, and clair-voyance, it calls upon every ounce of ingenuity, skill, and training to weed out and excuse or challenge those prospective jurors who, in the opinion of counsel, would not—or could not—for innumerable reasons render a fair, legal, and just verdict. Even with all the safeguards present and the right of both state and the defense to exercise challenges for cause and peremptory challenges, every now and then a juror weathers the barrage of inquiries and is accepted by all concerned—although it later develops that he or she is emotionally unstable and completely unfit to decide the issues and render a legal verdict.

This was going through my mind as the clerk escorted the first prospective juror into the courtroom. A lady.

For a brief and bewildered moment she stood looking about at the crowd, and then, when requested by the court, sat on the edge of her chair, the picture of stage fright and despair. I actually felt sorry for her.

The prosecutor asked many questions concerning her marital status, length of residence in the community, children, their ages, her husband's occupation, whether she knew the deceased, was acquainted with the accused, and then, "Have you read about the case or discussed it with anyone?"

"I have," she told the prosecutor.

"From what you have read or discussed with others, have you formed an opinion as to the guilt or innocence of this defendant?"

The judge interrupted to say that under no circumstances was she to indicate what her opinion was but merely to answer whether or not she had formed such an opinion.

"I do have an opinion in this case," said the juror.

"Is it a fixed opinion which you could not lay aside in order to try to decide this case only upon the evidence and testimony you hear in this courtroom and the law given to you by the court?" the prosecutor asked.

The lady didn't hesitate.

"I have," she said, "a fixed opinion and I could not lay it aside."

My challenge for cause was granted and the juror was excused.

A sidelight on that juror, however: It is a matter of record that although this juror was not permitted to voice her opinion in court, immediately upon leaving the courtroom she stated to a reporter that she believed Lyons was guilty and that he should be convicted. This statement was published that afternoon and the following morning in the press—and was available to all citizens, including prospective jurors.

Juror number two was questioned by the prosecutor. She, too, was excused because she said she had also formed an opinion as to Lyons's guilt and that it was a fixed opinion which could not be laid aside.

Juror after juror was called and excused for the same reason.

Until we reached juror number nine we had not found one who had no fixed opinion. Juror number nine, however, cleared that hurdle. The prosecutor next queried him on the death sentence.

"I believe in capital punishment," the juror replied.

I looked over my reports on the juror. It was then two-thirty in the afternoon, the gray wet day outside was filled with gloom, and the spectators were getting restless. Jury selection was, for them, a bore. Thus far I had not asked a prospective juror a single question. To ask had not been necessary. But there was juror number nine.

My report showed him to be thirty-six years old, married, the father of three children, and a machinist at General Electric, where he had worked eight years. He drank moderately, was well liked in the community, belonged to a bowling team, had a propensity for gambling, was a Catholic, attended church regularly, and had graduated from Withrow High School. So far so good, but there were other matters upon which the prosecuting attorney had not touched.

"Are you," I began, "acquainted with the prosecutor or any of his assistants?"

"I am not," he said.

"Have you ever sat on a jury before?"

"No," he said.

"Does the mere fact that the Hamilton County Grand Jury has returned an indictment charging Robert Lyons with first degree murder influence you against him?"

"I don't think so," he said.

"If you are selected as a juror in this case," I said, "the court will instruct you that an indictment is the formal means of bringing a defendant to trial and should not be considered as evidence for or against him. Will you follow that instruction?"

"I will."

"It is not my duty," I said, "or province to give you the law, but I am permitted to comment upon it. In any criminal case a defendant is and must be presumed innocent at the outset of the case. Will you presume Robert Lyons innocent?"

"I will," he said.

"Do you understand that this presumption of innocence is not an idle presumption but a substantial one and remains with Robert Lyons unless and until the state proves him Guilty beyond a reasonable doubt?"

"I understand," he said.

"Will you," I said, "demand of the State of Ohio before you join in any Guilty verdict that it produce evidence and testimony satisfying you beyond a reasonable doubt of Robert Lyons's guilt?"

"I will," he said.

"If the state should fail to prove Robert Lyons Guilty beyond a reasonable doubt would you have any hesitancy in voting him Not Guilty?"

"I would not."

"Do you go to church?" I said.

"I attend church regularly," he said.

I finally reached the real test questions. Each trial has its own set.

"Do you," I said, "know any members of the police force?"

"No," he said.

I read him a list of names of policemen. He did not know any of them.

"Do you know Don Roney of the prosecutor's office?" I said.

"No."

"In this case I'm positive you'll hear many policemen of different ranks. Assuming they do take the stand, would you as a juror give to a policeman more credence merely because he was a policeman than you would give to another witness?"

"No, sir," he said.

"You would not," I repeated, "give to the police officer more credence because he was a police officer and not an ordinary citizen?"

"I would not."

"Is there anything we have not covered in our questions or is there any reason that you know of that would prevent you from becoming a fair and impartial juror and giving to both sides a fair trial?"

"I would be fair," he said.

I looked out the window. I wondered, almost detached, when the drizzle would stop. I could picture the soft rain falling on my garden.

But that was another world.

"That will be all," I said—and took my seat.

We had, at least, got one juror that day.

This may surprise you but in the remaining two hours of the afternoon six more prospective jurors were examined and tentatively accepted, making a total of seven persons—four ladies and three gentlemen. Then the court adjourned for the day.

At ten the next morning, we began again. Our luck continued. By noon recess, four more prospective jurors had been seated. It didn't take long to qualify twelve jurors. Next came peremptory challenges.

Peremptory challenges. A tricky business. Ticklish. Frankly I was pleased with the panel we had, but I had butterflies in my stomach. Suppose the prosecutor challenged and removed sufficient jurors to change the complexion and mood of the panel? Only two jurors did not meet my complete approval, so I took a gamble. I challenged one. He was replaced. Again both the prosecutor and I questioned his replacement. He was sent to the jury box to sit with the others.

Juror number one was challenged and when his replacement strolled into the courtroom, I sat at the table, shaking my head in dismay. He was Elmer Hess.

Now, let the record show that Elmer Hess is a successful businessman. A vice-president, no less, at the Hess Blueprint Company. But let the record also show that this gentleman is not only a friend of mine but, in addition, he is my fraternity brother. We had been classmates at the University of Cincinnati where we both were members of Sigma Alpha Epsilon fraternity. The prosecutor questioned him, then turned him over to me.

I questioned him up one side and down the other.

In spite of our earlier relationship, the questions and answers developed that he would not favor me or my client and that, if selected, he would give both sides a fair and impartial trial. I still don't know why the state passed him.

What I mean is, the trouble with Elmer Hess was, he was too damned honest. I was confident that he wouldn't favor me over the state. What frightened me, frankly, knowing Elmer as I did, was the possibility that, in an abundance of caution, he might inadvertently lean toward the state's argument.

I stood before him, bewildered. I wanted to challenge him for another reason: he fit none of the specifications I had laid down for prospective jurors. He certainly wasn't living from hand to mouth. But to challenge him and send him packing? I wondered what effect that might have on the rest of the jurors. They might figure that if I was afraid to submit the life of Lyons into the hands of my fraternity brother, I must be in bad shape and had evidently no confidence in my case.

So I quizzed Elmer Hess for an hour. I asked him every conceivable question I thought might disqualify him, but he fielded them all and assured me—over and over again—that he would be fair and impartial and would not be embarrassed in the least to sit on the jury.

With misgiving I finally passed Elmer. He took his designated place in the jury box, from where he sat grinning at me, as if to say, "No hard feelings, pal."

This had been a crazy case from the beginning. It was running true to form. After all, what was so wrong in having a fraternity brother on the jury? If worst came to worst I could always sing our fraternity song, "Violets," in my final argument. It might help.

We exercised our second peremptory challenge by excusing juror number five. Her seat was filled by a male juror who passed the ordeal with flying colors.

Once again, if only temporarily, the jury panel was intact. For the moment, however, it was the state's turn to challenge. I waited—with impatience—for the prosecutor's decision. He had four peremptory challenges left and could, if he desired, change the makeup of the jury by exercising them. I was satisfied with the jury as it was.

Hover didn't hesitate.

"We pass this jury," he told the judge.

I was elated, but pretended not to be.

I had reason for my elation, too. Nine of the jurors were exactly the type I had prayed for. The other three—though not on the economic level of Lyons—were far from wealthy and, besides, they struck me as fair men with above-average intelligence. I first felt like jumping up and announcing to the world my pure pleasure with the jury, but I didn't. To do so, you see, would have given the jurors the wrong impression. If I accepted them too quickly, they might get the idea I considered them pushovers. I felt that the longer I made them sweat, the more they would become convinced that I had reservations concerning their qualifications.

So I played for time.

I asked the court's indulgence—and then Lyons, Harvey, and I shoved our chairs back from the counsel table. For a full ten minutes we talked among ourselves. From time to time, we would stare at the jurors. The jurors caught on fast. They appeared self-conscious and, in fact, they appeared downright uneasy the longer we conversed.

We finally resumed our places at the defense table. I stood and said, "If your Honor pleases, we are satisfied with this jury as it is now constituted."

The jury looked at me and I looked at them.

If I had been a college professor and had announced that my entire class had received passing grades upon a tough examination, I could not have expected a more favorable reaction. The jury actually seemed to heave a collective sigh of relief. Then they all settled back into their chairs, pleased. I had not found them wanting.

The jury consisted of eight men and four women. Their occupations were: vice-president of a blueprint company, assistant maintenance chief of Western Union Telegraph Company, wife of a post office employee, farmer, machinist, wife of a factory foreman, board of education janitor, foreman at General Electric, General Electric employee, wife of a mail carrier, wife of a truck driver, and an insurance agent.

At exactly 4:15 P.M. Frank Kispert commanded the jurors to stand and raise their right hands.

"Does each of you," said Kispert, "solemnly swear that you will well and truly try and due deliberance make between the State of Ohio and Robert Lyons, the defendant, so help you God?"

A chorus of "I do's" rose from the jury box.

Thus twelve men and women, for the duration of a trial, became wedded to our American system of justice.

And it to them.

III

"Your Honor, and ladies and gentlemen of the jury," the prosecutor began, "at this point in any criminal case, it is the duty of the State of Ohio to outline to you in some detail the evidence which the state expects to present in support of the charge which the grand jury has brought against the defendant Robert Lyons . . ."

The day before the Presidential elections—an Indian-summer kind of day, mellow and sweet—the more active part of the trial began. The courtroom was filled to capacity, but there were no standees. Those who could not get in waited, with and without patience, in a line in the corridor. C. Watson Hover, the prosecutor, had first crack at the jury. He read the indictment. Then, he said:

". . . The night before the murder Audrey Pugh had attended a club meeting in Fort Thomas, Kentucky. She was, at the time of this killing, suffering mildly from that type of periodic ailment of a young woman; she was not ill, she was just not feeling her very best. She got home at about two in the morning and went to bed without awakening her husband. The following morning, after she and her husband arose, Mrs. Pugh threw on a robe and went out to the kitchen to prepare her husband's breakfast. He left home at eight forty-five and Mrs. Pugh went back to bed for additional rest. That is where the state, and that is where everybody with the exception of one man, the defendant Lyons, loses track of the actual detailed life of the Pugh household, up until one o'clock that afternoon. At that time the defendant Lyons visited the house . . ."

Some spectators, leaning forward in their seats, had been at the courthouse since dawn, the better to witness the circus from a favorable vantage point. They had waited outside till seven-thirty. They had waited on the first floor till eight. When the courtroom doors had opened, five minutes before ten, the line had broken and stampeded. They had come to see a free show—and were getting their money's worth. I could see it in their eyes.

Hover explained to the jury that the meter reader carried a meter book which contained instructions as to how to gain entrance to each house on the route. The instructions for the Pugh residence required him to use a small side door near the front of the house and adjacent to the garage. Lyons, said Hover, had not done so. He had, instead, gone to the basement door.

"According to the Lyons statement," Hover went on, "he knocked and called until Mrs. Pugh admitted him at the basement door. According to the Lyons statement, Mrs. Pugh was upset and a small altercation ensued. We do not know how serious it was; only one person knows how serious it was; that is the defendant himself. The evidence will show that Lyons is a peculiar sort of person. He has some distinctions which the psychology people would call definite personality defects and deficiencies. In any event, his social life was restricted. While Lyons was reading the meter, Mrs. Pugh returned to the upper floor and at that point, for reasons best known to himself, Lyons started on a course of action that led ultimately to the murder of Mrs. Pugh . . ."

I stared at the ceiling during this presentation. I tilted back in my chair, appeared relaxed and unconcerned, but inside—out of sight— I suffered a storm of butterflies. My brother is wise, I thought. There are no butterflies in civil law. Only words—and ten thousand polite gestures of little consequence.

Hover went on and on.

". . . The combination of circumstances with which the man Lyons was confronted will be fully developed to you by the evidence. The combination, first arising from an argument with a housewife and the defendant's own preoccupation with job security which provided him with his only pleasure by virtue of copious consumption of beer as a hobby and recreation, provided possibly the only pleasure this man knew as an individual; you couple that with his own personality peculiarity, traits, and deviations, which the state will show, top that off with the bare, just the faintest suggestion of erotic interest in a woman who is slightly disheveled from lying in bed and dressed in a bathrobe, and you have a combination of facts and circumstances which are sufficient to change an ordinarily mild-mannered individual into a man bent on mischief and finally tragedy . . ."

I closed my eyes and tried—in my mind's eye—to picture that

sentence on paper. I tried to parse it. I gave up and opened my eyes again. Hover was in good form—in, that is, the best syntactical condition of an Eisenhower paragraph.

"We will present," he was saying, "not only a formal written confession of the defendant but in addition many other admissions which he made from time to time indicating his connection with this killing. If you believe his own statement confessing this murder, and in addition, the physical evidence of all the other witnesses over which he has no control and which he cannot influence, then there will be no doubt but that your verdict must be one of first degree murder and which will deserve for the defendant everything that the law provides by way of punishment for that crime."

There it was: Hover had asked for the death penalty.

My turn. I stood.

"In a case of this nature," I told the jury, after the usual opening remarks, "I believe it is highly important that you know the type of person you are about to try. I feel further that you should be advised as to the type of person that Audrey Pugh was. Our investigation disclosed that Audrey Pugh was a decent, moral, and God-fearing young woman. Her activities were normal and there is nothing in her background to suggest one breath of scandal or censure. She deserved and had earned the respect of those who knew her. And she enjoyed a very high reputation in the community at large. I am sure that she has been judged by the powers that be and that she has not been found wanting.

"Our evidence will show that Robert Lyons is a man forty-three years old and that he was born in Cincinnati. That he attended school here, the Lincoln Public School, where he remained through the eighth grade. He next attended Electrical Trade School, where he was a good student. At sixteen he graduated from that school. He was in sandlot baseball and played against Lieutenant Martin, who is head of the homicide squad. He also played in a small band. The evidence will show he was drafted into the army, that he served honorably in England and France, and was mustered out three years later with an honorable discharge. Our evidence will disclose that Robert Lyons has been a meter reader for the City of Cincinnati for some twenty years— and during that time he has read meters in some seven hundred thousand homes in this community without one complaint being registered against him. Our evidence will further show that seventeen years ago

Lyons married and that one daughter was born, but that a divorce ensued and that he was awarded the custody of his child. This is the man you are going to try for his life and this—if you please—is the woman who was murdered: two people with unimpeachable reputations . . ."

I paused, studied the twelve faces, read nothing, and went on. So much for the amenities, I thought. I launched into the heart of the case, saying I would prove "that the investigating officers of the City of Cincinnati under the direction and full approval of Chief of Police Stanley Schrotel and Chief of Detectives Henry Sandman aided and abetted by Don Roney of the county prosecutor's office did . . . obtain from this defendant, Robert V. Lyons, a false and untrue statement confessing the murder of the deceased, Audrey Pugh. We charge further that said statement confessing the murder of Audrey Pugh was obtained by premeditated and deliberate chicanery, subterfuge, lies, false statements of facts, promises not kept or intended to be kept, and by the manufacture and use of fake and fraudulent evidence, all intended to mislead Robert Lyons and to cause him such confusion of mind and mental anguish, apprehension of personal safety and well-being, that he in desperation and mental fatigue finally made and signed an involuntary statement admitting to a crime he did not commit.

"We charge further that said Don Roney to obtain this false statement lied to and misled Robert Lyons by false promises and threatened dire results and the electric chair if he, said Robert Lyons, did not cooperate. We charge further that the police together with Don Roney gave this defendant, Robert Lyons, a brainwash of some six weeks' duration which finally resulted in an untrue confession and an innocent man standing trial on a first degree murder charge . . ."

I told of the lengthy interrogation—from lunch one afternoon straight through till the following dawn—to which my client had been subjected by Don Roney and detectives Moore and Stagenhorst.

"The evidence will disclose," I said, "that these men produced a blown-up picture of a fingerprint and advised Lyons that it had been lifted from the entrance hall where Mrs. Pugh met her death and that it was his print. All denials by Lyons that it was his fingerprint met with the statement, 'Fingerprints don't lie.' We will demonstrate to you that the officials were lying to Lyons and that the fingerprint which they exhibited to him was not his print and had not been lifted from the entrance hall and was in fact a complete fake supported only by the false statements of the officials . . ."

Whether the officials when cross-examined would admit to employing a fake fingerprint I did not know. But I did know that Hover had not mentioned any fingerprint when he made his opening remarks. I had every reason to believe that the print then was pure fabrication. Otherwise Hover would have used it as one more nail in the coffin he was trying to construct for my client.

I watched the jury closely as I told them about the fake fingerprint. I was searching for some—any—manifestation of personal reaction to the trickery of the police and whether they—the jury— shared the indignation that I—as a citizen—felt at such unfair tactics.

The reaction of the jury was not long in presenting itself.

Every juror seemed visibly impressed by my accusation; several stared at the table where the prosecutor sat.

Magic moment.

My butterflies had flown away to light in the digestive organs of some representative of the state. I went on:

"Our evidence will establish that Lyons had been questioned some fifteen hours without letup. Time after time they told him he was going to the chair if he didn't do as they demanded. He had been without sleep nearly twenty-four hours. He was physically exhausted. He was completely demoralized. And, due to mental harassment and fatigue, he became befuddled in his thinking. He had reached the point where he was no longer a free agent. He no longer cared. He had been brainwashed. So, at Roney's suggestion, he confessed to a murder he hadn't committed and they reduced it to writing and he signed it . . . they drove him to the Pugh residence where, still without sleep and still under police direction, they had him reenact his 'crime' before a movie camera."

Again I scanned the faces of the jurors. I was not disappointed at what I saw.

When finished, I resumed my seat and the court announced a fifteen-minute recess. I glanced at my wristwatch. That I had been talking an hour and a half did not seem possible.

Lyons left the courtroom with Wiggeringloh, Harvey stepped away from the defense table to see a friend, and Ginny Heuser came to check with me during the break.

"Nice going, Foss," she commented. "I only hope they admit using a faked fingerprint. The jury's not going to like it."

We two sat, talking in low tones, when for some unknown reason I happened to glance at Lyons' empty chair and the area around it. There was a heavy concentration of semitransparent particles which, upon closer examination, resembled white flakes or scales. I am sure that if Lyons had not chosen that moment to rejoin us the matter would have remained an unsolved riddle which, in the rush of more important matters, would have been forgotten. But Lyons *did* return.

I pointed to the floor by his chair.

"Bob," I said. "Have you any idea what that stuff is?"

His face reddened. His eyes dropped. For the first time since I had known him, he seemed embarrassed. I have no idea why I pursued the subject; the gentleman in me said no, but some sixth sense in me said yes.

He finally answered me. "That's skin dropping from my legs," he said. He showed me his hands, palms down. At several points the skin was cracked open. "My legs are in even worse shape," he said. "You see, I have ichthyosis."

"The snowman!" I muttered. For some reason I started laughing.

Ginny, Harvey, Lyons, and Bill Wiggeringloh looked at me in disbelief. Those closest to us in the courtroom stared in our direction. We had worked for months preparing the case for trial and here was the answer in our laps all the time.

Lyons remained silent, but Ginny, Harvey, and Bill were talking at once.

"Foss, are you feeling all right?" Ginny said.

"What the hell's ichthyosis?" Harvey said.

"Who in the hell is the snowman?" Bill said.

I regained my composure but Judge Hoy had resumed the bench. Their queries for the moment would have to go unanswered. The judge ordered the prosecutor to call his first witness.

The prosecution called several police officers who established that a crime, indeed, had been committed where it had been committed—an essential fact to place on the record, however obvious that fact might appear. To show that the crime was committed established that the trial was in order—and to show where the crime was committed established which geographic area had the right to prosecute the accused.

Then the court adjourned for two days to allow everyone time to vote for either Ike or Adlai. Ginny, Harvey, and I did not join the rush for fresh air. We went with Lyons to the consultation room of the county jail upstairs.

"First things first," I said, when we were established in privacy. "Bob, I want you to stand on that chair."

He did so—and stood towering over us, sheepishly awaiting my next order.

"Now," I said, "pull up the leg of your trousers."

Again his face turned red, but he obliged, exposing his legs to his kneecap. Harvey and Ginny stared at the rough, fishlike scales which covered the exposed leg.

"That, my friends," I said, "is ichthyosis. It is a congenital disease in which the epidermis continuously flakes off in scales."

"How did you know that?" Harvey said.

"There's more to the practice of law than playing the banjo," I said. "Anyway, this is where the snowman comes in. When I was playing freshman football at the University of Cincinnati we had a halfback who had the same thing. In front of his locker on the floor would be that concentration of flakes shed from his legs. In other words, he left a trail. So we christened him the Snowman. Any comment?"

None, so on Election Day, as it will in Cincinnati, it rained four-tenths of an inch, Eisenhower won by a landslide, and the Hamilton County Courthouse—a Republican stronghold since the days of Noah's Ark—was in grand spirits waiting for the trial to begin again.

The elevator operator no longer announced the floor where our courtroom was. He simply called out, "Lyons Den!"

As soon as court got under way, the state continued its stream of witnesses. Mike Bogosian was called. He testified that he was a patrolman and had on the day of the killing accompanied his partner to the Pugh residence. His testimony, in reality, was the same as his partner's, but this time I had some questions I had not had before.

"Surrounding Mrs. Pugh's body," I asked him, "with the excep-

234 ::   MURDER

tion of this one blood spot and with the exception of the two buttons from the pajama top that you found on the floor, did you find anything else of a foreign nature there?"

"We found two blood spots on the floor," he said.

"But I am asking you, did you find anything else of a foreign nature there in the hall?"

"No, sir."

"Did you have occasion when you went down into the playroom to come back up those steps in the main part of the house?" I said.

"Yes," he said.

"When you came up those steps, will you tell the court and jury whether you saw or found anything of a foreign nature? Do you know what I mean by a foreign nature? That is something that you could not possibly expect to find on steps."

"I understand your question," he said. "No. I did not."

Homicide Lieutenant Erwin Martin was sworn next as a witness for the state. On cross-examination, I said: "Did you examine the floor in the den for any foreign things?"

"I did not notice anything," he said.

"Walking back along the hall where Mrs. Pugh was lying," I said, "did you examine the rug?"

"I did not see anything," he said.

"You did not see anything of a foreign nature?"

"No," he said.

We talked of other things, including the husband of the deceased. He told how, during that first investigation, he took Mr. Pugh into the bathroom and examined him with care.

"For what purpose?" I said.

"I was looking for a weapon or to see—well, just what he had on him. I examined his hands. There was a small amount of blood on one finger which I asked him about. He had what appeared to be —not a scratch but a slight reddish mark near his Adam's apple on the neck, and I asked him what that was caused from. I saw no other blood upon him and no weapon at all, but I did examine him carefully."

"Lieutenant, while you were there on this particular day, were any fingerprints taken?"

"You mean was the scene dusted for fingerprints?" he said.

"Yes," I said.

"Sam Eckler of our Bureau of Identification dusted the immediate area, which would be the outside of the front door and the inside of the door, and he made other searches for fingerprints but I do not know where."

"Do you know, Lieutenant, of your own knowledge, whether or not any fingerprints were obtained at that scene at that time?"

"There were some, in what we call fingerprint terminology 'smudges' or maybe some very partial prints obtained, but they were not identifiable prints," he said.

"Well, you used two terms there which I think you can explain. One is the word 'smudges' and the other is the word 'identifiable.' "

"A smudge," said the lieutenant, "is an impression that is left by a finger after it has moved. The lines are not distinct. In a partial print, you can see the lines but it's very minute. In some instances, some partial prints can be identified under good conditions."

My cross-examination of the lieutenant was lengthy. I covered the ground—over and over.

"You said you found some blood on one of Mr. Pugh's fingers?" I said.

"That is correct."

"And did you take a sample of that blood?"

"No," he said. "I did not."

"You didn't take a sample of it?"

"No, sir."

"You didn't test it for type?" I said.

"No. I did not."

We talked on and on about that. Then I swung back to another subject dear to my heart.

"Now, did you at any time find any fingerprint of Robert Lyons in the Pugh home?" I said.

"There were none found that match Lyons's prints," he said.

"Did you examine the rug Mrs. Pugh was lying on?"

"Yes," he said. "I did."

"Did you find any foreign material on that rug?"

"Only what I have already described," he said.

"Did you examine the dining-room rug?"

"Yes, I did."

"Did you find anything that you considered evidence on the floor there?" I said.

"No, I did not."

"Then did you examine the steps going from the kitchen to the basement?"

"Yes, I did."

"Did you find anything that you would consider evidence?"

"No, I did not," he said.

"No further questions," I said—and walked back to the defense table.

"Call your next witness," the court directed.

"We will call," said the prosecutor, "William Worthington Pugh."

The spectators—and those of us at the defense table—watched with interest as this new player entered upon our deadly stage. Our curiosity was justified. The prosecution had kept the husband of the deceased cloistered till that moment. This marked the first time that I laid eyes on him. I was curious—in a detached way—to see what kind of man this was who, they say, sat in the study of his home that early morning when in another room the meter reader was enacting before the camera the murder itself. He had chosen not to attend. He had remained closeted in the house, yet removed.

The husband proved to be a thin and prematurely bald young man, staring out at the world through the thick lenses of his glasses, and looking much older than his stated age of thirty-four. My client had been labeled a peculiar sort with odd mannerisms—the papers never had Lyons "walking" to a place, he "shuffled." As I looked at William Worthington Pugh I thought that he—under different circumstances—might be tagged with the same labels the press had given Lyons. Pugh seemed cold, remote, and beyond what was going on. I had the feeling it was a condescension on his part even to participate in such a public display as a trial.

He was well dressed. He was sure of himself.

I listened as he testified that he and his wife had eaten breakfast together, then he had gone to work. He said he remained at the office, the Pugh Printing Company, until noon, had gone to the University Club for lunch, had stopped at a jeweler's, had returned to his business around two, and had gone home around four-thirty. He told of entering the house, seeing his wife, calling a neighbor who was a doctor, then calling the police and asking that the life squad be dispatched.

My cross-examination of Pugh took several hours. I explored and reviewed every facet of the testimony he gave on direct examination, and other matters which I felt were germane.

"You knew your wife was dead, didn't you, when you called the police?" I said.

"No," he said, "I did not."

"Now, you formerly were a Boy Scout, were you not?"

"That is correct," he said.

"You had training in first aid?"

"Yes," he said. "I did."

"Your wife was lying there and there was a big pool of blood, was there not?"

"There was."

"You looked and you felt for her heartbeat," I said. "You saw certain lacerations such as stab wounds around her throat and left breast, did you not?"

"No," he said. "I didn't notice the lacerations."

I looked at him the longest time, then I looked out the window at the snow gently falling.

A white Thanksgiving, I thought.

"You didn't notice the stab wounds and lacerations?"

"No. I didn't."

"You saw that her mouth was open, did you not?"

"Yes," he said.

"You saw that her eyes were open and that they were staring, didn't you?"

"Yes, I did," he said.

"But you did not know that she was dead?"

"No, I didn't. I thought she was alive."

"That was your belief?"

"Yes, it was," he said. "I had seen people in stroke before. My father had several of them when he was alive and he looked sometimes like that and I ran across an experience in the White Mountains where a person passed out from insulin shock and she looked the same."

"But they didn't have a pool of blood or wounds around the neck?"

"No, they didn't," he said. "But I thought she was alive."

"When you found your wife lying in the entrance hall, was she wearing slippers?"

"She was not."

"Was your wife in the habit of walking around the house at any time without slippers?"

"I object!" said the prosecutor.

But the judge overruled him; the question stood.

"No," said Pugh. "She normally did not go around without bedroom slippers."

"In other words," I said, "you would say then as a rule she wore bedroom slippers, or at least slippers in the house when she walked around. Is that right?"

"Yes, it is."

"I think you made an answer to a question that the bed appeared as if your wife had jumped out in a hurry?"

"Yes," he said. "That is true."

"You said, 'The bed covers were thrown back as if my wife had gotten up in a big hurry.' Is that your phraseology?"

"Yes."

"What," I said, "did you mean by that answer?"

"Well, if my wife had gotten up in the normal course of events she would have straightened the bedcovers and so on and perhaps even made the bed because she was neat and orderly."

"That's the reason that you made the statement that she must have gotten up in a hurry?"

"That," he said, "plus the fact her slippers were still by the side of the bed."

"When you found your wife's body there were no slippers on her feet. Is that right?"

"No, there weren't," he said.

The slippers were important. In his alleged confession, Lyons had stated that when he stepped into the kitchen Mrs. Pugh was at the sink, peeling potatoes. This, if true, would tend to establish that Mrs. Pugh would have been wearing slippers—and not left them beside the bed.

"When did you call your lawyer?" I asked Pugh.

"It was after Lieutenant Martin came. I asked his permission."

"Did you tell him who Mr. Bullock was?"

"Yes," he said. "I did."

We talked of other things. Then I asked him, "In answer to one of Mr. Hover's questions, you said you had a drop or two of blood on the cuff of your shirt?"

"Yes."

"Was that a white shirt?" I said.

"Yes."

"I think there was some blood on one of your fingers, is that right?"

"Yes," he said.

We talked on and on.

"After the police left your home, where did you go?"

"I went over to my sister's home," he said.

"And then where?"

"The police were at my sister's home when I got there. They asked me to come to headquarters. My lawyer drove me down to the police station."

"What happened there?" I said.

"Well, two detectives—I think it was Young and Stagenhorst—took a tape recording from me. My lawyer wasn't in the room but he was in the building."

"Did you take a lie-detector test?"

"No, I didn't."

"Did you stop any place on your way to the police station?"

"Yes," he said. "I stopped at a drugstore to buy a toothbrush and some toothpaste."

"You did *what?*"

"I stopped to get a toothbrush and some toothpaste," he said.

"You weren't going on a visit, were you?"

"I wasn't going to spend the night in the house," he said.

"And this was approximately two hours after you found your wife's body?"

"It was."

I looked at him. A cool study. Detached. I wondered if I, or anyone else, would have been so detached under such conditions as to think of such purchases. We looked at one another for the longest time.

"That's all," I said.

But I made a mental note. I was not through with William Worthington Pugh.

I made a note to subpoena him for the defense.

The state's eleventh witness was Coroner Frank P. Cleveland.

The prosecutor, after qualifying the doctor, said: "Now, as the result of your examination, do you have any opinion as to the cause of death of this body?"

"It is my opinion," said the doctor, "that Audrey Pugh died of severe external hemorrhage resulting from multiple stab wounds of the neck and chest."

"Now, doctor, I take it that you noted the shape, the location, and the nature of each individual wound, did you not?" the prosecutor asked.

"That is correct, sir."

"Now," Hover went on, "after you noted those, I will ask you whether or not you had caused to be made any model or object to record the nature, extent, and location of these wounds?"

"Yes, sir," he said. "I did."

Hollywood couldn't have timed it better. Right on cue, as soon as the doctor had spoken, the door to the right of the judge's bench opened wide. Framed in the doorway, standing proud and erect, her head high, with an attentive male on either side, stood a female nude from the waist up, wearing only a petticoat. No strip artist at the height of her routine could have created a more intimate effect. The jury and spectators alike craned their necks and shifted their positions to gain a more advantageous view. Propelled by her two escorts, the store window mannequin glided silently into the courtroom and —without so much as a "Good morning, Judge!"—took up her position two feet from the witness stand, where she stood shamelessly facing the jury.

"Now that is what I call show business," one of the courthouse attachés muttered. "Only, on the other hand, I'm a fanny man myself."

"Hover sure outdid himself on this one," was Harvey's comment.

Someone had painted red markings upon the throat, chest, and left breast of the mannequin to indicate the size and location of the stab wounds found upon the body of Audrey Pugh. At the request of the prosecutor, the mannequin was marked Number 16 for identification.

Starting with the neck and moving downward, the doctor pointed out and discussed in great detail some twenty separate wounds found on Mrs. Pugh's body.

"One more question," said the prosecutor. "Based upon your autopsy of the body, your observation of the wounds which you found upon it, your observation of the body in the Pugh hallway, and the circumstances surrounding it there, do you have an opinion as to the lapse of time between the attack and the subsequent death?"

"Yes," said the coroner. "I do have an opinion."

"What is that opinion?"

I gazed at the ceiling, pretending unconcern, but this was what I had been waiting for. I glanced at the jury. The eyes of every jury member were focused on the doctor. Each juror was leaning forward —ever so slightly—as the doctor answered.

"It is my opinion," he said, "in consideration of the extent and the severity of all the wounds present upon the body, that Mrs. Pugh would have died within a matter of a few minutes. I would say five to ten minutes, or that the maximum she could have survived with such injury would be a period of an hour."

"A minimum of five minutes and a maximum of an hour?" said the prosecutor.

"That is correct, sir."

"No more questions," said the prosecutor.

Again I glanced at the jury. Disappointed, they had settled back, their attention no longer riveted on the coroner. I knew what they wanted: they wanted the time of the attack fixed exactly. I felt that it was mandatory to get that fact on record but I hesitated to reopen the questioning because of certain information I possessed.

Time magazine of May 7, 1956, had carried this item:

A new method of determining almost exactly the minute of death has been developed by Drs. Herbert P. Lyle and Frank P. Cleveland of the Hamilton County, Ohio, Coroner's Office. Old methods relied on stage of rigormortis, state of putrefaction, and rectal temperature changes in the corpse. The Cincinnati doctors told the American Association of Pathologists and Bacteriologists last week that a thin thermometer inserted into the brain will produce a series of constant readings for 24 hours following death since heat loss in the brain tissue occurs according to a predictable formula.

Because of the new method I knew that the doctor could establish the definite time of Mrs. Pugh's death and that the jury would accept his opinion as the gospel truth.

Years ago I knew a Chicago gambler, Denny Buford, who was a philosopher of the Damon Runyon school. Denny, proficient with dice and cards alike, on many occasions told me that "there are some bets you gotta go broke on." If Denny had been alive during the Lyons case, I am confident he would have characterized my position as a situation where, come hell or high water, the gamble had to be taken. I had no choice.

"You say that Audrey Pugh in your opinion lived for five or ten minutes after receiving the mortal wounds, and could have lived an hour at the extreme?" I asked.

"That is correct, sir," he answered.

The jury sensed that I was going to attempt to fix the time, for once again everyone leaned forward and listened with rapt attention to the doctor's answers.

I took a deep breath. My hands were cold and those damned butterflies returned to haunt me as I asked the question.

"Doctor, can you give this jury an opinion as to what time Mrs. Pugh was attacked or what time she received these wounds?"

"Yes, sir, I believe I could."

"Will you indicate that?"

The doctor did not answer for a moment. It seemed like an eternity.

"It is my opinion," said the doctor, "based upon the postmortem examination and observations made in the Pugh residence, and at the Hamilton County Morgue thereafter, that the death of Mrs. Pugh occurred in the region of 2 P.M. on April 11, 1956, and that the attack based upon the reference that I have made to the length of survival would have occurred in the neighborhood of 1 P.M."

"Hallelujah!" Chalk one up for Denny. If I had known where to find his grave I surely would have knelt and paid homage for as far as

I was concerned Denny had Socrates backed off the map. Once again my butterflies had departed for some unknown destination.

I looked at the jury, the jury looked at the prosecutor, and the prosecutor looked at the floor. "What gives here?" the jury seemed to be saying. "Aren't you giving us all the facts?"

"I have no further questions," I said . . . and sat down.

It was four-thirty and Bailiff Gray adjourned the court until ten the following morning. I turned to Harvey.

"Well?"

"I wet my pants," he said.

IV

"We questioned Lyons until shortly before midnight. At that time we showed him a fingerprint. We told Lyons that it was his and that we had found it on the second floor of the Pugh home."

"Had you found his print there?"

"No, sir. We had not."

The jury looked from Eugene Moore, city detective, who was on the witness stand, to the prosecutor who was questioning him. Disapproval of such police conduct showed in their eyes. So did indignation at such trickery.

And so the trial went on. Witness followed witness until they at times became a blur and until the days themselves ran together without true meaning.

My first question to Detective Moore, a handsome young officer precisely the sort Hollywood usually casts in such roles, concerned the visit Lyons made to the police station. After close questioning we established, for the further indignation of the jury, that Lyons had been questioned eleven hours without letup by many detectives.

"What you were really doing, Mr. Moore," I said, "you were questioning Lyons in relays of detectives, weren't you?"

"I would say so," the detective answered. "At least we were questioning him at different times."

"After that eleven hours of questioning," I said, "I want you to tell the court and jury what happened at or about six o'clock that evening?"

"We knew that this man had never been arrested before in his life," the detective said, "that he was a city employee, and we felt that we had to have further evidence and that what evidence we did have had to be weighed. It was decided then by Colonel Sandman and Lieutenant Martin that Lyons would be returned to his home."

"The point I'm getting to is this," I said. "When you told Lyons that you were positive that he had killed Mrs. Pugh, didn't he say to you, 'If you think I killed Mrs. Pugh, go ahead and arrest me'? Didn't he say that to you?"

"He didn't use those words."

"What words did he use?"

"He said, 'Well, I guess you will have to charge me.' "

"He was not charged with anything, was he?"

"No sir," the detective said. "He was not."

"And at one time," I went on, "when you and Stagenhorst were questioning him, didn't he say, 'I couldn't have done it.' Isn't that what he said to you?"

"Yes, sir."

"Didn't he say to you and deny to you that he was ever on the first floor, that is, the floor where the murder took place?"

"Yes, sir. He did."

I turned to the day the detectives and Roney, the prosecutor's investigator, had picked Lyons up and taken him to Dr. Lyle's office for lie-detector tests which lasted over six hours, and I asked: "And then Dr. Lyle came out and told you the tests were over?"

"That is correct," the detective said.

"It was then that you said, 'Robert Lyons, you are under arrest for the murder of Audrey Pugh.' Is that what happened?"

"That is the time we officially informed Lyons that he was under arrest for the murder of Audrey Pugh."

The detective told how, after that, Lyons was driven to City Hall and to the police interrogation room.

"Around 11 P.M.?" I said.

"Yes, sir. That is correct."

"Now, I think you said that you had decided you were going to have to take an approach here of sympathy, of kindness, and so forth, in your questions to Robert Lyons. Is that correct?"

"That is correct."

"Living up to your oath as an officer, right?"

"Yes, to conduct this in a legal manner," he said.

"Everything in a friendly and sympathetic way?"

"Yes."

"Did you send for a lawyer for Robert Lyons while this questioning was going on?"

"Lyons never asked for a lawyer. We never sent for one."

"Was there any representative of Mr. Lyons—an employer or anybody to look out for his interest?"

"No, sir. There was not."

"It is true that Lyons told you he did not kill Mrs. Pugh and that he had never been on the first floor of that Pugh residence?"

"Yes, sir. That is correct."

"And finally—after midnight—in the same kind and understanding and sympathetic manner, you showed him a fake fingerprint and told him it was his print and that it had been lifted from the upstairs hall, didn't you?"

"Yes, sir. We did."

"But you didn't have his fingerprint from upstairs, did you?"

"No, sir. We did not."

"You lied to him, didn't you?"

The prosecutor objected—quickly. His objection was sustained. I shrugged.

"Is that," I went on, "following your police duties?"

Again Hover objected. Again, he was sustained.

But I had been watching the jury. The jurors were angry—and their expressions left no doubt about it. This, they seemed to be saying, is our *honest* police department?

When I was a young lawyer trying an automobile theft case in Judge Thomas Darby's court, I had been given several answers by the witness, who indicated that my client might be innocent. Flushed with success I had continued my examination and, to my dismay, received answers which not only erased the innocence of my client but opened for him the gates of the state pen. Following this debacle, the judge had sent for me. "Young man," he said that long-ago day, "when you get what you want from a witness, desist."

There were a thousand other questions I ached to asked Detective Moore, but I had got what I wanted.

"That's all," I advised the court, and Moore left the stand.

"At least," Ginny told me during one recess, "public opinion is beginning to change a little. I can tell it from the way the spectators are talking out there in the hall. And in addition to the obscene letters, we're getting some for our side."

"But no Christmas cards yet," Harvey offered.

I would have commented on *that,* but the trial began again.

The prosecutor asked and was granted permission to read the alleged confession to the jury.

I sat there, gazing at the ceiling. After only a token fight, I let the prosecutor have his way. Why? Because, corny as it may sound to you, I needed to have the alleged confession heard. My case was built on the lies and miscalculations it contained.

"I am reading," said Hover, "from State's Exhibit 27, entitled Statement of Robert Lyons, taken Saturday, May 26, 1956, at 4:05 o'clock A.M. at City Hall, Cincinnati, Ohio . . ."

At *five after four* in the morning? Even that helped us. It proved that Lyons had been questioned for hours without letup. No one should confess at four in the morning. That hour is only good for sleep or lovemaking or, if you're so inclined, breaking into neighborhood grocery stores.

No matter. For the next hour Hover stood before the jury, slowly and methodically reading the fairy tale.

The members of the jury were an interesting study during the reading. On several occasions I detected quizzical expressions on their faces. Mrs. Pugh was in the kitchen, peeling potatoes? But her husband testified she had got up from bed in a hurry and had left her slippers there. The state's case was beginning to fall apart at the seams. There was the time element. Lyons said he visited the Pugh residence at noon. The confession said he visited at one.

Relaxing, I studied the jury. This was, I felt, the first murder case on record where a defendant's confession would prove his innocence.

But I had other axes to grind and other points to make. Another witness for the state was Chief of Detectives Colonel Henry J. Sandman, the twenty-first witness. His testimony on direct examination corroborated testimony that the state had offered before. But on cross-examination I explored several areas the state seemed to be avoiding.

"On April 12," I said, "when you got inside the Pugh home with Lieutenant Martin, did you personally make a search of the premises?"

"No," he said. "I did not."

"Did you see a rug in the front hall?"

"No, I did not."

"Was the rug missing when you got there?"

"Yes, sir."

"Do you know what happened to the rug?"

"It was submitted to Kettering Laboratory for examination."

"Was that rug returned by the laboratory to you?"

"No, sir."

"Do you of your own knowledge know what became of that rug?"

"No, sir."

"Have you seen that rug since you turned it over to the laboratory?"

"Yes, sir," he said. "In the Pugh residence about a month ago."

"I want you to tell the jury whether or not the rug had the same blood spots on it as when you first saw it."

"No, sir."

"In observing the rug, could you tell whether or not it had been cleaned?"

"I had some doubts," said the detective chief, "as to whether it was the same rug."

"Were you advised that it was the same rug?"

"Mr. Pugh told me it was the same rug."

Damn, I thought, but I tried my best to keep a poker face. So the rug on which Audrey Pugh and her slayer had engaged in a death struggle and where her butchered body had been found drenched in blood had, with the permission and blessing of the prosecutor and the police, been released to Pugh who in turn had it cleaned and thereby destroyed any opportunity for defense experts to explore the rug and record their findings.

I was angry. The longer I thought about what the authorities had done, the more angry I became. The horror of their unwarranted and unheard-of action sent chills down my spine. It could have resulted in the conviction of an innocent man. Here was a vital piece of defense evidence which had been destroyed. Did they believe their

findings alone were infallible? Had they vainly concluded that no
other expert would differ from them? By what right had they arrived
at this divine conclusion?

The jury at that moment had no way of knowing the importance
of the state's *faux pas* in returning the rug to Pugh. I looked forward
to the proper time when the jury would be advised of Lyons's ichthyosis and the importance of the rug as defense evidence—evidence now
gone forever.

I went on to another matter: the decision of the cops to nail
Lyons.

"So the plan was made that Moore and Stagenhorst and Don
Roney were to make contact with Lyons, is that correct?" I said.

"Yes, sir," said the detective chief.

"And were there any other things discussed at the conference?"

"We pooled our thinking and we decided Lyons was our man."

"This was the man who was guilty of murder?" I said.

"Yes."

"That's what you all *agreed*—at the meeting—that Lyons was
guilty?"

"That is right."

"Since you came to this conclusion that Robert Lyons committed
this murder," I said carefully, "were you the one who came up with
the idea to trick him by a fake fingerprint?"

Hover objected. The court sustained the objection.

"Were you," I went on, "the one who came up with the idea, if
you couldn't get a confession any other way, of telling Lyons, 'Here's
your fingerprint and we found it on the first floor,' when you knew it
was a lie?"

Hover again objected. Sustained.

"Did you have any conference," I said, "about the use of a fake
fingerprint?"

"Yes," said Sandman. "I did."

"Who did you talk to?"

"Detective Stagenhorst, I believe."

"And did you agree that was good police work, to lie to this
man?"

"Objection," said Hover.

Sustained.

"And, of course," I said, "you didn't have any fingerprint of Robert Lyons from the first floor, did you?"

"No, sir."

"All right. I want to ask you two more questions. Have you the murder weapon in this case?"

"No, sir."

"Did you order a lie-detector test for William Pugh?"

I never got an answer because, again, the prosecutor objected and, again, the objection was sustained.

Witnesses—and still more witnesses.

Then a movie projector and screen were set up in the courtroom. The blinds were drawn tight. The lights turned off. Lacking everything but the popcorn and previews of coming attractions, we all sat in semidarkness impatiently awaiting the sneak preview of a real-life murder thriller played to a very exclusive and limited audience whose verdict would decide the fate and future of the main star.

Quietly erect against the far wall and scarcely visible was the seminude mannequin that had created a stir at its initial appearance. In the dim light of the courtroom the figure representing the murdered woman, standing aloof and apart, assumed ghostly and ethereal proportions. Here was the kind of evidence prosecutors dream about, for who had ever heard of a defendant on trial for his life reenacting the murder of his victim for a jury that is to decide his fate?

The projector started and an officer gave a running account as the silent film spilled onto the screen. The movie's first shot showed Lyons coming down the outside steps and knocking on the door. The next sequence showed him entering the basement, going directly to the water meter, and then walking to the foot of the steps that led up-stairs. As the film recorded his slow ascent, my mind went back to the original interview with Lyons at the county jail. I could still hear him saying, "When I got up the stairs, I turned left. There was a detective at the top of the steps. The guy at the top of the steps grabbed me and turned me around so I would go into the kitchen. The way I turned they told me went into a garage. I don't know if this shows in the movie but it happened just as I am telling you."

There, on the silent screen, Lyons ascended the steps. The ascent seemed an eternity. Then, there he was on the landing. I pretended unconcern but my soul was trembling as I watched for what came next—and there, just as Lyons had said, appeared Detective Lytle Young, who reached out, swung Lyons around, and headed him for the kitchen.

"Hot damn," was Harvey's comment.

My interest in the movie waned after that. The actual reenactment of the murder as scripted by the police made little impression. Anyway, the camerawork had been only fair, the acting amateurish, but the *directing* had been superb.

I looked at Harvey.

"Well?" I said.

"I like musicals better," he said.

More witnesses for the state, and then Hover faced the court.

"At this time, if the court pleases," he said, "the state will rest its case in chief."

"Are you ready to proceed, Mr. Hopkins?" the court asked.

"Yes," I said. "We will call Mr. William Pugh," I added.

The jury came to attention. Although this was William Pugh's second appearance, this time he was being called as a witness for the defense. I had waited—patiently but with little hope—for the state to produce the rug on which Audrey Pugh's body had been found. But due to its return to Pugh and its subsequent cleaning, I knew—deep down—that the prosecutor and police had realized the enormity of their mistake, destroying possible defense evidence. Thus, following the state's failure to introduce the rug I had instructed Harvey to issue a subpoena for Pugh *duces tecum,* which directed him to produce the rug in open court.

"I ask you," I said to Pugh, "whether or not you were served with a subpoena *duces tecum* to bring with you a rug?"

"That is correct," said Pugh, the soul of detachment and correctness.

"As the result of that subpoena, I will ask you whether or not you brought into court today the rug on which your wife's body was found?"

"Yes, I did."

"Where is it?"

"I left it in the judge's chambers. I don't know where it is now."

The judge said that the rug, indeed, was in his chambers. An attaché brought it into the courtroom. I cut the string around the rug and unrolled it on the floor directly in front of the jury.

I told Harvey to lie on the rug and then requested Pugh to place Harvey's body exactly as Pugh had said he found his wife on April 11. Pugh left the stand and stood at the side of the rug upon which a red-faced Harvey—at Pugh's direction—twisted and turned until the witness was satisfied that Harvey's prone position represented a reasonably accurate duplication of that of Audrey Pugh's body as it lay on the rug on the day of the murder.

"You may resume the stand," I told Pugh. "Now, do you recall whether or not this rug was taken from your home following your wife's death?"

"Yes," he said. "It was taken from my home."

"Will you state whether or not there were any blood spots on the rug on April 11 when you found your wife?"

"Oh yes, there were. They show on the pictures."

"Now, in looking at the rug, do you see those same spots?"

"No, I don't."

"When was this rug returned to you?"

"On May 25."

"Who returned the rug to you?"

"The National Carpet Cleaning Company."

"Did you send this rug out to be cleaned?"

"After I was notified by the police that I could have the rug, I called the company to pick the rug up at Kettering Laboratories and clean it."

"Who told you that you could have the rug?"

"I believe it was either Lieutenant Martin or Colonel Sandman."

"I have no further questions," I said.

Later I would bring this matter up, I told myself. Not then.

There followed fourteen "reputation" witnesses for Lyons—each of whom had had the opportunity to observe and evaluate him; without exception they testified that his reputation for peace and quiet and honesty in the community was good. All were cross-examined by the prosecutor. Such witnesses—one after another—create a kind of tedium which you never view on a Perry Mason teleplay.

Then we introduced other witnesses to prove that Lyons was not

at the Pugh home when the police said he was and when the murder
was committed. Lords of the manors testified—and so did the kitchen
help. You who like society names and who attach more importance to
them than even their owners do would have delighted in this part of
the trial. Socialites testifying for a meter reader accused of murdering
one of the socialites' own. The prosecution cross-examined—but could
not shake the testimony that favored my client.

Each witness testified as to his or her contact with Lyons that
fateful day and specified the time at which Lyons had read the individual meter. Their collective testimony accounted for Lyons's whereabouts between the hours of 12:45 and 2:30 in the afternoon—and
each succeeding witness placed Lyons farther and farther away from
the Pugh residence as he continued along his route.

More interesting, it developed upon cross-examination of my
witnesses by the prosecutor that both the police and the investigators
of the prosecutor's office had also interviewed them right after the
murder and had received the same information we had brought out in
the trial.

Why or how the prosecutor and the police chose to ignore this
vital information, which was diametrically opposed to their theory of
the case, will always be a source of great wonder to me. As I had told
the jurors in my opening remarks, the authorities had woven a cloak
for Lyons—but woven into it all threads of guilt, discarding all threads
of innocence.

By the time the last witnesses had been cross-examined, it was
late in the day.

"If your Honor pleases," I said to the court, "we are within
thirty minutes of the time of adjournment and since I have only one
more witness before we rest our case, I would like to suggest that we
adjourn until tomorrow morning."

"Will the witness take some time?" the court said.

When I had mentioned "one more witness," representatives of
the news media had become alert, shaking off their afternoon doldrums.
For days reporters had—with no success—questioned Ginny, Harvey,
and me to see if we planned to put Robert Lyons on the stand.

Well, this was their moment, I thought.

"My last witness," I told the court, "will be the defendant,
Robert Lyons."

Bailiff Gray struck one sharp blow of the gavel to silence the murmurs of excitement.

The judge admonished the jury, whereupon Gray adjourned the court till ten the next morning.

The news media made one mad, noisy dash to advise the world that Lyons would testify.

"Well, Bob," I said, "tomorrow's the day you have been waiting for."

He smiled a slow and lonesome smile.

"It's been a long time in coming," he said.

"Anything you want to go over or talk about?" I said.

He hesitated. "They're going to get the truth right down the line," he said. He didn't sound braggadocio or overconfident. I got the feeling he was merely stating a fact. "The jury will believe me. I've got nothing to worry about . . ."

The next morning Ginny greeted me with an extra-cheerful Hello but I could sense that she concealed the same inner turmoil I concealed. She walked along Main Street beside me, her high heels clicking loudly, and she talked faster than she usually did. OK, so there you are. We both realized that the chips were down. The fate of Lyons rested—that day—squarely on his own shoulders.

As the courthouse elevator opened onto the third floor, I couldn't believe the mob scene. Compared to that bedlam, anything I had seen before during the trial was second-rate. The corridor was one mass of spectators. As we struggled through the crowd, one of the men spotted me and shouted, "Give 'em hell, Foss!"

We were fifteen minutes early in the courtroom, but every seat was filled.

A few minutes later Wiggeringloh brought Lyons into the room and to the defense table. Harvey and I stood and shook hands with the meter reader. The door to the judge's chambers opened, the judge entered, and—exactly at ten—court opened.

"We will call the defendant, Robert Vernon Lyons, to the stand," I said.

Lyons pushed back from the counsel table, unwound his rangy body, stood erect, and, upon the order of the clerk, raised his hand.

"Do you swear to tell the truth," the clerk asked, "the whole truth, and nothing but the truth, so help you God?"

In a clear, firm voice, Lyons said, "I do."

He was led to the stand, he sat, and the microphone was adjusted to his lips. His shirt was clean but unironed (the jail would not permit him an iron and this saddened him), his tie was slightly askew, and his ill-fitting suit—worn thin from long use—reflected the shininess of the courtroom lights. It may sound silly but that suit reminded me of a shining suit of armor.

"Will you state your name?" I began.

"Robert Vernon Lyons . . ."

And so I questioned him, first about his life prior to his arrest, and then in detail—all of which you have heard—about what happened afterward. Via word pictures he actually relived his ordeal on the night he was questioned without rest until, exhausted and confused, he had confessed to the murder he did not commit. I saw—and the jury saw—everything relived in his eyes: the shock, the exhaustion, the indignation, the fright, the desperation, the hopelessness.

He gave us the impression, also, that he was ashamed of having been human and having weakened, of confessing a crime he did not commit. His testimony was something that I cannot forget. Even as I write this I can still see him on that stand: the picture of the disintegration of a man's will.

As Lyons testified I had, from time to time, studied the jurors. I was not disappointed in what I saw.

Then it was time for the clincher.

I looked at Harvey at the defense table. The lad could hardly contain himself because he knew what was coming. He grinned at me and blew on his hands as if he were cold. He knew it was going to snow. We had guarded Lyons's ichthyosis well and I was positive no one in the courtroom with the exception of Lyons, Harvey, Ginny, and me had the slightest suspicion of what was about to happen. So the stage was set, the actors were on cue, and the members of the audience were settled in their seats. At long last the time had come to administer the coup de grace.

"Harvey," I said, "will you bring that chair over here?"

Harvey picked up a chair and—with loving care—placed it directly in front of the jury. I unfolded a handkerchief and methodically dusted the seat of the chair clean.

"Bob," I said to Lyons, "will you step over here a moment?"

Lyons stood and as he walked toward the chair, irrepressible Harvey in a soft whisper chanted into my ear the ancient cry of the midway pitchman—"Hold your hat and Hallelujah, Bobbie's gonna show it to ya!"

"Bob," I said. "I want you to stand on the seat of this chair."

Lyons did so. There he stood, some nine feet tall, sheepishly surveying the jury and waiting for my next command.

"Now," I told him, "I want you to pull up your trouser legs."

He was embarrassed but he was game. He lifted both trouser legs above his knees, exhibiting to the world the most beautiful ichthyosis since the beginning of time. His legs were scaly and rough, bluish-red, and fishlike in appearance.

The tattooed man from carnival land never created more stir and interest than Robert Lyons on the day he stood on a chair and raised his pants legs.

I don't know whether the jury—or Hover—had ever viewed ichthyosis before, but the jury sat in rapt attention and poor Hover stared with wonder and disbelief. I didn't give the prosecutor time to recover. I told Lyons to return to the witness stand and I addressed the bench.

"If your Honor pleases, I would ask permission for the jury to leave the jury box and view the seat of this chair."

The judge granted permission. The jury marched in single file by the chair where Lyons had just stood.

On the polished surface which moments before I had carefully dusted now rested hundreds of skin flakes fallen from Lyons's legs.

The jurors, puzzled, looked at me questioningly, but there was more to be done first.

"Now, if your Honor pleases, I am asking permission for the jury to view the floor of the witness stand."

Again permission was granted. The jurors headed to the stand, where each took a long hard look. Thousands and thousands of flakes had fallen from Lyons's legs during the time he had been testifying. These flakes covered the entire floor area.

Hover himself got up and stared at the "snowfall." His expression mirrored his incredulity.

I stood.

"I have no further questions."

Hover blinked at me, then at the witness stand where Lyons was. And so the prosecutor took over the cross-examination. The prosecution hammered at Lyons for two hours. It was a thorough and searching examination, but when it was completed the state had failed to shake the testimony Lyons had given on direct examination.

At one point, Lyons was asked, "After you got down from that chair there was something on the chair, wasn't there?"

"Yes, sir," said Lyons. "There was."

"What was the reason for coming over here, Lyons, and standing on the chair?"

"Well, Mr. Hopkins asked me to come over and stand on the chair, and so I went over and stood on the chair."

"Other than that, you do not know?"

"Well, If I would have been on the first floor of the Pugh home, I imagine particles of the skin would have been on the floor."

"Tell them what you wear summer and winter under your pants."

"I wear shorts."

"You wear long drawers, don't you, Lyons?"

"No, sir."

"Did you tell the police department that you wear long drawers?"

"No, sir," said Lyons. "My dad wears long drawers," he added.

"Lyons, I will show you a pair of long drawers marked for identification 42. Did you ever see those before?"

"Yes, sir," Lyons said.

"Isn't it true you had those on on April 11, 1956?"

"No, sir."

"Isn't it true you told Lieutenant Martin you had those on on April 11, 1956?"

"No, I did not."

"Isn't it true that you told Lieutenant Martin that you wore long drawers summer and winter?"

"No, sir."

"Isn't it true that you do wear long drawers?"

"I do not."

"Did Colonel Sandman talk to you about long drawers?"

"No sir."

"Did anyone show you this pair of long underwear which is marked for identification 42?"

"No, sir."

"No one spoke to you at any time at police headquarters regarding the long drawers?"

"No," said Lyons. "They did not."

At times in his cross-examination the prosecutor had become somewhat agitated and even angry, trying to get my client into long drawers and shoot holes in the snowfall theory. But Lyons fielded each question perfectly and—in contrast to the prosecutor—remained polite, cooperative, and composed throughout the ordeal. Lyons had conducted himself magnificently. He had been a lawyer's dream: the perfect witness.

"That's all," said the prosecutor—and Lyons left the witness stand.

"If your Honor pleases," I said, "at this time, on behalf of the defendant, Robert Lyons, we will rest our case . . ."

"Now what?" said Lyons.

"Rebuttal witnesses for the prosecution," I told him. "But relax. You're the greatest."

The state called, as rebuttal witnesses, Lieutenant Martin, Colonel Sandman, and Detective John Green in an attempt to prove that Lyons wore long drawers. But each was digging a hole for the prosecution to be buried in. I could see it, and soon I would show it to the jury. I was amazed at Hover. Was he blind? Had he missed it completely?

All three witnesses testified that Lyons, on diverse occasions, had told them he wore long drawers all the time. On cross-examination, Lieutenant Martin testified that he himself had been at the Lyons' home early on the morning of April 28.

"Isn't it true that Lyons was in bed when you got there?" I said.

"Yes, I believe that he was," the officer said.

"Now, I want you to tell this court and jury, didn't he get up and get dressed in your presence and didn't he put on a pair of shorts, April 28?"

"I recall him getting out of bed, but I don't—I don't know whether he had his long drawers on then or not. I really don't know."

"Didn't he have a pair of shorts on?" I said.

"I don't recall what he had on," the officer said lamely.

My cross-examination of Colonel Sandman was short and sweet.

"You were on the stand for some length of time before when there were direct questions and then cross-examination by me?" I asked him.

"Yes, sir."

"Did you at any time during that examination, even when asked by me to relate the entire conversation you had with Lyons, mention anything about this conversation about long underwear on your appearances before in this case?"

"No, sir."

Upon cross-examination of Detective Green, he admitted he had not searched for shorts nor had he questioned Lyons's father in reference to the long underwear.

"You didn't mention any conversation concerning long drawers in your prior testimony?" I said.

"I was not asked," he said.

"I didn't ask you that," I said. "You didn't mention it?"

"No, sir. I didn't mention it."

"Call your next witness," the court told the prosecution.

"We have no further rebuttal testimony your Honor," the prosecutor said. "At this time, we would like to offer the long drawers in evidence."

I could hardly believe my ears. I fully appreciated poor Hover's dilemma, though. He had to offer some "explanation" for the lack of snowfall.

"What do you say, Mr. Hopkins?" asked the court.

"I have no objection to the exhibit," I said.

"In that case," said the Court, "they will be received and will be noted Exhibit 38."

I stared blandly at the ceiling, trying not to grin. The long drawers which the state claimed my client had worn were at least six sizes too small for him. He couldn't have got into them with a greasy shoehorn. Hover, the police, and the gods had delivered me the icing for the cake.

The stage was set for the final act.

V

It was agreed by and between counsel with the approval of the Court that the prosecution would make its opening argument and then Court would be adjourned until 9:00 A.M. on Friday, November 23, at which time the defense argument and the state's final argument would be made. Melvin Rueger, assistant prosecuting attorney, opened for the state. He talked for one hour and eighteen minutes and when he finished I was convinced the state wasn't throwing in the towel until the final curtain descended and that I had better keep my guard up at all times.

Rueger reviewed the evidence at great length and then asked the jury, "Are you going to believe Lyons or the men of the police department, Colonel Sandman, Lieutenant Martin, Moore, Stagenhorst, Donald Roney and the others that testified against him?" The state, he said, had brought out all the evidence it had in the case, some positive and some negative, "but several times in the last few days every move the state made was turned into a sinister one, one with something meant to deprive the defendant of the rights to which he is lawfully entitled.

"This is Operation Big Lie or the case of the Red Herring," he continued. "That is what we have here, a deliberate, planned attempt by the most capable criminal lawyer in this section of the country to lead you down a cold trail."

Rueger again asked the jury if they were going to believe the police officers or Lyons, "who said they made up the words in the signed confession.

"The evidence in this case," he argued, "provides no basis for a verdict carrying mercy.

"I am asking you for a verdict of Guilty of first degree murder as the defendant stands charged in the indictment."

So they were shooting the works. I understood the state's strategy for I had witnessed it on many other occasions but I wondered what effect this demand for the chair would have on the twelve good people in the jury box who were to decide Lyons's fate. They had never before participated in a knockdown, drag 'em out murder case and could not realize the prosecutor's demand for the electric chair was only par for the course.

At the conclusion of the judge's admonishment to the jury, he wished them a happy Thanksgiving. Court was adjourned until 9 A.M. on Friday, November 23.

We bade Lyons good night. Wiggeringloh escorted him from the courtroom. Ginny had joined us at the counsel table.

"Well, what do you think?" she asked.

"I think they're asking for the moon and hoping for a piece of cheese," I said.

We left the courtroom and went outside. The air was colder than when we had gone to lunch. Dusk was falling. The sky was gray and forbidding.

Ginny looked at the heavens.

"It's going to snow," she said.

Thanksgiving Day was overcast and cold. Lyons, I noted from the press, was served a Thanksgiving dinner of roast beef, lima beans, cole slaw, celery, whipped potatoes, gravy, cranberry sauce, apple pie, oranges, apples, and coffee. He shared the dinner with the county jail's 275 other guests. Outside, while he ate, snow dumped down on the city. Nearly five inches fell, clogging the city streets and byways with white.

I spent Thanksgiving half in celebration of the day and half in preparation for the next. Thelma had outdone herself in the preparation of our Thanksgiving meal and as Henry, Anne's parents, Anne, and I gathered around the festive board we all agreed we had much to be thankful for.

By nightfall, Anne's parents had left. Henry watched television. Anne went to bed at ten. I got undressed, put on a robe, and retired to my den, where once again I reviewed the evidence of the trial.

Outside, except for the occasional moan of wind, the world was dark and silent. And crisp.

A pool of official court reporters had, during the three weeks of the trial, alternated the courtroom duties and miraculously managed to keep abreast of the testimony. Every morning when I had sat down at the defense table, resting before me was a transcript of the preceding day.

Now these were all accumulated in my den.

How court reporters do their job I'll never know. They work in silence and swiftly. They seldom—if ever—complain. Every word uttered in every trial finds its way through their fingers into printed record for future reference and possible appeal. I looked at my wristwatch. It was 1 A.M. This night would never end.

After Reuger's opening argument I had been keyed to the proper pitch. I had been ready to answer him and to anticipate any new matter that might be advanced in Hover's final argument to the jury. I had been foolish to agree to the Thanksgiving continuance but there wasn't anything I could do about it now. Where everything had been so crystal clear, it was now difficult to concentrate or to marshal my thoughts. I felt as if I were going to explode.

I went to the front door and looked out. We were snowbound. A foot of snow covered the ground. Some drifts were as high as my head. As Harvey would say, "Think of the poor sailors on a night like this."

It was 2 A.M. when I went to bed. I must have dozed off only to awake with a start. I had been standing before a jury in a packed courtroom arguing a case and my attire had been a suit of long underwear. I looked at the clock beside my bed. Six o'clock. I got up, took a shower, and dressed. I awakened Anne and we left home at seven forty-five.

Tons of snow had fallen on Hamilton County that Thanksgiving. By Friday, despite the efforts of hundreds of maintenance men during the night, most roads and streets remained impassable. It was a wild and woolly ride but we managed to negotiate the fourteen miles to the courthouse and arrived safe and sound.

Ginny and Harvey were in the courtroom when we arrived and every spectator seat was occupied. Several hundred disappointed men and women milled about the hallway outside the courtroom, awaiting an opportunity to gain admittance.

"You remember," said Harvey, "what you said about Hover buttoning up his overcoat for it was going to snow? Well, it snowed inside and boy, oh, boy, did it snow outside. Talk about a good omen. That man upstairs is sure on our side. I'm impressed."

Jurors skidded into the city from their various hilltop homes. The judge, who had left his home in Mount Healthy at 7:45 A.M., did not reach the courthouse until the last minute, but he noted that "the traffic was bumper to bumper all the way." It took Hover two hours to travel the snow-clogged traffic jam from Ridgewood Avenue into the city. One juror rode a bus and darned near froze his feet. He arrived late. The snow and traffic did not deter the spectators, however. They were there—in crowds.

Court opened that morning two hours late.

As I sat waiting for the missing jurors to arrive, my mind began to function again and everything fell into place. By the time the jurors all assembled, the judge was ready, and so was I.

"Before I resume my seat," I said, "I feel confident that I will establish to your satisfaction that Robert Lyons is an innocent man and that your correct verdict in this case is Not Guilty . . ." I took exception to the prosecution's inference that I had tried to mislead the jury. "The prosecutors in this case," I said, "are the two most confused lawyers in the community. They have swallowed the sinister interpretation the police have made in this case. In my opening statement, I indicted the police. I now charge that the police have told lies, used fake fingerprints, and tricked Robert Lyons—and I say to you this is not good or acceptable police work. I say to them, put your own house in order before charging us with pulling 'Operation Big Lie.' "

I paused, studied the jury, then went on in a low, calm voice.

"Now, ladies and gentlemen, there is only one basic fact in this case and that is: Did Robert Lyons on April 11 enter the Pugh home, go upstairs, struggle with Mrs. Pugh, and cause the wounds shown on that replica of Mrs. Pugh?" I indicated the seminude mannequin still charming the courtroom. "You have heard the testimony, but I am going to review some of it for you . . ."

I discussed the occasion when the police, in shifts, questioned my client for eleven straight hours. "Colonel Sandman for three and a half hours subjected him to questions," I said. "Sandman got tired and Stagenhorst and Moore took over. Moore and Stagenhorst got tired and were relieved by Sandman. Who in the name of God was relieving Bob Lyons?"

I discussed the final evening of Lyons versus the entire police department.

"We all know of Cardinal Mindszenty of Hungary," I said. "He confessed to terrible crimes against the state. We all know his confession wasn't true. He was brainwashed. Psychological warfare. I leave it to you. Robert Lyons signed the confession in the greatest fear he ever felt in his life: fear of the electric chair. That was the one reason. Another was that he had faith in the officers and because he was told it meant only a year or two in some hospital . . ."

I turned to the confession itself. "The state says it has a confession. But, says the state, he didn't do it that way. I am mixed up myself.

"Now, here is a vital point and I'm talking especially to the four ladies on this jury. Men don't know too much about kitchen knives. I don't believe you have ever seen a kitchen without a paring knife. Have you ever seen a set sold unless it was a set of carving knives without a paring knife? The state says the weapon did not come from the Pugh residence. The only person who tells you there wasn't a paring knife in that house was William Pugh. I tell you a paring knife was missing and there was one there!"

The time element was child's play.

"According to Dr. Cleveland," I said, "Mrs. Pugh was attacked and died between 1 and 2 P.M. on the afternoon of the eleventh. Our investigators went to 138 homes and thank God we were able to bring in witnesses to indicate the time. It would have been physically impossible for Robert Lyons to have committed this crime . . . It would have been physically impossible for this man to be in two places at one time. The prosecutor and detectives also checked this information but they didn't bring it in . . .

"You may smile at the H & H Social Club but these clubs are the core of America. That club is just as important to Bob Lyons as any club would be to me. They are all decent, hardworking Americans. His boss, Mr. Tierney, told you Lyons was an outstanding meter reader and had a perfect record . . ."

I sighed. "The state," I said, "says it is chicanery to have Lyons pull up his pants legs to show you his skin disease. I hadn't heard underwear mentioned at all until we showed that. And can you imagine taking the rug Audrey Pugh was slain on and being so egotistical after their so-called expert had examined it as to send it back to Pugh and have it cleaned before we had a chance to examine it for flakes of skin?"

Then I went over to the court reporter's table, picked up those long drawers the prosecutor had introduced as an exhibit, and I told the jury:

"Robert Lyons told you these were not his. He told you that he washes his clothes and his father's clothes and that his father puts dirty clothes in his room . . ."

I motioned to Lyons, who got up from the defense table and stood beside me in front of the jury. I took the long drawers and held them up against my client. If it had not been a murder trial, the sight would have been funny. The drawers were so outlandishly too small they were a joke.

But the joke was on Hover.

"And these, if you please," I said, "are going to send my client to the electric chair! These are the drawers he wore on April 11? These are the drawers that kept the flakes of skin from falling to the floor? You can believe it if you want to.

"Thank God for our jury system. Thank God that we Americans do not accept the dangerous philosophies of some foreign countries.

"Thank God we have liberty which permits us to go down into the bowels of City Hall and lift from this room of Brotherly Love, where fair play, friendship, sympathy and good fellowship prevail, this stinking mess and bring it into this courtroom and give it a public airing which it so sorely needed.

"Thank God that although it has taken some three weeks to purify the air after its contamination, the last semblance of lies and deceit have been obliterated and the truth, the whole truth, at last stands revealed for all to behold.

"To you Robert Lyons, I, as a citizen, want to offer my most humble apology for what has happened to you. Here in America it couldn't happen, but it did happen. You have been arrested and thrown in jail. You have been indicted for a heinous crime and you are standing trial for your life. You have borne your cross, mental anguish and ridicule, and you have somehow withstood the pitiless spotlight of public condemnation. You have somehow withstood the torture of the damned.

"You have borne your cross and taken it on the chin in a manner that should demonstrate to all that—here is a man.

"I don't know whether or not you can find it in your makeup to forgive society for this terrible and despicable wrong. I, at least, as a member of society, can humbly apologize and beg your forgiveness.

"Paul Lawrence Dunbar, the great colored poet, wrote a beautiful poem which should from this day hence be your motto and guide your future life.

"Paul Lawrence Dunbar wrote:

> For I have suffered loss and grievous pain,
> The hurts of hatred and the world's disdain,
> And wounds so deep that love, well-tried and pure,
> Had not the pow'r to ease them or to cure.
> When all is done, say not my day is o'er,
> And that thro' night I seek a dimmer shore:
> Say rather that my morn has just begun,—
> I greet the dawn and not a setting sun,
> When all is done."

Court was adjourned until two-fifteen, at which time Hover would make his final argument for the state and then the judge would charge the jury.

Not a spectator moved, for seats were too hard to come by. Lyons stood and shook hands with me. "Thank you," he said.

I stepped outside. The crowd was increasing in size and a double line of hopeful spectators extended for several hundred feet down the hall. They didn't have a Chinaman's chance of getting into the courtroom but at least in later years they could relate to acquaintances, their children and grandchildren that they were present at the Hamilton County Courthouse when Robert Lyons was tried for the murder of Audrey Pugh.

Court reconvened promptly at two-fifteen and Hover arose and began his address to the jury. He talked of the confession, the honesty of the police, and many other matters. But may I suggest that his arguments failed to impress me? And I am confident that what he had to say did not enhance the cause of the state nor endear him to the jury because juries are outrageous and beautiful animals, sensitive as teen-agers, and hardheaded as old men. Hover made one more mistake. He had ignored all the evidence given by the residents along the route the meter reader took. Ignoring this not only insulted the intelligence of the jury but greatly detracted from any impact which might otherwise have been present.

Judge Hoy immediately charged the jury concerning the law applicable to the case.

With one exception, there was nothing extraordinary about his charge. It included the three degrees of homicide, the definition and legal meaning of each degree, the presumption of innocence, an explanation of the term "beyond a reasonable doubt," and both direct and circumstantial evidence. I sat at the defense table, completely relaxed, listening to the judge rambling on.

But, then, out of the blue, the judge said:

"You are also instructed that the mere fact that a confession is made to law enforcement officers while the accused is in custody does not in and of itself render such confession involuntary. Nor would the fact that a police officer or others may have advised the accused that it would be better to tell the truth be sufficient to exclude the confession. Furthermore, the mere fact that police officers may have made false or untrue statements to the accused as to fingerprints or any other evidence of the defendant's guilt which they did not have would not invalidate a confession made by the defendant if it appears that the only effect of the fraud practiced was to elicit the truth from him."

I stared in disbelief. I was hearing a judge put his stamp of approval on the conduct of Moore, Stagenhorst, and Roney in their use of fake fingerprints. In my opinion, the remarks of the judge were uncalled for. They would be declared prejudicial error in the event of an appeal. Why the judge gave such a charge I'll never know, but I did know this: His charge made the trial a brand-new ballgame. We were in trouble.

I was more than upset. I did the only thing I could do: I took exception to the judge's charge. It was so noted.

At 4:14 P.M. that Friday the jury retired to the jury room.

Ginny joined us at the table. Worry was in her eyes.

"I didn't think we could lose this one," she said, "but now I don't know. Did you ever hear a charge like that before?"

"I don't like the charge any more than you and Harvey do," I said, "but we have one thing to be thankful for. If the case goes against us, we've a built-in insurance policy for a new trial."

Bill Wiggeringloh had long since taken Lyons back to his cell to await the verdict, so we sat around in the courtroom, talking to newsmen and acquaintances about anything and everything that came to mind.

The wake had begun.

Each time, I swear to God that the wake will be my last one. On the surface, to others, I suppose I appear reasonably cheerful and—as far as I can unbend—carefree. But I am not. I am at an enforced cocktail party of the damned. We must make small talk and we must never allow a moment's silence—or we will never be able to talk again.

I also feel sorry for my clients who wait in jail. They go through hell. All they can do is sit in that cell and sweat and pray. The only difference is that my clients haven't any choice. They have to go through with the trial but I don't. I have a choice, for I, at least, can refuse employment. But the more I considered my lot the more it became clear that I too had no choice for this was my chosen profession, my business, my life: This was the way it was and I couldn't do anything about it.

At exactly 5:45 P.M. the jury buzzer sounded. As I waited for the bailiff to answer the jury's summons, I died a thousand times.

When he returned we knew the jury had no verdict but a question, for folded in the bailiff's hand was a piece of paper which he carried to the judge's chamber. But Lyons had to be brought from the cell and back into the court. As the jury sat again in the jury box, all the players were in their places, and the judge said: "I have received the following note signed by the foreman of the jury, 'Was Robert Lyons right-handed or left-handed?' I will say to the jury that the court does not recall any evidence in the trial touching upon this subject. At this time I would like to inquire of all counsel whether or not any of you has any recollection of any evidence which might answer this question put by the jury?"

Hover and I indicated no.

"Ladies and gentlemen of the jury," the judge said, "it will be impossible for the court to answer your question for the reason there was no evidence adduced in the trial of this cause covering this subject. You may retire to your jury room and continue your deliberations."

Again the wake began.

At 6:30 P.M. the court sent the jurors through the snowy streets to a local hotel for their evening meal. Bailiff Gray and Wiggeringloh were in charge of the dinner party to see that the jurors remained together and that no one else communicated with them in any way. After they left the courthouse, we left, too. My wife Anne, Harvey, Ginny, and some personal friends went out into the icy evening to the Terrace Plaza, high above the city, for dinner. We occupied a large table—and never have I heard so many subjects discussed so avidly by so few people. We talked of everything but what was on our minds.

I tried to eat, but couldn't. I wasn't hungry. Soon the meal was over. We returned at once to the courthouse, where we learned that the jury, preceding us by fifteen minutes, was again locked in the jury room and back at its deliberations.

Sitting in the courtroom, my shirt soaking wet and plastered to my back, I made small talk.

I had expected an early verdict but since the jury had been deliberating for over four hours I wasn't sure of anything. At such moments I play little games in my mind. "If," I tell myself, "the jury comes back right away, we've won." "If," I will tell myself another time, "the jury takes five hours, we're ahead."

The buzzer.

Upon the bailiff's return from the jury room, he carried another note.

"Oh, God," I thought. "Not again . . ."

Lyons was recalled, the players assembled, the ritual began.

Said the judge, "The court has received a note signed by the foreman of the jury, reading as follows: 'Will the court explain the difference between second degree murder and manslaughter?' Does the counsel for the state have any comment or objection to the granting of this request?"

Hover said no. The judge put the same question to me. I said no, so the judge explained.

Once again the jury retired.

"I'll be goddamned, we blew it," Harvey whispered. Harvey was more disappointed than I was. "Just as soon," he said, "as this case is over I am going to re-enlist in the navy where everything is quiet and peaceful. Fighting Japanese submarines is child's play compared to this."

At the moment, I believe, he meant every word he said.

I turned and came face to face with a distraught Anne.

"What do you think, Foss?"

"We're dead," I answered, "and you know it as well as I do. The only thing I can't figure out is where I made the mistake."

I walked out to a drinking fountain. I drank deep but still had cotton in my mouth. I returned to counsel table but didn't talk to anyone. I was too sick. All I wanted was for the jury to bring in a verdict —any verdict—so I could get the hell out of that courtroom. I glanced at Hover at the prosecutor's table. His face showed elation.

The buzzer.

Exactly 11:16 P.M.

But this time my heart didn't skip a beat. For me there was no anticipation. A few moments later, Wiggeringloh appeared with Lyons, who gave me that slow, shy smile, but I could not respond.

The jury filed in. I heard the shuffling of their feet as they passed behind me. I heard the sound of chairs being moved about as they settled in the jury box. But I couldn't bring myself to look at them. I was so filled with emotion I felt I was going to explode. I wanted to scream, but the dance does not permit such luxuries. I sat with my head bowed and my eyes fixed on the floor.

"Have you arrived at a verdict?" the judge said.

"We have, your Honor," said the foreman.

"You will hand your verdict to the clerk, who shall read and record same," said the judge.

The clerk moved past me to the jury box, received the verdict, moved from the jury until he stood directly opposite me, and paused. I could hear the paper crinkle.

He cleared his throat and read:

"We the members of the jury find the defendant Robert Lyons— *Not Guilty . . .*"

Since 6:00 P.M. on Friday, November 23, 1956, the H & H Tavern on Eastern Avenue had been packed. All the regulars were there, as were others in the neighborhood who had never before frequented the café. There was, however, one regular missing, and his name was Robert Lyons.

Lyons had lived just around the corner from the tavern and up to six months ago had been a frequent customer. He was single, forty-four years old, a meter man for the city of Cincinnati, and universally respected by his friends and neighbors as a hard-working and law-abiding citizen.

In fact, Lyons's absence from the neighborhood was the cause of the gathering of the clan.

Some six months prior to November 23, Robert Lyons had been arrested and charged with the murder of one Audrey Pugh.

He had been indicted for first degree murder, and his trial had commenced on November 1. It was now 6:00 P.M. on Friday, November 23, and the jury had been deliberating Lyons's fate for some two hours. The patrons in the tavern either stood or sat in small groups drinking their beer and in hushed tones discussing Bob Lyons and his trial for his life. Gone was the usual hilarity. Time stood still, and as the evening wore on a tenseness and suppressed excitement permeated the barroom.

Dance music flowed from a radio on the bar. Whenever the music stopped, every eye was focused on the radio and ears were strained to guarantee that every word might be noted and digested. On three separate occasions programs were interrupted for special bulletins from the Hamilton County Court House. Each time the patrons steeled themselves for the verdict, only to be advised that the jury was merely asking another question of the Court.

At exactly 11:17 it happened.

The music stopped.

"We now take you to the Hamilton County Court House," the announcer stated. "Stand by." Then another voice: "I am standing just outside the courtroom where Robert Lyons is on trial for the murder of Audrey Pugh.

"It has just been officially announced that the jury is ready to report and that they have arrived at a verdict."

Every man and woman in the tavern stared at the radio in hypnotic fascination as the announcer continued:

"It will be a few minutes before the verdict will be read. It is necessary that Lyons be brought to the courtroom from the County Jail, and all counsel must be located."

Some five minutes elapsed, and then the announcer again: "Lyons was just taken into the courtroom, and here comes the jury. The foreman has just handed the verdict to the Criminal Clerk. He is reading it—*Not Guilty*. Robert Lyons has just been found Not Guilty."

For a brief moment the full impact of his words Not Guilty did not seem to register, and then a rebel yell of victory split the air. The announcer's voice droned on and on but his words were lost to posterity. Cheer after cheer echoed throughout the tavern. It was as if the emotionally drained patrons had collectively gone berserk. Some sobbed, but the sobs were drowned out by the laughter and cheers. There was much backslapping and handshaking. Women hugged and kissed men and men hugged and kissed women in a display of unrestrained and uninhibited gaiety and relief. The drinks were on the house and glass after glass was raised in toast after toast to Robert Lyons and his acquittal. Yes, Bob Lyons was coming home!

I did not hear the bailiff adjourn court nor did I observe the judge and prosecutors leave. The first I remember I was in the middle of a shoving, pulling, crazy, beautiful crowd. Lyons was there. The world was there. People were shaking hands and hugging one another. The way television cameras saw it, there wasn't a dry eye in the house. Radiomen were pleading for statements. So were reporters. Flash bulbs popped—and popped again and again and again.

We would have probably been there all night if Bill Wiggeringloh hadn't announced that he had to take Lyons back to jail to officially check him out. As the two left the courtroom, I shouted:

"If you don't have him back in ten minutes I'm going to file a writ of habeas corpus!"

I heard Wiggeringloh's cheerful answer, "Leave it to me, counselor. He'll be back."

"On second thought," said Harvey, "this law practice isn't so bad. I think I'll stick around for a while."

"Who's going to sink all the Jap submarines?" Ginny asked.

"Don't you worry. The admiral will send for me if things get too tough," was Harvey's rejoinder. Harvey started to whistle "I'm Dreaming of a White Christmas" as he left the counsel table and headed for the hall.

"That boy," said Ginny, "is going to love snow the rest of his life. The Abominable Snowman of the Himalayas wouldn't frighten Harvey. He'd love him."

We were all gathered in the hall awaiting Lyons's arrival from jail when I noticed that I, in the excitement, had forgotten my hat. I stepped back into the courtroom to retrieve it. The only light that filtered through the frosted glass of the courtroom doors caused familiar objects to take on strange shapes and sizes. Where moments before there had been excitement, a silence now prevailed.

I had an eerie feeling I wasn't alone. As I picked up my hat I came to a dead stop. Against the far wall, in command of all she could survey, stood the dim form of the mannequin in Audrey Pugh's blue robe and red gown. As I looked at her a strange and unbelievable thing occurred. It had to be an optical illusion or some trick of my imagination but I swear she winked at me.

I couldn't blame you if you didn't believe me for you and I both know it couldn't have happened, but—I blew her a kiss and softly closed the courtroom door.

When we all left the courthouse it must have been near zero. I adjusted my muffler and buttoned up my overcoat for the half-square walk to the lot where I had parked my car.

Lyons was walking beside me and for the first time I realized he was hatless and not wearing an overcoat. Mildred Miller, Cincinnati *Enquirer* columnist, who accompanied us, had this to say in her paper the following morning concerning that short walk to my car:

> It was near midnight Friday. The man in the blue serge suit stepped out into the clear, cold air. His slender body shivered as wintry winds whipped through his thin garments. But his gentle face glowed with an inner warmth. He turned his gaze toward the star-studded heavens. The reverence in his eyes bespoke—better than words—his gratitude to his God. Robert Lyons was a free man.

"You must be freezing," I sympathized to the tall thin man at my side.

"Oh, I don't mind," came his reply. "I—I'm just glad to be here!"

Together we walked down the Court House steps to William F. Hopkins' waiting car. The defense attorney in the Pugh murder trial was filling a promise of many weeks ago—to drive his client home to his 85-year-old dad. There had never been any question in the noted criminal lawyer's mind that Robert Lyons was innocent.

"It is the first time in 37 years of law practice," the attorney had declared, "that I've predicted a verdict of 'not guilty' in a murder trial."

Mr. Hopkins, his wife, his secretary, Virginia Heuser, and his assistant, Harvey Woods, sat in the front seat on the drive to the Lyons home at 240 Setchell Street. Lyons, his brother Bill and I occupied the rear seat.

After some difficulty I started the motor and we headed for Eastern Avenue. For a few moments nobody spoke. The only sound was the soft purr of the motor and the continuing crunch of the tires as they bit into the snow.

Suddenly everybody started to talk at once. For the life of me I can't remember a single word that was said during our trip to the East End. I will never forget, however, the blanket of snow that covered every object and stretched in every direction. It was almost as if Jack Frost had waved a wand to transform Eastern Avenue into a winter wonderland. Tired, old buildings, proudly wearing their mantle of snow, became objects of temporary beauty, glistening and sparkling as my headlights sought them out.

Shrubbery and trees alike, in courtly and graceful curtsies, paid tribute to the weight of their new-found jewels with a magnificent display which defied description. Snow was everywhere. I remembered my statement when I learned of Lyons's ichthyosis: "Hover better button up his overcoat, there's going to be one hell of a snowstorm." Well, there had been quite a snowstorm both inside and outside the courtroom.

I couldn't help but feel the deluge of snow outside had to be a salute to Robert Lyons and his acquittal and to the "flakes of snow" inside, which had played such an important part in that acquittal.

As we drove along Eastern Avenue I had, from time to time,

observed Lyons in the rear-vision mirror. He had been continuously craning his neck to peer through the windshield and as we reached Setchell Street a bright neon sign loomed in the distance. His face spread into a wide, boyish grin. "That's the H & H Café," he exclaimed.

I made a right turn into Setchell Street and brought my car to a halt directly in front of Lyons's modest two-story residence.

"Come up on the porch a minute," Lyons said to me. "There's something I want to show you."

We both got out of the car and I followed him up the short walk to the front porch. He pointed to the door. "Take a look at that," he said.

Attached to the door and printed in large and uneven letters was a cardboard sign stating "I'LL BE BACK." It was signed Robert Vernon Lyons.

Before I could comment he said, "I told you just as soon as the jury heard the evidence we would prove I didn't do it."

This man never ceased to amaze me and I could only marvel at the faith he had in his fellow human beings.

"How in the name of heaven did you manage that?" I asked.

"I gave it to my brother Bill down at the jail and he put it up for me," he said.

"I'll wait in the car," I said, as Lyons opened the door and disappeared into the dim interior.

In a few moments he returned and climbed into the back seat.

"Everything all right?" I asked.

He blew his nose and then in a hoarse whisper said, "Dad said to thank you."

This simple, direct message, sans flowery embellishments, brought a lump to my throat. The cold must have gotten to my eyes for as I started the car my vision had become somewhat impaired.

I drove back to Eastern Avenue, made a right turn, and pulled up to the H & H Café. The place was jumping. Lyons alighted. I slid from behind the wheel and joined him on the sidewalk where we stood just a few feet from the entrance to the café. He held out his hand.

"I don't know what anybody else thinks but I know I've got the most beautiful legs in the world," he said.

"I agree with you," I replied. "They are beautiful, but you better keep them warm and put on some long underwear."

"I will if I can borrow a suit from my father. Won't you come inside?" he asked.

"No," I said. "These are your friends. This is your homecoming. It belongs to you and you alone."

"Well, thanks for everything," he said. "I'll be seeing you." He opened the café door. A scream of joy split the air as he disappeared behind a wall of human flesh.

As I pulled away from the curb I could hear men's and women's voices raised in a mighty blood-tingling salute.

"For he's a jolly good fellow,
For he's a jolly good fellow!"

And then, as the distance lengthened, the singing faded into the night.

The next morning the newspapers would be angry that Lyons had gone free. Some would question the police tactics used. Hover would do a slow burn—in full view of the voters. Perhaps Al Segal, writing as "Cincinnatus" in the *Post,* said it best:

Suppose the victim of this murder case had been some Mrs. Smith who lived in a tenement house on upper Race Street, instead of one whom the newspapers described as being a socialite? In such case, how many pages of the newspapers would the trial have been given? The trial would have had no more than a few paragraphs a day, and wouldn't have lasted as long as it did.

CHAPTER 13
the lady was not
for burning

I

For the several of you who delight in the macabre, I note that, in addition to men who have died in the Ohio chair, three ladies have danced the dance electric.

In 1938 Anna Marie Hahn, convicted of dispatching old men with poison, was carried limp to her electric doom. In 1954, two other ladies died in that awful seat. Dovie Dean, convicted of poisoning her farmer husband, walked calmly to the chair and death as one walks to the front door to meet a long-lost friend. Edie Butler, convicted of drowning another lady, walked mumbling to the chair; in her hand she clutched a crucifix. Electricity respects neither sex nor race. Edie Butler was black. Anna Marie Hahn and Dovie Dean were white.

May I tell you of one woman candidate who cheated the chair of its victim? True, she lied to the police, to me, and to the world. As the result of these lies she duly achieved the hollow honor of being the fourth woman in Ohio to be sentenced to electrocution. But her sentence was never carried out.

Here is the story of a bizarre murder case: The State of Ohio versus Edythe Margaret Klumpp. In many ways, however, it is much more than that; it is several stories wrapped into one. It is the story of a prosecutor so intent on victory that he proved, and the jury believed, that a murder took place where it did not take place, that a murder was committed by a person who did not commit it, and that the victim's body was burned by a person who did not burn it. It is the story of my efforts as Mrs. Klumpp's attorney after her conviction and death sentence to save her life. It is the story of a prosecutor who made up his mind and inexorably refused to budge from an untenable position. It is the story of a humane and conscientious Governor who, despite public abuse and large-scale criticism, stuck to his guns and prevented a miscarriage of justice but in the process laid the groundwork for his own political demise.

It is a story that couldn't happen but did.

On Thursday, October 30, 1958, Mrs. Louise Bergen, thirty-two, later described by the press as "an attractive brunette," left the Stillpass Transit Company, where she worked as a secretary. She drove from the company parking lot at 5 P.M., vanished in the rush-hour traffic that makes Spring Grove Avenue a bumper bedlam, and was never seen alive again.

Later that night, in an apparently unrelated incident, Deputy Sheriff Irwin Schulte recorded that Anderson Township Rangers had delivered to him a pair of glasses and a portion of a necklace, plus a pair of child's shorts which had been bloodied. The report indicated that these objects had been discovered in the Cincinnati suburb of Mount Washington by a man named Bayes. The sheriff forwarded the items to the Kettering Crime Laboratory, where they remained until transferred to the office of C. Watson Hover, the Hamilton County prosecutor. In the prosecutor's office, these items were tagged as unmarked evidence and put into a file that contained oddments of other such evidence to which the prosecutor's office could attach no meaning.

Now let us move from that Thursday to Saturday. On the Saturday morning following the disappearance of Mrs. Bergen, three duck hunters shivered in the cold and fog in their little boat on Lake Cowan, a state park in another county. As far the the duck hunters were concerned, their outing wasn't going well at all. Their motor had conked out, wouldn't start, and there they drifted in the gloom. They managed to row their boat to the nearest shore: a lonely stand of trees partly hidden by the fog. One of the hunters got out to get the car and bring it back to that location; they planned to haul the boat out of the lake and kiss the outing a chilly good-bye.

After the first hunter vanished in the mist and gray, the two others searched the wilderness shore for the best place to pull their boat out of the lake. One of them came across a pile of charred ruins, the leftover debris of a fire. He thought at first that vandals had set fire to a store-window dummy which, by then, was only charcoal from the waist up.

But as he looked closer, he felt sick. What had been burned was no mannequin.

Because the body had been discovered on state park property, enter the state police. The officers shot many pictures of the melancholy scene. Then, as best they could, they collected the crumbling body and removed it from the park. Under the body they found the rest of the necklace which had been found in Mount Washington, a piece of red cloth, a small remnant of a green dress, a penknife, and keys on a key chain. But the body itself had been so badly burned that identification was impossible. Having stripped the death scene of its victim and its evidence, the state police left. Once more the only sounds were water lapping and the honk of ducks, flying free in the fog.

Now, as in television, let us move to another scene.

We find ourselves in Cincinnati's new police building, a modern plant that lacks the smells and the antiquity of the catacombs of City Hall. The office of the chief, for instance, has wall-to-wall carpeting and soft lighting, the very feeling of an office occupied by a high muckity-muck of big business, which some say is the way the chief then wanted it. No matter. The rest of the building, while less magnificent is nonetheless clean and bright and efficient. We watch as an emaciated Lothario walks into the main lobby, blinks, then heads toward the counter and the uniformed officer behind it. Our visitor is tall, lean, partially bald, and—at least in his own estimation—one of Cincinnati's greatest lovers. His name? William Bergen.

"May I help you, sir?" the officer asks.

Our balding hero unfolds his tale: his estranged wife has been missing for some time.

The officer nods. He brings forth a form and writes upon it the essentials: Bergen's wife was thirty-two, weighed 135 pounds, had dark hair, brown eyes, and when last seen had been wearing tortoise-shell glasses, green knit dress, red coat, black leather pumps . . .

Efficiency—and the zeroing in on a thousand reports.

The sergeant completes the missing-person report and, as he bids Bergen good day, assures him that a thorough investigation will immediately follow.

The clues found by the state police at Lake Cowan had been broadcast to all law enforcement agencies within a three-state radius. They matched perfectly the clothing described by Bergen. Now if the keys found by the charred corpse fitted the missing lady's car, Louise Bergen had been found.

The keys did fit.

Later the same day the victim was positively identified as Louise Bergen and the hunt was on for her killer or killers. Lead after lead was explored, digested, and discarded by the homicide squad in a futile effort to track down the guilty party or parties.

It was not, however, until some two weeks later, when Edythe Klumpp was scheduled to take a polygraph test, that the investigation finally struck pay dirt.

Mrs. Klumpp drove to her rendezvous with the police in her own car and parked just outside City Hall. Unbeknown to her, as she faced the challenge of the lie detector her automobile was being searched and checked by crime experts for blood and other evidence. For three hours Mrs. Klumpp and the polygraph squared off, but it was an unequal contest. The final result was inevitable. The polygraph won, for the machine indicated that Mrs. Klumpp was lying and that she had some guilty knowledge of Louise Bergen's death. Thus, Edythe Klumpp—with whom Bergen had been living—was quickly arrested.

She was now ready to talk—and what a fairy tale she spun for the police and the prosecutor.

Mrs. Klumpp told the police that in March, while working as a waitress at the Sky Galley Restaurant at Lunken Airport, she had met Bill Bergen. Some four weeks later they had started dating, became intimate. Soon Bergen moved into her home in Mt. Washington and several months after that he gave her a wedding ring, whereupon she and Bergen announced that they were man and wife.

Mrs. Klumpp continued. "On Thursday, October 30, Louise called me about ten minutes to five. She wanted me to meet her and talk to her. I had the Girl Scouts there (six of them), teaching them to sew so they could get their sewing badge. I do not get paid for this. The kids all know me as 'Aunt Edythe.' I asked her if I could meet her later, around six-thirty, and she said she had an appointment for later. The girls left around five. I called Bill at the office but he wasn't there.

"The first time I saw the pistol was when Bill moved into my house. He brought it with him. Then one Sunday when we were down at the airport with some friend of his that had a place for target practice, they decided to go out and shoot a little bit. Bill was going to give me lessons. First he had me shoot a rifle. Then he'd let me shoot the pistol. He was going to join this shooting club at the Hotel Alms and he was intending to take me with him. Bill always kept the shells in the trunk of his car. A couple of weeks before this happened, I decided to take some of the shells and try to shoot a few times before we went down there. I took four of them and put them in my purse. I was going to practice down by the river where I was sure I wouldn't hit anything. He always kept the gun in his drawer so the kids couldn't get it. On Tuesday afternoon I went to the Farmer's Mart to get some vegetables. I went down by the river by the waterworks. There are a lot of old boats down there. I loaded the gun one at a time. I had put the fourth shell in. I had no reason for not shooting it but I didn't. Later I forgot it was loaded. I know it looks stupid when I tell you I loaded it one at a time but that is what I did. I wrapped it in the white cloth that Bill kept it in and put it in the glove compartment of my car. When I got home, I took the vegetables in and forgot about the pistol.

"On my way over to meet Louise at Swifton Village the night

this happened I opened the glove compartment to get a Kleenex and I saw the pistol. I thought to myself—I forgot to put the pistol back and I better put it back when I get home because Bill is so particular about it, so I laid the gun on the seat beside me. I did not unwrap it. It was there when I met Louise. She got in the front seat. I met her by Urmetz Jewelers. She did not see the gun. My purse was right there too, kind of over it. I picked Louise up in the middle of one of those lanes. There was no place to park. We started up North Bend Road and I was going to park at the bottom of North Bend but there was a lot of traffic so we went to Caldwell Park. On the way there, we talked about the kids and Hallowe'en and stuff like that. She wanted to know if Bill had made up his mind what to do. I told her I had asked him to wait until after Christmas because of the kids. She had made up her mind to get a divorce and she was not going back to him.

"It was just getting dusk when we drove into Caldwell Circle. She told me that she had said to Bill, 'That girl loves you, don't make her as miserable as you made me.' When we got there I wanted to push the seat back so I could sit sideways and talk to her. I said, 'Wait a minute, the seat is stuck, probably something under it.' I got out and got into the back seat to see what was holding it and there was a Coke bottle under it. It seems to me I just pulled it out and left it lay there. I probably took it out when I cleaned the car the next day. When I straightened up she had the gun in her hand, pointing it at me. She was smiling. Nothing was ever said about being mad or anything like that. I made a grab for the gun. When we were struggling over the gun it went off. She slid down and her head was by the steering wheel. When the gun went off, the blood started coming from her mouth. I just remember it gushing out of her mouth. I remember that blood and that she made a gurgling sound. I don't remember hitting her at all. (Several times I have suffered from blackouts. I just come to and I'm some place. I went to a doctor about this and I remember telling him that I would get real dizzy and pass out.)

"The next thing I remember I was sitting on the edge of the back seat and I realized what had happened. I felt her heart and her pulse and couldn't feel anything. First I thought I would call Bill and then I thought he wouldn't believe what had happened. I was going to pull her out and leave her there but I thought something would be connected with me. I was scared to death. I went to the right side of the car and pulled her out. She was quite a bit bigger than me, weighed about 150 pounds. I weigh between 125 and 130. I have been having trouble with my arms for some time. Hardly able to use them.

"Her head hit the car and then the ground. I just dragged her by her feet. It was beginning to get dusk. There was nobody around. I opened the trunk of the car and had an awful time trying to get her in. Her legs would flop out. I couldn't seem to get all of her in at one time. I could hardly lift her—I would get one part in and the other part would fall out. Finally, I got her in the car. She was on her left side with her legs curled up. I had to kind of push her legs together. Then I drove home real quick. Parked the car in front of the house. My daughter was there when I got home. I cleaned up right away and went over to teach my sewing class. I was a little late getting there. The body was in the car when I drove over there. It was about seven twenty-five when I got there and I was there until nine twenty-five.

"I called Bill when I got out of school and asked him why he was not waiting for me and he said he saw that I had the car. I asked him if he wanted me to come over and he said, 'No, I'll be home in a few minutes.' When I got home I parked the car in front of the house. It just didn't seem like it had happened. It seemed like someone else had done it. That night I could hardly pray about it. Bill and I were sleeping together and I thought about telling him a couple of times during the night but he was asleep. The next day I washed the car in the driveway. It was still wet and I put a towel over the seat and went to get the two kids that I keep during the day. It was after ten o'clock when I started for Lake Cowan. At first I thought I would drive somewhere and put her out. I was thinking about the river or some place where I could put her. I don't know why I went to Lake Cowan but I had been there a few years ago. I had to take the kids with me. I couldn't leave them alone. They are one, two, and three years old. The baby was in the front seat with me and the other two in the back. Lake Cowan is about fifty miles from here. I bought some gasoline here in Cincinnati. I thought if I couldn't get her in the water, I would just burn the body. I parked in a spot that was not too secluded. I thought about leaving her alongside the road.

Then I drove down this road and decided to leave her there and burn her. The trunk lid was up, the kids couldn't see what I was doing. The baby was asleep. I parked the car up as far as I could. I had to flop her over a couple of times to get her out. Then I poured gasoline over the body and threw some rags on it and lit it with a match. I got in the car as soon as I lit the match and drove away. I didn't look back. Then I went home and finished cleaning the car. I didn't get all the blood out."

At the conclusion of her statement, Detectives Eugene Moore and Wilbur Stagenhorst argued with Mrs. Klumpp about the alleged struggle over the pistol and her statement that Mrs. Bergen sustained a mortal wound in the throat. The coroner's finding did not mention such a wound, nor had the autopsy produced any bullet or metal residue which might support Mrs. Klumpp's contention. It was the coroner's finding that Mrs. Bergen died of fractures of the skull; injuries to the brain; and epidural, subdural, and subarachnoid hemorrhages—or as a result of multiple impact to the head.

The coroner had released Mrs. Bergen's body, which was at the moment on a midnight train headed East for burial.

It took immediate action on the part of the police to reclaim the body, which was accomplished at the Union Station in Columbus, Ohio, where, once again, Mrs. Bergen's danse macabre was interrupted by the omnipotent hand of a murder investigation in order that the coroner might examine it again. Upon reexamination of the body, an embarrassed coroner reported that metal residue was found in the area of the badly charred throat tissue. The finding established the fact that Mrs. Bergen had sustained a gunshot wound in her throat and threw grave doubt upon the authenticity of the coroner's original report as to the cause of death.

This new finding made no difference to the police and prosecutor, however. Their attitude remained inexorable. They had absolved Bergen of any connection with his wife's death. Mrs. Klumpp had given them a confession, and they had reconstructed the facts and had formed their own interpretation of what she had revealed. No further investigation was necessary. No different interpretation could be advanced.

Unfortunately for Mrs. Klumpp, the police and the prosecutor swallowed her story hook, line, and sinker. The public did too. It never occurred to the police to check further the truth or falsity of her confession. Not once did the police and prosecutor subject her to further polygraph tests, nor did they employ other means to ascertain what credence could be given to her statement. They were satisfied and sure that they had the guilty party and stated so to the press and all who would lend an ear.

And if anyone should imagine that I may have strayed from an objective path or that I am not stating facts, hear this from the answers of Detective Gene Moore when cross-examined by me at the Klumpp trial. I am quoting from the official transcript of the Klumpp trial, page 786:

> Q. Did you say to her or explain, or did Mr. Stagenhorst say to her what her constitutional rights were at that moment?
> A. No, sir, we did not. We knew it was not necessary.
> Q. Now you say you knew it was not necessary. Will you explain to the court and jury what you mean by that statement?
> A. We had a nasty crime on our hands. We knew we had the guilty party and as I understand the Ohio law it is not necessary to inform a defendant while the investigation is under way of all his constitutional rights.

Any evidence coming to the attention of the police and prosecutor which fit their interpretation of the facts was woven into a cloak of guilt being prepared for Mrs. Klumpp's adornment at her trial. Any evidence which did not meet these standards and specifications was discarded and held for naught. It had to be spurious for it was incongruous to the "known facts."

Mrs. Klumpp was charged with first degree murder and the following morning appeared before Judge Clarence Denning to answer that charge.

When I was called into the case I had already known Edythe Klumpp because our firm had been instrumental in getting her divorce. Although she had asked for me the night she was questioned, I had a difficult time getting to see her. The next morning when I arrived at Central Station, where she was supposed to be caged, she was not there. Detectives had secretly whisked her to the alleged murder scene, pumping her for all they were worth, before she could enjoy the benefit of counsel.

I was not permitted to see my client until that afternoon at Central Station. There we held a quick conference: she on one side of the bars and I on the other.

When I saw her through the bars that afternoon, I could see that she had changed since our last meeting. Gone was the fat which had rendered her undesirable. She had slimmed to the point of being svelte. But I could still see that she remained the exasperating female whose personality alternated between girlish foolishness and those ice-cold moments when she worried about keeping her family financially afloat. As she gripped the bars that afternoon she was not the silly giggler; her face was solemn, white, and drawn.

Also, she was frowning at me.

"I asked for you yesterday," she complained.

I nodded.

"And they told me," she went on, "that I couldn't see you until I confessed the murder."

"Listen," I said to her, equally irritated, "I telephoned Colonel Sandman and told him I wanted to see you at eight-thirty this morning but when I got here they'd taken you somewhere else. What the hell is going on here? It's now three in the afternoon, Mrs. Klumpp. You've been talking to them twenty-six hours—and they haven't booked you yet!"

We didn't chat long. There was little privacy there.

I do not usually try murder cases in police court. In the case of first degree murder I find it more efficient to have the grand jury first return an indictment, to have my client released on bond or deposited in the Hamilton County Jail, and then proceed in the proper manner in the proper court. But that morning at City Hall there were some things I had to get straight. That's why I said to the judge: "Normally, your Honor, I would waive preliminary hearing. And though I don't wish to go into all the details, I would like to hear at least some of the testimony on the cause of death and the venue. I want to be sure I'm in the right court. I understand from the newspapers that a first degree murder warrant is also being filed in Clinton County where the body was found."

I didn't have to explain why I wanted to know the cause of death. Thanks to the many interpretations of the coroner, I think the court was as confused as I was. Had the victim been shot? Burned to death?

Clubbed to death? Or had Mrs. Bergen been a victim of carbon monoxide?

I asked for and was granted a five-day continuance in order that I might check the court's venue and the cause of death. But the court held that these were matters that could be explored if and when Mrs. Klumpp was indicted, and thereupon bound her over to the grand jury without bond.

Mrs. Klumpp was guided back down the stairs to Women's Detention. Flash bulbs popped. Photographers had a field day. Edythe Klumpp was then removed to the county jail atop the Hamilton County Courthouse.

That afternoon in the county jail's little consultation room, where you and I have been so many times before, Ginny, Harvey, and I awaited the appearance of my client.

"This is going to be another one of those," Ginny said. She seemed sad about something.

"Another one—like what?" I said.

She shrugged.

"While you were at court this morning," she said, "we had six obscene calls."

"There'll be more," I said.

"I know," Harvey said.

Obscene calls—the applause a criminal lawyer gets from his appreciative fans. No wonder few lawyers seek the courtroom arena. Some of their wives would be shocked at the kind of calls a criminal lawyer gets—at home as well as at the office. I remember once, before I was married, coming home and finding my mother crying.

But I had no time to brood upon these melancholy facets of the enlightened public. Edythe Klumpp had entered and taken a seat opposite me.

"Before you say anything, Mrs. Klumpp," I said, "I want to explain a few things to you. You are going to be tried for your life. I know what that means. I've been through it hundreds of times. The only clients of mine who don't get a fair verdict are the ones who lie to me . . ."

As you know, the first time around, I let my clients talk—without interruption. Mrs. Klumpp talked for three straight hours and spun me a fairy tale. All it lacked was for her to begin it with "Once upon a time . . ."

I couldn't believe my own ears. I was supposed to be hearing a confidential statement between client and attorney. Her life was at stake. Yet she sat across from me, smug and sure of herself, repeating practically the same statement—and confession—she had given the police.

Finally I became angry. It couldn't have happened the way she said it had.

"Are you quite finished?" I said.

She nodded again.

"Now," I said, "I'll tell you why you're a liar."

She looked as if I had struck her, but she listened.

"First," I said, "do you mean to tell me that you burned the body of Mrs. Bergen in broad daylight in a state park—the fire must have lasted at least three hours—and that no one in that time noticed anything?"

She nodded. That's the way it happened, her eyes said.

"Do you mean to tell me that you, unassisted, lifted a body weighing more than 135 pounds into the trunk of that car?" I demanded. "I know for a fact you had to quit your waitress job because you lacked the strength to carry trays!"

But again she nodded. That's the way it happened, her eyes said.

I argued with her. I pleaded with her. I begged her to trust me and to relate the true facts.

"Someone else had to be there," I said, "helping you."

She shook her head.

And I knew instinctively who that someone had been.

But she said nothing—and there was nothing I could do.

I warned her that if she persisted in the fairy tale, she was headed for the chair.

She shrugged.

Well, that was that.

As Ginny, Harvey, and I rode the cab back to the office, I seethed.

"If I don't believe her, and I don't, you know damn well a jury won't believe her."

"What do you do now?" Ginny asked.

"Defend her against herself," I said.

I didn't worry too much at that point. Time, I believed, was on my side. I was certain in the ample time that remained that Edythe Klumpp would tell the true story.

I was never more wrong in my life.

It was near the end of February when Mrs. Klumpp was indicted for first degree murder. After her arraignment and formal plea of Not Guilty, we renewed our efforts to persuade her to tell the truth. We argued with her by the hour, and on two occasions I walked out on her, but it made no difference. She stuck to her lies.

"Someone had to help you," I kept hammering.

She insisted she had lugged the dead body around by herself.

One day I was more fed up than usual.

"What goes on here, Mrs. Klumpp?" I demanded. "According to what I hear, Bergen has been visiting you here at the county jail at least three times a week."

She nodded.

"And he stays forever each visit," I raved. "What the hell is going on?"

"He believes my story even if you don't," she said. "He's giving me moral support."

"Well," I said, "don't hold your breath waiting for him to show up again. He just quit his job and took off to Washington, D.C., with a girl half his age."

We noticed a change in Mrs. Klumpp after Bergen's departure. She was tense and continually depressed. Her face became pale and drawn. Time after time I felt that she was about to break and tell me the truth but at the last moment a look of fear would come into her eyes and her lips would lock in two bloodless lines that no probing of mine would release.

The time had come for me to make a decision.

I finally realized that Mrs. Klumpp was not going to change her cock-and-bull story and that if I continued to represent her it would have to be according to the alleged facts set forth in her original statement to the police and prosecutor and later repeated to me. I was convinced that she was lying but there seemed to be nothing that I could do about it.

I could withdraw from the case, but I was so intrigued and consumed with curiosity I just couldn't let go. I decided to see it through with a hope and prayer that the real facts might develop at the trial. So the die was cast and although Mrs. Klumpp was her own worst enemy I decided to attempt to save her—in spite of herself.

II

In May the special murder jury was drawn from the jury wheel. Seventy-five names were drawn, twelve of which would finally be selected as the jury that would try Mrs. Klumpp for her life.

To defend anyone on a first degree murder charge where a life is at stake is a Herculean undertaking and soul-searching experience. It is difficult enough to prepare and try a first degree murder case when you have all the facts available and you have a client who is truthful and cooperative. But to defend a woman who tells you one falsehood after another is to have embarked upon a hazardous undertaking which is doomed from the very outset.

After the jury was impaneled, the first order of business was a tour of the various sites: the scarred earth where the charred body had been found, the home of the accused, the exact spot where the car of Mrs. Klumpp was supposed to have parked when the foul deed was done, plus here, there, and everywhere. The jury traveled in an air-conditioned city bus. Edythe Klumpp traveled with a deputy in a car in the wake of the huge bus. Though a crowd had assembled outside the courthouse to see the junket off, Mrs. Klumpp averted her eyes. She pretended that no one was there.

A pleasant day for a drive in the hot sun.

One of the stops was near the water's edge at Lake Cowan. There—in tangled underbrush—duck hunters had found the body. As we pulled up, sun-tanned swimmers paused in their play to watch the jurors step down from the bus. The country air smelled of lake water, plowed fields, fumes from the diesel bus, and the blacktop road which bubbled in the heat. The jury studied the site in silence. The only sounds were the idling of the bus engine, the sounds that splashing and distant swimmers made, music from a picnicker's transistor radio, and the buzz of insects as they swarmed about in concert. Where the death fire had been, the willows were burned black. Then in silence the jurors turned and walked back to the bus. The swimmers—leggy girls and handsome young men—had long since returned to their splashing games.

Another stop was at the former home of Mrs. Klumpp—before her divorce—now occupied by her ex-husband. When the bus stopped a block from the house itself, the jurors dismounted in the heat and straggled like Coxie's army up the hilly road. Since her arrest Edythe Klumpp had sold her half-interest in the house to her former husband, who lived there with three of their four children. But when we visited the house, no one was about. While the jurors wandered round the yard, I paused, sat at the deserted picnic table, and watched a cat lap water from a miniature swimming pool.

Frank Gusweiler, the judge, had already instructed the jury that on the tour it must not play detective nor search for new clues.

"It is not the function of the jury," he had said, "to try to gather evidence. The purpose of the visit is so that the jury might better understand evidence and testimony it will hear later."

Again the jurors boarded the bus, this time heading for Mariemont Inn, where they had lunch. Edythe Klumpp did not attend.

The newspapers played up the Edythe Klumpp trial. Some spectators arrived at the courthouse four hours before court opened and the prosecution began. Some actually brought sandwiches and cold drinks to have a picnic—a modern Roman holiday!—whenever the court recessed. Elderly ladies carried cushions, the better to sit on the hard benches. Those who did not get into the courtroom itself gathered in a crowd outside its doors or lined the stairs.

Everyone was in attendance but a carnival bum selling balloons.

County Prosecutor C. Watson Hover joked that "We would all be rich if we hired the Cincinnati Gardens for the trial. But I'm afraid Foss Hopkins would object to the venue."

I said nothing. What was there to say to this man—and, indeed, what is there that I can write here now that Mr. Hover has gone on to his own reward? C. Watson Hover was of small physical stature but a pleasant and amiable fellow with an easy grin and a solemn manner. Whether he was unhappy because, only the year before, he had lost the Pugh murder case to me, I cannot and will not say.

Now the trial began in earnest.

Harry C. Schoettmer, assistant prosecutor, delivered a powerful opening statement in which, among other things, he said: "Three duck hunters found the body after the motor on their boat conked out . . . one of the boys spotted the charred remains . . . he'll tell you that from the waist up it was nothing but charcoal. You'll see a picture of that scene!"

Schoettmer said that state highway patrolman Robert Dunbar found under the body half a necklace, a piece of red cloth, a key chain, and a penknife. On that chain, he said, was a key that fit the Oldsmobile Mrs. Bergen had left at the Swifton Center. The luggage key fit Mrs. Bergen's luggage. The knife was the same kind of knife that the president of Stillpass had given to each employee.

Schoettmer went on to tell of the affair my client was having with Mr. Bergen, husband of the dead woman. He told how each time Bergen said he wanted to go back to his wife, my client had pretended pregnancy. He described the murder struggle, as, in his estimation, it had taken place. He told how Edythe Klumpp had gotten into the back seat, "crawled behind Mrs. Bergen—and fired the shot. The body toppled. Mrs. Bergen's head went under the wheel. Edythe Klumpp battered that head. She slugged it with a gun . . ."

From the spectators came murmurs of approval. This was better than television. They clutched their sandwich bags, leaned forward in their seats, and listened in awe and pleasure.

"We know she placed the body in the trunk," the assistant prosecutor was saying. "We will have the skirt of Edythe Klumpp, which was well saturated with blood. When she got home, her daughter Jill noticed the blood, but Mrs. Klumpp explained it by saying that she had a nosebleed . . ."

On and on he went.

Then, in that hot stuffy courtroom, it was my turn at the jury.

I turned first to Mrs. Klumpp.

"Unless you tell the truth," I said, "you're as good as dead. Tell me who was with you?"

But she said nothing.

She refused to look at me.

As I rose from my chair beside her at the defense table, before that crowd of one hundred spectators, all of whom were the enemy waiting for the kill, I felt older and more tired than I have ever felt before or since. I was in an *Alice in Wonderland* world—drowning in gobbledygook—but for once the looking glass was real. As I faced the jury I could not think of one thing to say.

I looked at the jury a long time before I began.

"All right, Foss," I told myself gloomily, "do the best you can. Work with what truth you have but to hell with the lies."

But tell the jury what?

I didn't know, but they were waiting. I had to say something. I cleared my throat and began.

"After listening to two hours and fifteen minutes of Mr. Schoettmer's statement," I said, "I have reached the conclusion that my client must be a monster."

Murmurs from the spectators were gaveled to silence.

"If the state can establish and prove what it claims," I went on, "you'll find her Guilty of murder in the first degree. From the picture painted here, if proven, she must indeed be despicable."

I let that sink in. Then I continued in a gentler tone.

"But I want to give you some of Mrs. Klumpp's real background," I said. "Edythe Klumpp was born January 15, 1918, in Cincinnati. She graduated from Hartwell High School when she was seventeen. She met George Montgomery in 1936. She fell in love with him and had a son by him, a son who has been in the air force for two years now. In 1939 or 1940 she got a divorce and custody of the child. Her first husband did not contribute to that child's support. So she went to work. In 1940 she married Robert Klumpp and four children were born of that marriage. One died in infancy and the others, Jill, Joan, and Jan were living with Mrs. Klumpp at the time of this tragedy. She worked at Rollman's, the Big Store, the Sky Galley, and had sewing classes. Her home was rated as one of the outstanding foster homes in the county. She sang in the choir at church. She was president of a youth group. And of the Mr. and Mrs. group . . ."

I paused. "This," I wanted to say, "is your monster!" I didn't. I went on in a logical manner.

"As fate would have it, one day Bill Bergen came into the Sky Galley. Bergen plays a very important part in this trial," I added. I knew he played the most important part. But I had no proof. I had only intuition.

"Approximately six weeks later, Bergen called Mrs. Klumpp and there was a date. The evidence will show that Bill Bergen came to her home and they watched the late movie. Bill Bergen told Mrs. Klumpp that he and Mrs. Bergen had not been living together as man and wife for over a year and they were going to separate. For a period of two weeks Bergen had a date with Mrs. Klumpp every night. He professed his love and asked her to marry him. We will establish the fact that two months after the first date Bergen and Mrs. Klumpp became intimate. It was only shortly thereafter that Bill Bergen moved into Mrs. Klumpp's residence. Then we come to that fateful day, October 30, 1958."

I paused, walked over to the defense table, shuffled some papers, and turned again to the jury.

"We are trying Edythe Klumpp for murder," I said. "Not for burning a body. She, on that day, conducted a sewing class for girls. About ten before five, the telephone rang. On the other end was Mrs. Bergen. Mrs. Bergen said, 'I want to see you and discuss this matter of Bill Bergen and myself.' When they got to Swifton Center, Mrs. Bergen got into Mrs. Klumpp's car. It was Beggar's Night. There was no animosity. They discussed Hallowe'en, at first, and the kids . . ."

On and on I went but my heart was not in that opening statement. There was no way to free me from the looking glass.

As I sat down, finally, Edythe Klumpp nodded as if in approval of my words.

It was a strange trial as murder trials go. Everything was too pat. Mrs. Klumpp had set the tempo when she dictated the script. The police duly recorded her story and passed it on to the prosecuting attorney, who in turn placed his own interpretation upon her statement and directed its production. The magnificent and deadly production was not unlike some mythological tragedy with Osiris, the god of death, hovering in the wings patiently and inexorably waiting for the curtain to fall to claim his own.

All during the trial the spectators craned their necks, looking first at Mrs. Klumpp, then at the cardboard box from which the prosecuting attorney and his helpers pulled object after object recovered from the death site.

Said one newspaper account: "Every spectator interviewed has an opinion of Mrs. Klumpp's guilt or innocence and an idea of the outcome of the trial."

You could see those opinions glistening in their eyes.

When the pictures of the death scene were shown to the jury, the coroner sat in the witness box and used a small spotlight as a pointer to emphasize the different portions of the burned body. His testimony was as simple as it was shocking. He made the point that the body was so badly burned it could hardly be identified at all.

It was during the direct examination of the pathologist that the prosecutor, over my objection, was permitted to exhibit an enlarged colored slide of Mrs. Bergen's burned and partially destroyed body. To support my objection, I had argued that to permit the jurors to view this exhibit could only inflame their minds against Mrs. Klumpp to a point where they could not render a fair and impartial verdict. One only had to witness the looks of horror and disbelief on the juror's faces as the gruesome picture was thrown on the screen to understand that the exhibit had inflamed the jury beyond recall.

There could be no doubt nor could one misinterpret the fatal message that the juror's eyes conveyed as they gazed at Mrs. Klumpp. It was there for all to hear and see. The day of reckoning was close at hand. The coup de grace was only a matter of time.

Mrs. Klumpp got the message for she was never quite the same thereafter. She became listless and resigned to her fate and no amount of pleading on our part seemed to help.

The prosecutor asked the coroner if any foreign matter—a bullet?—had been found.

"There was complete destruction of the neck and neck organs," the coroner testified. "There was a depressed fracture of the bone of the skull."

The prosecutor persisted. Could any of these injuries, he wanted to know, have been caused prior to death?

I objected.

But I was overruled.

The question stood.

"Yes," the coroner said. "They were sufficient to cause death."

At one point in my cross-examination, though, I produced a human skull from a hatbox and asked the coroner to point out where the fractures had been. The coroner promptly announced that a sliver of metal was found on the left side of the under surface of the jaw near the jawbone.

"You didn't mention that piece of metal," I said, "when Mr. Hover questioned you. Why not?"

The coroner gave me a look.

"I wasn't asked about it," he said.

Only once during the trial did I dare allow myself the luxury of hope. That was when Bill Bergen himself was on the stand and with his testimony strapping my client securely into the electric chair. Edythe Klumpp, by then, had become a listless participant in the spectacle.

But she listened with interest to what her lover had to say. His testimony, of course, was derogatory. Her eyes never left his face as he babbled on, telling his whereabouts on that evening of death and his association with my client the remainder of that awful night. I could hear Edythe's breath quicken. I watched her closely. Anger was in her eyes.

Bergen told the jury that in February he had first met Edythe Klumpp while she was employed as a waitress at the Sky Galley Restaurant at Lunken Airport. Shortly thereafter he had phoned her and they had dated. He further testified that some months later they had become intimate and after that saw each other almost every night. On May 29 he and his wife had separated and he took up residence at Mrs. Klumpp's home in Mt. Washington. He told how in June he had purchased a ring for Mrs. Klumpp and that they had announced to the neighbors they were man and wife. Going on to October 30 Bergen testified that he finished work about four-thirty, at which time he drove some three blocks to Stillpass to see a friend, one Mel Abrams. He and Abrams talked for a short time, he said, after which he returned to his place of employment, Colonial Stores.

From the record at the trial:

Q: Then you went back to Colonial Stores?
A: I did.
Q: What time did you finally leave Colonial Stores?
A: Some time after seven.

Bergen then testified that he drove out past Woodward High School to check on whether or not Mrs. Klumpp had driven her car to the school where she taught a sewing class on Thursday nights.

Upon seeing her car, Bergen testified that he drove immediately to Abrams's home where he remained until he received a call at about nine-thirty from Mrs. Klumpp advising him that she was finished with her class. Bergen told the jury that he then drove to Bloomingdale Road in Mt. Washington, where Mrs. Klumpp's home was located, and that Mrs. Klumpp was home when he arrived.

From the record at the trial:

> Q: Was Edythe there when you arrived?
> A: Yes, she was.
> Q: Did you stay at that residence that evening?
> A: Yes, we did.
> Q: Then did you two go to sleep together?
> A: Yes, we did.
> Q: What time did you leave for work on October 31?
> A: About eight o'clock.

Bergen admitted that after Mrs. Klumpp's arrest he had visited her at the county jail over a period of some three months.

At the next recess, Ginny, as is her custom, came to the defense table to discuss with me the notes she had taken. Mrs. Klumpp turned to Ginny and said: "I don't know how he can lie like that when he knows what I can tell on him."

Here was the break we had been waiting for.

"Go on," I said.

But she retreated back inside herself and said nothing.

The glimmer of hope had come and just as swiftly gone. We were again in Wonderland.

The prosecutor next called Detective Eugene Moore to the stand. After a few preliminary questions, Judge Gusweiler, upon my motion, excused the jury to hear testimony concerning the facts surrounding Mrs. Klumpp's alleged confession. Moore, upon cross-examination, admitted that he had not advised Mrs. Klumpp of her constitutional rights, stating, "We knew we had the guilty party. It wasn't necessary."

Homicide Detective Wilbur Stagenhorst, who followed Moore on the stand, corroborated his testimony in its entirety.

It developed on cross-examination that Mrs. Klumpp, on many occasions during his interrogation, had asked for a lawyer, but that the officers had refused to cooperate until their investigation was over.

According to the official transcript of the Klumpp trial, page 862:

> Q: I want you to tell the jury what you told her when she asked how soon she could have a lawyer.
> A: I told her she would have an opportunity to contact a lawyer in due time.
> Q: In due time?
> A: Yes, sir.
> Q: What did you mean by that?
> A: Well, when the investigation was completed.
> Q: When the investigation was completed?
> A: Yes, sir.

With the court's permission I called Mrs. Klumpp to the stand for the sole purpose of challenging the interrogating officer's testimony.

> Q: What was said to you after you took the lie test?
> A: They said I had run a bad chart on the lie test and that I had lied to them. They said there were blood spots in the car and a certain type of grass at Lake Cowan different from the kind they have around here, and that some of that grass was on the bottom of my car. They said they had found tire tracks by Lake Cowan that matched mine. I said, "You couldn't have."
> Q: When you were under arrest, were you advised of your constitutional rights?
> A: No.
> Q: Prior to that, had you asked to see a lawyer?
> A: I think after I was under arrest I believe I asked to see my lawyer and they said I couldn't until after I had made a statement. I kept insisting I wanted to see you. There were three of them in there and they kept pounding questions at me, one after the other.
> Q: How many times did you ask to see me?
> A: Quite a few times.
> Q: Were you taken to your home?
> A: I kept asking to go. I was worried about it. That it would get in the papers and I said, "I can't hear you. All I can think of is getting the kids out of town." They said, "After you make the statement we'll take you to the kids and you'll

have time to make arrangements." Then they said, "If we take you to see the kids, you'll make a statement?" I said yes.

Mrs. Klumpp testified that the next morning she was first taken to "show up," then to Lake Cowan. She said, "I said that my attorney was supposed to be there early. I kept insisting that I wanted to see you. I didn't want to go out there. They said, 'His early means noon. We'll be back before he gets here.'"

After she had been cross-examined, I launched into what the press labeled "an impassioned speech to the court maintaining that the written statements of Edythe Klumpp had not been given voluntarily." Inducements had been held out to her to make these statements. The inducements were leniency and the promise that she could see her children.

I told the court:

"To get Edythe Klumpp to change her story she was told: 'If you tell the truth about the gun, we'll see to it that you're charged with manslaughter and released on your own recognizance.' Do you think a woman can make that up? What does she know about being released 'on your own recognizance'? That's something lawyers and policemen know about. Either I had to put these words in her mouth or a policeman did. And *I* did not do it!"

I acknowledged that under Ohio law the interrogating officers were not bound to advise Mrs. Klumpp of her constitutional rights. Their failure to do so was, in my opinion, morally wrong but not legally wrong. They had, however, by their actions, violated the mandatory provisions of two sections of the statute law of the State of Ohio and used every trick known to the trade in obtaining Mrs. Klumpp's statement. I pointed out to the court that the interrogating officers' failure to comply with Mrs. Klumpp's request for a lawyer violated Section 2935.16 of the Revised Code of the State of Ohio in that "no officer having in charge any person, suspect, accused or charged with the commission of a crime or offense shall upon the request of such person prevent such person from consulting immediately and privately with any attorney at law or for the purpose of enabling such person to employ such attorney at law."

"When Mrs. Klumpp asked, 'When may I see a lawyer?' it was

the mandatory duty of the interrogating officers to advise her *at that very moment* of her rights insofar as legal counsel was concerned," I told the court. "The interrogating officers instead employed subterfuge and outright falsehood in utter disregard of the defendant's rights and their mandatory duty under both state law and the federal Constitution, when they advised her that she could see a lawyer in 'due time' and that she could not see a lawyer until their investigation was completed. The legislature felt so strongly concerning the subject matter contained in Section 2935.16 it provided a penalty of twenty-five dollars to one hundred dollars or imprisonment of not more than thirty days or both for any officer violating the mandatory provisions of this statute."

I argued that the officers had also violated Section 2935.05 of the Revised Code of the State of Ohio:

"When a sheriff, deputy sheriff, marshal, deputy marshal, watchman or police officer has arrested a person without a warrant, he must, without unnecessary delay, take the person arrested before a court or magistrate having jurisdiction of the offense, and must make or cause to be made before such court or magistrate a complaint stating the offense for which the person was arrested."

I told the court: "The officers' false statement and illegal actions not only usurped and held for naught every state and federal guarantee of a citizen but violated both Section 2935.05 and Section 2935.16 of the Revised Code of the State of Ohio and violated and held for naught the defendant's constitutional guarantees as set forth in the Fourteenth Amendment to the federal Constitution and in Article 1, Section 10 of the Constitution of the State of Ohio."

But the judge ruled against the defense—and the Wonderland continued. With the introduction of Mrs. Klumpp's "confession," the state rested its case.

The irony was that just a short time after the Klumpp trial, the United States Supreme Court, in a similar case (*Miranda* v. *Arizona,* 384 U.S. 436) held that "the prosecution may not use statements stemming from custodial interrogation of a defendant unless it demonstrates the use of procedural safeguards effective to secure the privilege against self-incrimination."

The rules that the Supreme Court announced, and which must be followed, are as follows:

(1) At the outset, if a person in custody is to be subjected to interrogation, he must first be informed in clear and unequivocal terms that he has the right to remain silent. (2) The warning of the right to remain silent must be accompanied by the explanation that anything said can be used against the individual in court. (3) The person in custody must be clearly informed that he has the right to consult with a lawyer and to have a lawyer with him during interrogation. (4) There must be effective and express explanation to the person that if he is indigent a lawyer will be appointed to represent him. (5) If the individual indicates, in any manner, at any time prior or during questioning, that he wishes to remain silent, the interrogation must cease.

Any statement, the Supreme Court held, obtained as a result of interrogation of a person in custody or otherwise deprived of his freedom who has not been given the protections required by the Miranda decision may not be admitted in evidence in a trial. All this did not help Mrs. Klumpp one iota, for just a week after the Miranda decision, the Supreme Court held in *John* v. *New Jersey*, 384 U.S. 719 that its ruling in the Miranda case was not retroactive.

Yet the Miranda decision spelled out the law which I had advocated in the Klumpp case and was a complete reversal of the court's ruling admitting Mrs. Klumpp's statement into evidence at her trial.

Edythe Klumpp each day seemed to grow more thin and pale. Wrote Margaret Josten in the *Enquirer:*

Her blonde hair once curled precisely now straggles at the ends and hangs unnoticed over her forehead. Although her clothing is still fresh and uncrumpled, obviously she is no longer making an effort to wear new costumes each day in court. Nor is the accused woman bothering to hide animosity for those at the prosecution table. This was most evident as she glared at C. Watson Hover, prosecuting attorney, while he argued that Edythe's confession on the death of Louise Bergen should be part of the evidence. An observer remarked, "If looks could kill, Hover would fall dead . . ." On the witness stand, Mrs. Klumpp spoke in a husky voice and so quickly it was sometimes impossible to catch all she was saying. Her words tumbled out and a court reporter had to ask for a repeat several times . . ."

After a few preliminary witnesses had appeared, I called Mrs. Klumpp to the stand. She, in answer to my questions, related the same unbelievable and silly story that she had been telling and retelling since the night of her arrest.

It then became the prosecutor's turn to interrogate Mrs. Klumpp. They had selected Schoettmer to cross-examine her, and what a job he did. Mrs. Klumpp and Schoettmer faced each other but it was an unequal duel. She was vulnerable and lying. He was poised and experienced. She was a sitting duck as he fired question after question with the rapidity of a machine gun scoring a bull's-eye with every shot. It became apparent to all that the prosecutor was playing for keeps. Mrs. Klumpp looked worse and worse as Schoettmer, sensing the kill, showed no mercy. She didn't have a chance. He crucified her. He destroyed her.

And thus the trial dwindled to a conclusion.

When Schoettmer summed up for the jury, he pulled out every stop.

"I look upon this woman as a home wrecker," he cried, "who used physical wiles to lure this man to set himself up as her husband. Why do I say that? Well, for one thing, there was a wedding ring. There was this idyllic setting in which he mentioned undoubtedly the deep pools of fire in her eyes, the heavenly loveliness that she has, and slipped that wedding ring on her finger . . ."

Schoettmer talked for almost two hours, starting at quarter after nine in the morning.

He characterized Edythe Klumpp as "a mistress with certain physical charms and wiles. Edythe Klumpp went on the stand and said she was a religious woman. Yet she admits she burned the body and lived in adultery."

"Listen," Harvey murmured, "no one is perfect."

But he could not cheer me at that moment.

"She claims to be a truthful woman," Schoettmer went on, filled to brim with indignation, "yet admits lying to her mother, her daughter, Bergen, the community, the police. How many more? Now, as to her appearance. On Thursday Mrs. Klumpp testified for three and a half hours under direct examination. She had a meek, reticent approach. Her counsel literally screamed at her to keep her voice up.

She had the appearance of a fragile woman. That was her role on Thursday, but on Friday she came out of that role. She was fighting. She even asked the prosecutor questions. When she said, 'The Lord has forgiven me,' she didn't mean it at all. She was never close to tears. She wanted to be a fighting cat—and that is what she is. Yesterday again she played the meek, fragile role. Well, was she meek and mild on October 30—or a fighting wildcat?"

Bitter stuff.

He also labeled my defense as the "Hopkins Treatment."

What could I say in return? I didn't know. But there I stood, facing that jury.

"Tomorrow," I began, "will make the thirty-ninth anniversary of my start in criminal law practice. I have spent those entire thirty-nine years in the defense of men, women, boys, and girls charged with alleged commission of an offense. I have always felt that it was more important to fight over life and liberty than to fight over property rights. As long as I am able to draw a breath and stand on my hind legs, I intend to continue in my chosen profession . . ."

Yet, I thought ruefully, here I stand wishing I were somewhere else.

I made a motion with my hands as if to embrace the jury, the very courtroom and all its contents.

"I believe in the jury system," I said. "If we ever lost the jury system here in America we would have the most dangerous philosophies sweep over this nation, the sort that now run rampant in foreign countries . . ."

But the preliminaries were over. I was still in Wonderland—and I had to discuss the trial.

I looked at my hands, as if seeking the truth there. Then I looked straight into the eyes of the jury. "If," I said, "the Hopkins treatment means that I do not believe in mob rule; that I do not believe in permitting the arresting officers to determine my client's guilt or innocence; that I do not believe in permitting the prosecuting attorney—or his staff—to go unchallenged in their interpretation of a case; if the Hopkins treatment means that I believe in a fair and legal trial for all, regardless of race, color, or creed; if it means that I believe in trying cases on the facts without concealing testimony or without employing subterfuge; and if it means that I believe in utter frankness and do not believe in misleading juries—if the Hopkins treatment means all these things, I'm humbly proud that my efforts have not gone in vain . . ."

I talked of the evidence that had been presented and then said, "As I sat here for three weeks listening for the facts in this case to develop, I have come to the conclusion we are trying the wrong party. The man—and I use that term loosely—who caused this tragedy has been permitted to go scot free. This target-pistol Romeo, this aviator of sorts, by his deceit, subterfuge, and honey-dripping promises and vows has brought about the death of his wife and the trial of Edythe Klumpp upon the charge of murder."

The jury sat in stony silence.

I plunged ahead.

"This setup of his beats Social Security by a mile. A wife working to support herself and a child, a second wife furnishing home, food, and lodging to children—the children who, by dropping their dimes into a piggy bank, help pay for his second honeymoon. Here was a gravy train with biscuit wheels. Bill Bergen wasn't about to give it up. What a scene that must have been when the 'wedding' of Bill Bergen and Edythe Klumpp took place. Can't you see his sadistic smile when he lied, 'With this ring, I thee wed'?"

The Klumpp jury? They looked at me with disdain. Then juror number twelve fixed me but good. There I was, making my final argument, a plea for a fellow human being's life, and out of a clear blue sky she blurted out for all to hear: "Why, that's not true."

I stopped cold. That, reasonably, was enough for a mistrial then and there. I asked for an immediate recess and talked to the judge and the prosecution about her interruption. But the judge told me that he would not grant a mistrial. He said, however, that he would admonish the jury—and particularly number twelve—to keep quiet. So we trooped back into the courtroom to start again. I had only gone about another ten minutes when number twelve nudged the juror next to her and said: "I told you he would pull that!"

I turned to the judge.

"There is," I said, "no reason for me to proceed. This woman has made up her mind in direct violation of your Honor's instructions. She, by her actions, has prejudiced the defendant's case beyond recall. This is prejudicial error. I move your Honor to declare a mistrial."

But once again the judge overruled my motion. He warned the juror to keep quiet and then directed me to proceed with my argument.

I was outraged but there was nothing I could do but continue.

I indicted Bill Bergen as much as possible, but the attempt was useless.

"So," I said in one last attempt, "I repeat, we are trying the wrong party. Surely there must be some way for the law to clip Bergen's wings so as to protect other women he will come into contact with? From the stand he is a self-confessed adulterer. The State of Ohio would be remiss in its duty if it did not prosecute on this charge and give warning at least that such conduct will not be tolerated. But maybe because he testified against Edythe Klumpp, they will give him a gold medal. I don't know. All I know is, until this happened, Edythe Klumpp was a decent woman . . ."

My argument, as well as the charge of the court, was anticlimactic, however. The jury received the case at 4:09 P.M. July 1. At eleven that evening, when the jury was unable to agree, it was sent to a hotel for the night. The following morning it resumed deliberations again—but the day dwindled into twilight without a verdict. Soon street lights came on. At home, viewers eagerly watched the eleven o'clock news on the tube, but the reporters said the jury was still out. The waiting game continued. As the clock neared midnight, those of us still at the courthouse waited for the judge to send the jurors to their hotel.

Judge Gusweiler had just instructed the bailiff to inquire of the jury if there was any chance a verdict might be reached that evening. But before the bailiff could comply, the buzzer sounded.

The sound of a buzzer to some is an ordinary sound, but to those players in the drama that is criminal law the sound of a buzzer is the most hateful and beautiful and breath-stopping noise God ever allowed on the face of the earth. Many times it means merely that the jury has a question. But sooner or later it means that the jury has reached a verdict. Between the noise the buzzer makes and the reading of the verdict we live in suspended animation. We are, all of us, in limbo.

"If it's another question," one reporter complained when the buzzer sounded, "I'm hitting the hay."

Then word flashed into the room: "They've got a verdict! They've got a verdict!"

The reaction was electric. The press snapped to attention. Camera crews manned their stations. Courtesy and manners were flung into the darkness of the night as those lingerers in the corridors hurled themselves at the courtroom door, each fighting for the best seat in the house. They wanted to be present for the kill. The Roman holiday was nearing the grand climax. This was what the lingerers had lingered for—the sight of blood, real or imagined. Those frequenters of accidents, those in attendance at fires, they were in the courtroom as the clock neared midnight.

As the jurors entered, I knew the verdict. The reading of it was a mere fillip that the dance required. Each juror purposely ignored Edythe Klumpp, choosing to stare straight ahead. No longer were these the faces of men or women or mothers and fathers. The countenance of each member of the jury evidenced strain; their eyes appeared to be staring and sunken, their faces were drained of color and were frozen in grotesque masks.

Edythe Klumpp, who had been studying these faces, said in a haunted voice: "I actually feel sorry for them."

I shrugged, pretending to be impassive as the Great Stone Face. But inside I was sick. I realized that true facts had not been presented to this jury. I was sick because we had not been able to turn up evidence to support my theory that Mrs. Klumpp had not killed Mrs. Bergen. I felt I knew who the guilty party was, but with Edythe Klumpp herself steadfastly refusing to cooperate and steadfastly insisting—both in private consultation and in her testimony in the trial—that she had pulled the trigger, it was next to impossible to prove otherwise.

The jury was seated. Judge Gusweiler ascended the bench.

"Have you reached a verdict?" he said.

"We have," said the foreman.

"Hand the verdict to the clerk," said the judge, "and it shall be read and recorded."

The foreman stood and handed the folded paper to the clerk. The clerk immediately turned his back to the jury, marched some ten paces, did an about-face, and opened the missive.

"We the members of the jury," he read, "find the defendant—" and here he paused for a dramatic effect—"Guilty of murder in the first degree."

Pandemonium!

Bill Wiggeringloh, the genial criminal bailiff, but not genial then, ran interference for Mrs. Klumpp as he extricated her from the Roman holiday scene in the courtroom and started her on her first steps to the execution chamber.

Reporters, news photographers, movie and television cameramen, radio men with tape recorders at the ready, and the mob of courthouse hangers-on followed in their wake in the frantic scramble to record the gruesome and sensational data surrounding the verdict of a jury that had just decreed the death of a woman. They wanted to summarize in prose any word of anguish and despair—in order that you, while partaking of breakfast the next day might have the pleasure of murder as well as marmalade to round out your morning feast.

About an hour before the death verdict in the Klumpp case, I received a long-distance call from Hamilton, Ohio. It was from Harvey Woods, to whom I had assigned the job of representing a man by the name of Poindexter charged with first degree murder in that city.

It was a badly shaken young lawyer who advised me that a three-judge panel had just handed down a verdict of death, decreeing that Poindexter must die in the electric chair. I had temporarily recovered from the shock of the Poindexter verdict when the buzzer had sounded, heralding a similar fate for Mrs. Klumpp.

Two death verdicts in one day in two separate first degree murder trials in two separate cities, and both defendants represented by my office.

Ironically, this day, July 2, 1959, was my thirty-ninth anniversary in law practice. Instead of happiness and celebration there was nothing but demoralization and self-condemnation.

I sat alone at the defense table facing an empty jury box. The pandemonium of moments before had given way to peace and quiet.

There are some times in one's life, owing to happenings and circumstances beyond one's control, when one must be alone—when one must hold communion with one's other self; when one must reflect; when one must analyze and reanalyze, argue and reargue any contemplated affirmative action; when one must search one's soul to determine whether one has the intestinal fortitude, in spite of seemingly insurmountable odds, to rededicate oneself to the challenge lying ahead.

How long I sat there I do not know. I was startled when I heard a voice inquiring if I was going to stay all night. It was Al Schottelkotte, the News Director of WCPO-TV.

Al asked me if I had any comment on the verdict in the Klumpp case. I shrugged. I was thinking of C. Watson Hover, the prosecutor. When he had left the courtroom he had said:

"Thank God that's over!"

"How wrong you are," I was thinking. "It's only just begun."

I didn't know then, nor did anyone else, that Edythe Klumpp was about to change her story.

And that it would be a brand new ball game.

III

"You should eat something," Anne said.

Brave girl. Sitting through almost every awful day of the Klumpp trial, she would smile at me whenever I hit emotional rock bottom, and her smile helped. When, in the courtroom among the spectators, she heard others mutter that defense lawyers should not be allowed on the face of the earth, her eyes flashed with anger. Then, when that circus of a trial was over, she tried her best to cheer me, but I could not be cheered.

"Not hungry," I said. "Sorry." And went for a walk in the summer twilight. Peaceful—almost. Everything except my soul. Stars, struggling to shine, glittered from a thousand years before. As I walked my mind's eye went over the trial transcript one more time— but searching for what? I had reread that damned record so often I had every comma committed to memory. And, as I walked, I remembered the voice of Edythe Klumpp telling a newspaper reporter, "I told Bill to watch out for my mother and my children. She promised that if I had to go away, the children would be raised the way I wanted them to be raised. She promised that she would see that they would keep going to church. The trial? Actually, the state didn't prove a thing. The state's case was full of lies . . ."

"But our case was also lies," I told the approaching night. "The truth never emerged."

As I walked in the gathering darkness, the crickets began to sing love songs to one another. Lightning bugs turned themselves on and off, hundreds of unpolarized dots of green and yellow. From somewhere distant, over the next hill, came the screech of tires on asphalt. Everything—all noises—said freedom. But at that precise moment Edythe Klumpp was far from free. She sweltered in the cage atop the county courthouse, trapped there by a jury and the city heat.

Was she sewing? No. Not anymore, I told myself.

She would remain there, in the county jail, until Judge Gusweiler returned from vacation to hear my plea for a new trial. Then, if that plea was denied, she would be moved to Marysville Reformatory, the state prison for women twenty miles northwest of Columbus, where the flatlands of Ohio stretch out forever. She would spend her last hours on earth at Marysville until time came to transport her to the penitentiary at Columbus and her appointment with the chair. The Columbus lockup had no facilities for ladies awaiting death.

"But no more sewing for you, Mrs. Klumpp," I thought, as I walked on in the darkness.

Once convicted by the jury, she had been deprived of the tools of her pleasure: the pins and needles and scissors of the seamstress. Thus, while in the county jail, no more sewing for Edythe Klumpp. The papers made a big thing of that.

They made a big thing of something else, too. "Would she," one reporter wondered, "be allowed to make a new dress for her own execution, as she had turned out a new dress almost for each day of the trial?" The reporter had queried the state prison. Prisoners headed for the chair are allowed to choose the menu for their last meal, the query went; are they also permitted to choose their death costume? Said an official at Columbus, "Such a request of the condemned woman probably would be granted . . ."

Days came and went.

One day a surprise visitor appeared at my office.

"Who?" I said to Ginny.

"Minister," she said.

"You're kidding," I said. "What would a minister be doing here?"

"You'll never guess in a million years," Ginny said, and grinned at me.

She sent the minister in.

He was the Reverend Oscar Minyard of the Cincinnati Church of Christ and the chaplain at the county jail.

"I've talked quite a bit with Mrs. Klumpp before and during the trial," he said, when the preliminary courtesies were done.

I nodded.

"Frankly," he said, "I've been convinced for a long time that she was lying."

"Welcome to the club," I said.

"When I talked with her after the verdict," he said, "she was scared. She's scared to death, Mr. Hopkins."

"She has every right to be," I said.

"I've been urging her to tell the true facts," he said.

"She'll never do it," I said.

"No," he said, "after I urged her, she was silent for a moment, then it was as if a dam had broken, Mr. Hopkins. All the emotion and frustration she had been holding in during the trial . . ."

"Go on."

"Well," he said, "she admits now that she lied to the police, to you, and to the jury."

"Oh God," I whispered.

The minister nodded.

"Yes," he said with a slow smile on his face. "That's the name of the game."

And then the three of us—Ginny, the minister, and myself—sat in my office, grinning with what the theologians would, I suppose, classify as joy.

He went on to say that she had told him that Bill Bergen had threatened the lives of her children if she dared involve him in the murder. She told the minister that Bergen himself had fabricated the fairy tale she had palmed off on the rest of us. It seems Bergen had told her, "This way nobody gets hurt. Your children stay alive and the jury won't do anything to a woman."

As he talked, a dismal thought occurred to me.

"She told you," I said. "But you're a minister. Suppose she won't tell these things to me or to the court?"

"I insisted that she give me permission to tell you her new story," he said. "Otherwise, I told her it would do no good. After all, Mr. Hopkins, you're better at the legal trade than I am. That's your business."

Ten minutes later—as fast as a taxi could hurl us there—Ginny, Harvey, and I were closeted again with Mrs. Klumpp in that little conference room at the county jail.

How I managed to control myself after the misdirected effort I had put forth in her behalf, I don't know to this day. But instead of heaping a diatribe upon her head I merely asked her to repeat what she had told Reverend Minyard.

"When the police first started to question Bill is when the story I gave the police was first made up," she said. "He told me that if I stuck to that story everything would be all right, that everybody would know it was an accident and that I couldn't have done it, that it wasn't possible for me to have done it, and that I didn't have to worry because I would get out of it. After I gave the story at police headquarters and when Bill was brought down there, I told him I couldn't go through with it because of the children. He told me I had better think of the children and go through with it—because of them . . .

"Louise Bergen called me on October 30 in the afternoon about ten minutes to five. Bill was working and I called him and told him about the call. Louise said she wanted to see me and it was important; she wanted to see me right away. I asked her if we could make it later because I had to be at school. She said she had an engagement at six-thirty and wanted to talk to me that evening. So I said yes. I think it was about the lawyer. I believe she mentioned that after she was in the car. She said she was going to tell him to go ahead with the divorce. I called Bill and suggested that he pick her up and I would meet them behind the Mt. Washington Theater as soon as I could get there. I stopped to get gas and then ran into Albers. I guess I got there about five forty-five. They got out of his car and got into mine. They were arguing when they got into my car. Louise sat in the front seat with me and Bill sat in the back. The argument got so bad at one time that Bill slapped her. That was when she started telling me some of the things he had done and that ever since two weeks after they were married he had been running around.

"They were arguing about more money. She wanted another hundred dollars. When she called me, she didn't know she was going to see Bill. She just said that she wanted to discuss something with me. I started driving and I told Bill I wanted to look for a gas station because I wanted to go to the rest room. He was in a foul mood. This was right before we turned down Four Mile Road, when I said I wanted to look for a gas station. He said, 'Just pull back in that new subdivision and you can go there.' I stopped and got out of the car and went to relieve myself. I was away from the car about five minutes, I guess. I was very upset because of the way they were arguing. When I came back, she was on the front seat and he was leaning over her. I don't know what he was doing. I got excited and passed out. I went down on the ground. Her head was all bloody. I didn't see anything in his hand. I didn't see the gun. About a week before that Bill had been down on the riverbank shooting and when he finished he put the gun in the glove compartment. He was loading the magazine. I couldn't load the gun in court. I had never loaded that gun before.

"After I came to, I looked at her again and felt her pulse and then I started running down the road. I said I was going for help. Bill told me to get back there or I would get some of the same thing. I went back and got in the car and started shaking her. I was so upset I guess that is why I was shaking her. He opened the trunk and told me to help him. When I wouldn't, he started yelling at me that I had to help him. He said they were arguing and she was crying and she reached in her purse for a Kleenex and then she leaned over and opened the glove compartment. I thought it was locked but he said she opened it and pulled the gun out and he reached over and grabbed her arm and the gun went off under her chin and shot her. I didn't know the gun was loaded in there because I just wouldn't think it would be. When we were on the riverbank he was loading it, and when we finished he wiped the gun off. He even wiped the inside off.

"I drove Bill back to the show and he got his car. He said he was going to clean himself up and go to Mel Abrams's house and I should go to school. I didn't want to go to school but he insisted that I had to go. It would look funny if I didn't go is what he said.

After I taught school, I called Bill and he said I should go on home
and he would be there shortly. Bill was trying to figure out what to
do with her. We were talking about taking her down to the river and
putting her in but there might be people with boats. Then we tried
to think of other places where there was water and I suggested Lake
Cowan. Bill wore his dark trousers that night. There was blood on
them. I poured gasoline on them on the morning of the thirty-first,
Friday, and burned them. I don't know what time we left that night to
get rid of the body, about eleven or eleven-thirty I guess. I don't
know exactly what time we got back. He wanted me to help him but
I couldn't and I got back in the car. He is the one that poured the
gasoline on the body. I had the car started and I glanced back; it
made a terrific blaze. It never entered my mind at that time to go
to the authorities but I thought a couple of times later about telling
a fellow that I worked with on state patrol but I was afraid to."

What she said made sense. I listened, excited, because at long
last I had the information necessary to see that justice was done.
What she told us we kept secret until August 25, the day set for Judge
Gusweiler's decision upon a motion for a new trial.

But word was out that she had changed her story.

Reporters were everywhere, but all I would say was, "Sorry,
gentlemen. No comment."

Then came August 25 and there we were before the judge. I
asked, and received permission, to read Mrs. Klumpp's statement so
that the court should be fully advised as to the turn of events.

What hopes I had went skittering out the window.

Said Judge Gusweiler, "The court has considered your motion
for a new trial, the oral arguments, and the authority cited, and is
of the opinion that the motion is not well taken . . ." My heart sank.
"Only one of the grounds of error, I believe, needs commenting on
and that's the alleged misconduct of the jury. In the court's opinion,
there was no misconduct . . ." He went on and on but I had stopped
listening. As far as we were concerned, in his court, at least, the
matter was closed. I waited only for him to say the words I knew he
had to say. Mrs. Klumpp trembled at my side, still as if in a trance,
but tears brimmed in her eyes.

Said Judge Gusweiler, "Mrs. Klumpp, you know you have been
found Guilty of murder in the first degree without recommendation

of mercy. Is there anything you wish to say before sentence is pronounced?"

Silence—awful, awful silence.

My client shook her head. Then she stared at me in disbelief.

Said Judge Gusweiler, "I see nothing to alter the verdict which was based on the evidence and the law and was a clear and just one. Edythe Margaret Klumpp, you are to be placed in the custody of the sheriff and he, within thirty days, will deliver you to the warden of the Ohio Penitentiary and on December 15, the warden shall cause a current of electricity of sufficient intensity to cause death to pass through your body, and this application shall continue until you are dead . . . and may God have mercy on your soul."

My client was sobbing.

Said Judge Gusweiler, "And said defendant shall pay the costs of this prosecution."

To sentence any fellow human being to death is not only cruel and inhuman but is a barbaric and archaic ritual demonstrating once again that men and women can in the name of the law do collectively what one man or woman does not dare do individually. As we look back in horror upon the witch trials and the burning at the stake, we likewise will on a day not too far distant kneel and beg forgiveness for this vengeance and for our utter disregard of God's commandment: "Thou shalt not kill."

The sheriff and the court bailiff marched my distraught client out of the courtroom and straight to the elevator. She looked neither to the right nor to the left. The photographers and reporters gained nothing from her but the scent of her grief.

For those of you who delight in the tedious and have bookkeeper minds, I shall note here that Mrs. Klumpp's tab for the trial came to $3,927.70, according to the clerk of courts, Elmer Hunsicker. This broke down to lodging and meals for jurors, $405.42; taxi service to and from the hotel and courthouse for jurors, $14.70; meal for jurors at Mariemont Inn, $39.02; pay for jurors who sat nineteen days, $1,260.00; clerk fees, $65.45; sheriff fees, $39.94; municipal court hearing, $5.00; fees for 45 witnesses, $312.80; official stenographer, $76.00; transcript fees for both defense and prosecution, $1,596.37; and rental of one air-conditioned Greyhound bus, $95.00. The rule was that if she died or was imprisoned without funds, the county—generously—would not try to collect but would pay the tab itself.

Even the most amateur of Perry Masons, knew, of course, that my client would not die on December 15 as prescribed. Before she would be scheduled to keep that melancholy appointment, every legal avenue would be employed to divert her footsteps from that awful finality. Appeals would be heard. Yet, the joy one finds in a stay of execution is only temporary. The chair always waits.

After the hearing before Judge Gusweiler, I tried to get back into the routine of my days, but the routine did not come easily. For instance, that one morning—early and the dawn still young—I stared in the mirror to shave and I realized that elsewhere another drama was being enacted. At the precise moment I applied the razor, Edythe Klumpp walked out of the gloomy confines of the courthouse. As she departed, said the reporters, the sunshine was beautiful. She paused only briefly to allow the photographers to record her departure on film. Reporters noted that she wore a black dress with a white collar, which, they added, she had worn on several occasions during the trial. They noted that she carried with her a small pillow upon which to rest her head during the long drive to Columbus. This, you see, was before expressways. They noted also that the other female inmates of the county jail had gotten up at five to say good-bye to Mrs. Klumpp. They noted that as the car drove away from the courthouse, church bells tolled 6 A.M. and good-bye. Then, putting away their notes, they adjourned to pleasanter scenes for a cup of coffee and to talk perhaps of the weather.

All that morning, as I worked in my office, Edythe Klumpp was either en route to Columbus or there. The trip, I learned, had been a grim and silent affair. Muted conversation and the soft playing of the car radio turned down low. Edythe Klumpp added little to the conversation, but one going through the legal channels en route to a scheduled demise has little to say. To talk of yesterdays would have been sad. To talk of tomorrows would have broken her heart. At Sabina they stopped for a soft drink. The people they saw along the way expressed no interest in the car or the condemned passenger it contained. The stop at the Ohio Penitentiary, at Columbus, was brief and efficient. Mrs. Klumpp was given the number 108278, was further classified, made a part of the records, and then, just as quickly, the sheriff's stationwagon went from Columbus to Marysville. My client, during the entire trip, was not handcuffed.

I suppose that by the time the Cincinnati streets were clogged with noontime lunch seekers, Edythe Klumpp had been officially "processed" in Columbus and was then on her way to the Women's Reformatory. She told me later that as she traveled through the Ohio flatland, she did not stare out the window at the passing barns and stands of corn. And she expressed little interest in the gentle town of Marysville itself. As the car turned down the long lane on the edge of town, the lane that ended at the prison, the buildings of the prison were not visible. She saw only that single smokestack—tall, darkened with soot, and antique—which stuck up in the blue sky like a dirty finger, pointing to where Heaven is.

And I suppose that by the time the Cincinnati streets were filled with the quiet of the afternoon—everyone back at his desk, playing little games with pieces of paper and/or filing same—Edythe Klumpp was established in her second-floor quarters of the building called the Quarantine. This red brick structure is where new inmates are kept until they can be declared healthy enough to join the other damsels at the sewing machines and ironing boards and baking ovens for regular prison toil. But Edythe Klumpp would not be leaving Quarantine. She would stay on the second floor, far from the other incarcerated ladies, and there remain until the final drive back to Columbus and her death.

"You've been staring at that one legal brief an hour," Ginny said. "I think you've read it by now, don't you?"

Summer ended, autumn came. Then winter.

February 1, 1960. The First District Court of Appeals upheld the jury conviction of my client. In a twenty-page written opinion by Judge Bert Long concurred in by Judges Stanley Matthews and James O'Connell, the court said that my client had received a fair trial and that there had been no prejudicial error.

Edythe Klumpp heard the news of her appeal denied over a radio newscast. A nurse who had also heard the broadcast hurried to Mrs. Klumpp's side—and found her in tears.

"I don't really know why I cried that afternoon," she told me later. "For days I had actually been hoping that I wouldn't win the appeal for a new trial."

"Why?" I said, bewildered.

"Don't you see?" she said. "I don't think I could have stood going back to Cincinnati and going through the trial all over again. Yet, at the same time, I was afraid I would lose the appeal. Then when I heard the announcement over the radio, I couldn't help myself. I didn't feel sad exactly. I felt—well, not relieved but like something that I had been waiting for a long time had finally happened."

On May 18, 1960, the Ohio Supreme Court refused to review the case. My client was scheduled to die on June 17.

The court did, however, grant us a ninety-day stay of execution in order to appeal to the United States Supreme Court.

Spring came, then summer. Then autumn.

On October 17, 1960, the United States Supreme Court refused to admit the Klumpp case.

"Now what?" said Anne, pouring me a Scotch.

"We petition for a rehearing," I said. "And don't forget the twist of lemon."

Our petition for a rehearing was denied.

December 9, 1960, was the date set for Mrs. Klumpp's final car ride to Columbus, but Governor Michael V. DiSalle granted a thirty-day stay of execution in order that he and the parole board might review the case thoroughly.

Meanwhile, in Marysville, Mrs. Klumpp had fallen into a set routine: embroidering, drawing, painting, working puzzles, and reading. And crying. The radio—which brought her news of Christmas sales—was outside the bars of her cell, beyond her reach. She was not allowed contact with other inmates, although she could see them through the bars of her window as they moved in comparative freedom about the prison grounds. By day, she was in a day room—a vast room supposed to be a hospital ward, but she had it to herself. By night, she was locked in her small cell, the kind of quarters the other ladies enjoyed. The distance between the day room and her cell was several paces. This was her freedom.

Locked in her cell, she ate meals alone, always aware that someone watched.

Her visitors had been few: a clergyman, her mother, her four children, Ginny, myself, and once—without her knowledge—the Governor.

On the wall of her day room was a bulletin board clustered with cards and photographs and homemade greetings scrawled with lonely love from her children. A center strip of pictures featured her only grandson. Elsewhere there was a photograph of Mrs. Klumpp herself —younger, prettier, slimmer—in the red robe of a choir singer. Sweet, sweet days thumbtacked to the past.

Edythe Klumpp officially asked only one favor: that her execution, if it had to be, should not take place on the one day in January which was her oldest daughter's birthday.

Since the inauguration of Governor DiSalle, only one electrocution had been carried out in Ohio. The Governor once painted a vivid description of his emotions during that night that Walter Byomin was executed for killing a policeman. In a talk in Florida, Governor DiSalle told how during the electrocution he took a drive in his car, which had a mobile radio unit. Over the unit had come the radio message: "Detail completed, 8:07."

Said the Governor, "The next morning I woke with a very empty feeling."

Ten days before Christmas I was in Columbus before the parole board.

"Last chance?" said Anne.

"Just about," I said.

The parole board was composed of four men and one woman. In a hearing before this board there are no rules of evidence as in a regular trial. The prosecutor and I each argued our case, he for denying Mrs. Klumpp her life, I for saving her life.

This board faces only the most difficult of assignments: to grant or not to grant some form of freedom to its petitioners. The board members must set aside their hearts and be hard-shelled realists, for to have a board grant every petition is not to have an effective board at all. Such a board would fling open every cell in every prison and turn loose upon society not only those who deserve their freedom but those to whom freedom means only license to kill and plunder. So, let us know this: that the unhappy but necessary task of such boards is, at times against its own good will, to say no.

The board, agonizingly aware of its responsibility, heard me out, listening to me with great and lonely patience.

I suggested to this body that I myself would pay for a truth serum test to point up and establish my client's account of the slaying. I told them I would personally finance the test. "Not as a lawyer," I said, "but as a private citizen, because, as long as capital punishment is on the statute books, we had better be mighty sure what we're doing and certain that we have the true facts . . . because electrocution is irrevocable."

The board members listened, but I could not read their eyes.

"What has the state got to lose by giving her the test?" I said.

Mrs. Klumpp's mother appeared before the board, wept, pleaded for her daughter's life, and was led, sobbing, from the room.

The eyes before me told me nothing.

A sister of Edythe Klumpp appeared before them. "Her children need a mother," she said. "I can't take her place. Now they can go and see her. What will happen to these children?"

The eyes of the board were the same as before: remote, observing, and—human eyes, trying not to see human tears. The board does not judge on the basis of the quantity of tears. It judges on what it considers human justice.

I said what I had to say, that "Mrs. Klumpp's original yarn was a complete fabrication. I went through the first trial because my investigation could not bring forth one way or the other any proof as to its truth or falsity. You should recommend clemency. I feel that a man by the name of William Bergen is over his head in this crime . . ."

But I stared at eyes that said nothing back to me.

C. Watson Hover, who had prosecuted Mrs. Klumpp, said, "If this fantastic version is correct, this woman is innocent. She should not be commuted, but she should be pardoned."

He went on, though, maintaining her guilt.

Finally, the hearing over, Commission Chairman Joseph E. Doneghy of Toledo said, "We will decide whether to recommend mercy . . ."

Their decision: no. They voted against it three to two.

Two days before Christmas they forwarded the finding to the Governor.

Unknown to me at the time, however, my plea for a truth serum test had struck a responding chord with Colonel William M. Vance, a member of that board. He had cast the deciding vote in the three-to-two decision against executive clemency, but at the same time he had urged the Governor to try the serum on Mrs. Klumpp. He asked that the Governor stay the execution until the appropriate time—after the truth serum and other tests had been carried out. He also wrote to the Governor:

> It appears clear that the truth or falsity of this last-minute reversal of the account of death has never been tested by any of the means available to modern science. Because of the finality of death and the inability of society to correct an awful mistake and finite judgment after death has sealed the door, I feel that every precaution should be taken before taking the life of a person who might be innocent, however remote the probability of such innocence may be. I left the personal interview with Edythe Klumpp with the definite impression that she was not deliberately lying and was probably telling the truth. If more accurate means of ascertaining the truth than experience and intuition exist, they should be exhausted. If the results of such tests as proposed by the defense attorney at the commission hearing indicate Edythe Klumpp is innocent and William Bergen is guilty of the death of Louise Bergen, I am sure the prosecuting attorney of Hamilton County will prosecute William Bergen under his official oath and duty. Was Edythe Klumpp deprived of her constitutional rights of counsel by refusal of the police to allow her to communicate with an attorney before getting a statement from her? The courts have said no. I disagree, as is my right. I think in this point alone the case should have been retried and the so-called "confession" excluded from evidence as involuntary . . .

And, as I said, Christmas came and went. Cocktail parties, formal, informal, made up the holiday season. Church services. And here and there, talk over the punch bowl of law and justice and the rest. But my mind kept wandering up to central Ohio. No cocktail parties in the cage. No gaiety. Nothing but marking the days off on a calendar, waiting for New Year's Eve, and then waiting to die.

"Have you exhausted all the ways of saving her?" Anne asked.

"One left," I said. "A direct appeal to the Governor."

"Will that work?"

"Who knows?"

Shortly after Christmas I, together with Mrs. Klumpp's four children and her mother, appeared in Governor DiSalle's office at the state capitol and made a final effort to save the life of Mrs. Klumpp. The conference lasted two hours and was highlighted—mournfully— by the four children, whose ages ranged from eleven to twenty-two, begging for their mother's life. I made a more dispassionate plea, but to no avail. The Governor, courteous and attentive, gave us no indication what his final verdict might be.

As we stepped outside on the wide stone steps of the state capitol, the wind in that prairie flatland seemed to be colder than before and I had never seen the sky so gray.

"Did we do all right?" one of the four children said.

"You did just fine," I said—and wanted to bawl right there.

New Year's Eve came—and went.

On January 4, at 4 P.M., just forty-eight hours before Mrs. Klumpp was scheduled to die, I received a long-distance call from an executive assistant to the Governor, requesting my immediate presence in the Governor's office in Columbus.

"Why?" I said.

But no amount of questioning could elucidate the purpose of the meeting.

"Will Hover be there?" I said. "At least tell me that."

Yes, Hover would be there. The prosecutor and his staff had received a similar invitation.

I called Anne. "Want to go to Columbus?"

"Why?" she asked.

"I don't know, but the Governor wants to see me. You can bet your life it's about the Klumpp case."

"You don't suppose—"

But I interrupted her, "If you're going, you'll have to be ready in twenty minutes."

"Try to keep me home," she challenged.

The trip to Columbus was swift and filled with wonder.

The Governor's outer office was a madhouse. Reporters were there. Television cameramen were there. Radio newsmen were there. But we had to wait. The Governor wasn't there.

An hour later, the Governor walked into the room. Others, whom I did not recognize, were with him. He walked to his desk and without his usual cordiality—he was all business—began.

He said that he and Dr. Milton Parker of Ohio State University had just returned from the Women's Reformatory in Marysville, where Dr. Parker at his request had administered a truth serum test to Mrs. Klumpp. He said the test had been recorded and that he wanted both the prosecutor and defense counsel to hear it.

There was a murmur of suppressed excitement as the Governor nodded and a technician flipped the switch on the tape recorder.

The room fell silent.

Now, may I suggest here that I am not a dramatist nor am I a novelist. I did not create the characters who walk across these pages. God created them. I, in my limited way, try only to capture them with words.

I wish I could have invited you to join me in the Governor's office that winter night and hear that tape just as the rest of us heard it. It was a drama no playwright could have manufactured. You would have heard the voices of real people—Dr. Parker, Edythe Klumpp, and Governor DiSalle—as they sat in a room at the women's prison that gray afternoon. The doctor's steady voice, the Governor's gentle one, and the voice of Edythe Klumpp under the truth serum, her haunting voice, now strong and clear, now weak and almost but not quite unintelligible, retracing and reliving the happenings surrounding the evening of Mrs. Bergen's death.

It was as if someone had lifted a curtain and we were privileged to eavesdrop upon a very private and confidential matter not intended for our ears.

Mrs. Klumpp related the horror of the afternoon and night when Mrs. Bergen met her death. She repeated, but in greater detail, the same story she had told Reverend Minyard, Ginny, and me after her conviction and death sentence.

For most of us it was a weird, spine-tingling experience. But not for Hover. He sat chain-smoking in a chair much too large for him. His face was white and frozen. His eyes stared intently at the tape recorder as it spun out Mrs. Klumpp's account of Mrs. Bergen's death.

The tape played for ninety minutes, punctuated only by Hover's periodic snorts of disgust and outraged disbelief.

At the conclusion of the recording, Governor DiSalle advised us that both he and Dr. Parker were convinced that Mrs. Klumpp was telling the truth—*and that he was therefore commuting her death sentence to life.*

Prosecutor C. Watson Hover stared in disbelief at the Governor. The prosecutor jumped to his feet, moved his mouth, but no word came out. Then everything happened at once. Tempers flared. Shouts. Angry shouts. At one point an attaché had to restrain—physically—an assistant prosecutor who had approached the Governor in a manner that can only be described as threatening. Everyone was shouting at everyone else, everyone—that is—but the Governor. Dr. Parker and Hover argued with vehemence the merits and lack of merits of truth serum. All the while, spinning rapidly, the tape spun on the tape recorder, and having run its length, twirled uselessly with a flap-flap-flapping noise. Finally, someone remembered to shut off the machine.

Never once raising his voice above conversational level, Governor DiSalle explained—with patience as one might explain to an unruly kindergarten class the wonder of the stars—that Colonel Vance of the parole board had also recommended the use of the truth serum as well as, added the Governor, "any other scientific means to learn the true facts. Furthermore, Dr. Parker is one of the few experts on sodium amytal in the United States. He graduated from Ohio State University in 1943, served as a psychiatrist in the United States Navy, and later at Washington's St. Elizabeth Hospital administered sodium amytal to over two hundred criminals."

The prosecutor seethed, and so did his assistants. They listened in angry silence as the Governor, calling Bill Bergen in another state, requested that Bergen return to Ohio. The Governor advised Bergen that he believed that Bergen had accidentally killed his wife and, if Bergen would return, the Governor would help him in any way he could.

But Bergen, who had since married a teen-age girl, dodged the matter. He wanted no part of the fun-and-games.

The Governor then told us in the office that he was personally satisfied that Edythe Klumpp had been convicted of a crime she had not committed and he went on to ask us—myself and the glaring prosecutor—to work together to seek the true facts and to reverse the jury's decision.

The prosecutor and his staff left without comment. They didn't need to comment. Refusal glittered in their eyes. The others left, too, and in the office were just the Governor, Anne, and I. He looked at me. I looked at him.

"Long day," I said.

He nodded. Outside the city of Columbus slept. Midnight had come and gone.

"Governor?"

"Yes?"

"I've been a Republican and a Protestant all my life—up to now," I said. "But after watching you work and the way you conducted yourself tonight I am going to become a Democrat and I am going to join the Catholic Church."

"Welcome to the Democratic Party," he said seriously, but there was a twinkle in his eye. "But for God's sake," he added, "don't ruin our Church."

It was 1 A.M. when Anne and I started back to Cincinnati.

So Edythe Klumpp wasn't going to die after all.

I had no feeling of elation or the warmth of victory. It was rather that a great weight had been lifted from my shoulders and that I had been released from a responsibility which was almost too much for anyone to bear.

I had walked hand in hand with this death verdict for the past eighteen months. For the first time in my life I was near the breaking point. A feeling of peace and thankfulness descended upon me.

I wanted to get home and go to bed.

I was tired.

When Edythe Klumpp learned that her sentence had been commuted to life, she was beside herself. She had not been aware of what the Governor had really said during the session with sodium amytal. The session to her had been no more than a dream which one could not, afterward, piece together and make reality of. The next day, typically feminine, she settled down in a corner of her cell and began working on her hairdo. She made her jailers promise not to let anyone in to see her until she looked nice. She hugged herself with glee. She looked out the window as if seeing snow for the first time. Before, she had not watched it. She had suffered nightmares about that snow: it being shoveled aside in order that her grave might be dug. She beamed. She no longer need avoid the snow. She would see another spring.

When told that Bill Bergen had been asked to come back and perhaps take sodium amytal, too, she turned sad.

"He'd better not," she said, "for his own good." Then, still looking at the snow, she murmured, "Poor, poor Bill. He's so confused. I feel sorry for him . . ."

And worked on her hair some more.

Outside the beautiful, beautiful snow continued its silent white drenching of the flatland countryside.

Dick Kirkpatrick of the *Enquirer* summed up the dilemma that the new facts had created when he wrote:

> When *was* the body of Louise Bergen saturated with gasoline and burned at Lake Cowan? Was it burned by Edythe Klumpp around noon as she testified? Or was it burned some time the evening before, as Mrs. Klumpp now says?

The key to the dilemma: if the body had been burned as she said at the trial—at noon at Lake Cowan—Bill Bergen had a beautiful alibi. But if—as she said via truth serum—she and Bergen were with Mrs. Bergen right after work and he had killed Louise then, Bergen had no alibi at all. Nor did he have an alibi for later, when—according to Mrs. Klumpp—they both drove the body to the lake where it was burned.

But the next morning, after I returned from Columbus, the public was not concerned with these legal niceties upon which the life of a lady hung. The public seemed enraged that it had been robbed of the last act of the circus.

Cried the *Enquirer:*

> . . . Governor DiSalle not only has dismayed law enforcement throughout Ohio by his whimsical exercise of clemency, but he has insulted—we say insulted and mean it—the jury, the courts, and the whole modern system of criminology. Maybe the Governor himself ought to take a test of temperamental suitability to be Chief Executive of this great state. Or perhaps he just took it and flunked . . .

"Cold enough for you today?" Ginny said, bringing in the morning mail. She saw I had been reading the *Enquirer*.

"Quite chilly," I said.

And we both laughed but, at the same time, felt sad.

Juror number twelve in the Klumpp trial, and the self-elected spokesman for the jury, had this to say via the news columns:

> None of us had any doubt at all about Mrs. Klumpp's guilt. They say truth serum does not work on pathological liars. If ever there was a pathological liar, Mrs. Klumpp was one. There was nothing personal in our feelings toward Mrs. Klumpp. We wanted to see justice done. The Governor has undone all the real, conscientious work done by the law enforcement agencies, the prosecutors, and the judge and jury. We could tell Bergen was telling the truth.

"So speaks the self-appointed authority on pathological liars and justice," a courthouse wag grinned.

The attack mounted from all sides. Doctors, pseudo-psychiatrists, and those enlightened souls proclaiming special knowledge in the administration of sodium amytal had an amateur field day.

"But listen," said my favorite bartender, "they can't all be dumbos. What about this guy they call Dr. Gerber, the coroner up there in Cleveland?"

"What about him?" I said.

"Well, Mr. Hopkins, I read where he said DiSalle was way off base using that truth serum. He said something about it being an insult to the intelligence and the competence of the coroner, the judges, and things like the Supreme Court."

"If he was so against it," I said, "why did he himself suggest that truth serum be used on Dr. Sheppard?"

"The next one is on me," my favorite bartender muttered, pouring same. "I guess I'll stick to bartending and leave the law to broads like you had on the jury. That one loudmouth, I mean."

"You said it," I said. "I didn't."

I was, in fact, about the only one *not* saying anything.

Republican State Senator John W. Brown introduced a bill that would prohibit the use of truth serum to secure information that would bring about convictions, reprieves, commutations, and pardons. Said the Governor, "This is a cheap way to get some cheap publicity for a rather mediocre politician."

DiSalle bore the brunt of the attack. Although he said that his mail balanced out favorably, some of the letter writers from Cincinnati charged him with everything from sexual interest in Mrs. Klumpp to a sixty thousand dollar bribe. He indicated that Edythe Klumpp could never again receive a fair trial in Cincinnati.

Much of the hammering appeared in the newspapers. Also appearing was the word-by-word account by Edythe Klumpp under the truth serum. As far as I was concerned, the most important reader of that transcript was Deputy Sheriff Irwin Schulte. Mrs. Klumpp—on two different occasions under sodium amytal—had mentioned Mrs. Bergen's glasses and the new locale of the lady's death. The deputy, his memory triggered, looked up old records. Sure enough, there it was verifying Mrs. Klumpp's story. On the evening of October 30, 1958, Anderson Township Rangers had delivered Mrs. Bergen's glasses, a portion of her necklace—then unidentified—and a pair of child's bloody shorts to the deputy. Schulte, convinced that the Stratton Avenue location as described by Mrs. Klumpp under truth serum had to be the scene of Mrs. Bergen's death, called the sheriff's office advising him of his suspicions and inquiring the present whereabouts of the glasses and necklace. The call started an immediate investigation and the articles were finally located tucked away in a file in the prosecutor's office. The evidence that would have blown the case sky high had rested there throughout the trial. It is an amazing fact that at the time Mrs. Bergen's glasses were found, no official attempt was made to trace their ownership. To ascertain their origin would have been a comparatively simple matter requiring only minimum routine police investigation and probably would have resulted in the immediate piecing together of the true facts.

To say that the prosecutor and police were embarrassed would be the understatement of the year. The prosecutor blamed the laboratory for not identifying the glasses in the first place. Tempers again reached the breaking point as C. Watson Hover once more found his prosecution crumbling all about him.

But the circus wasn't over. The prosecutor, for some unknown and unexplained reason, left for Columbus to report the find of the "new evidence" and to show it to the Governor. When you consider that Hover, after DiSalle's commutation of Mrs. Klumpp's sentence, had in stinging terms publicly castigated and criticized the Governor, you can only come to the possible conclusion that the prosecutor may have panicked and that his weird conduct was only the result of running scared.

Upon his return to Cincinnati, the prosecutor proclaimed: "The new locale of the crime strengthens the case against Mrs. Klumpp. I do not intend to reopen the case."

The new evidence changed the time and location of the crime, shot Bergen's alibi full of holes, and meant a whole new ball game; but Hover shut his eyes and refused to acknowledge the facts.

"Now what?" asked Anne.

"This leaves it squarely up to the Governor," I said.

The Governor accepted Hover's challenge. He ordered the state patrol to reinvestigate the case, which the prosecutor should have done.

Seven months later, the state patrol report complete, the Governor again shook the state's moral timbers with its publication.

The report established that:

1. Mrs. Bergen's death took place at Mt. Washington and not Caldwell Park as had been alleged by the prosecutor and proved by him to the satisfaction of the jury.

2. Bergen had on many instances committed perjury at the trial.

3. Mel Abrams admitted that he was mistaken when he corroborated Bergen's testimony as to his, Bergen's, whereabouts between 5 and 7 P.M. on the day of the crime.

4. Mrs. Bergen's body had been burned during the night and not at noon as alleged by the prosecutor and affirmed by Mrs. Klumpp in her testimony at her trial.

Mrs. Klumpp in her alleged confession had stated (and later repeated at her trial) that she alone had driven to Lake Cowan on the day after Mrs. Bergen's death, and that she had doused the victim's body with gasoline, which she had purchased in Cincinnati prior to her trip, and attached a match thereto in an attempt to burn Mrs. Bergen's body.

She had stated that she had left Cincinnati at approximately 10 A.M. and had set fire to the body at approximately noon. These facts were contained in her original statement to the police and were later testified to and established as "facts" by the prosecutor at Mrs. Klumpp's trial.

These were the "facts" on which the prosecutor based his case and which were proved by him to the satisfaction of the jury beyond a reasonable doubt.

These were the most damning "facts" on which the jury based its death verdict decreeing that Mrs. Klumpp die in the electric chair.

Mrs. Klumpp in her sodium amytal test, contrary to her testimony at her trial, revealed that Bergen and she had transported Mrs. Bergen to Lake Cowan the evening of her death, and that Bergen had pulled his wife's body from the trunk of the car, soaked it in gasoline, and set fire to the corpse.

This was a vital point in the reinvestigation, for Bergen had sworn under oath at Mrs. Klumpp's trial that he had been with her from approximately 11 P.M. on the date of his wife's death until eight the following morning and that he and Mrs. Klumpp had occupied the same bed.

If it could be established that the body was in reality burned during the night while Bergen and Mrs. Klumpp, according to Bergen's testimony, were together, then a giant stride had been taken in uncovering the true facts as they related to the events after Mrs. Bergen's death.

The Ohio state patrol's report on its reinvestigation of the Klumpp case left no doubt in any mind that Mrs. Bergen's body had not been burned at noon the following day as testified to by Mrs. Klumpp at her trial but had in fact been burned during the preceding night as stated by Mrs. Klumpp while under sodium amytal.

The report also established the following facts:

1. Mrs. Bergen's shoes had been found in Clinton County by one Chester Davis long before the time that Mrs. Klumpp had testified at her trial she left Cincinnati to drive to Lake Cowan to burn Mrs. Bergen's body.

2. Employees of the State of Ohio had been working at Lake Cowan on the day indicated by Mrs. Klumpp when she testified at her

trial that she had burned the body between 12 noon and 1 P.M. These employees were interviewed by the state patrol and signed individual affidavits stating that they were working from 10:30 A.M. to 3:30 P.M. at this locale upon the day in question and at times were within thirty feet of the spot where Mrs. Bergen's body was later discovered. At no time, they stated, did they see a fire, nor was there an odor of burning.

The fire that partially destroyed Mrs. Bergen's body was not of short duration. Experts stated that it would have taken an intensive fire of some three to five hours to accomplish the damage to Mrs. Bergen's body as duly and faithfully recorded in the coroner's autopsy report.

Mrs. Klumpp in her truth serum test said that Bergen had been with her and Mrs. Bergen at or about 6 P.M. on the date of his wife's death. She had further stated that she had become ill and left the car and that when she returned, Mrs. Bergen had been shot.

At Mrs. Klumpp's trial, since she had assumed all responsibility and had absolved Bergen of any complicity, his whereabouts upon the day of his wife's death between the hours of 5:30 and 7 P.M. were of no importance whatsoever.

As matters at that time stood, since it couldn't help our cause, I saw no reason to challenge seriously his statements at the trial as to these fateful hours. Bergen had testified at the trial that he left Colonial Stores, his place of employment, at or about 5 P.M. and went directly to Stillpass, where he saw a friend by the name of Mel Abrams. That he and Abrams talked for a short interval, during which time he made arrangements to drop in at Abrams's home sometime later that evening.

He testified further that he again returned to Colonial Stores, a distance of some three blocks, where he remained until 7 P.M.

This recitation, if true, established an alibi for Bergen covering the time in which his wife had met her death.

Bergen's testimony together with Mel Abrams's corroboration was not challenged until Mrs. Klumpp stated under truth serum that Bergen had been with her during the time in question and had, in fact, shot his wife.

So Bergen's testimony, which had been incidental and of no import, now became of paramount importance. Bergen, because of

Mrs. Klumpp's statements and accusations, was contacted by the Ohio State Patrol and subjected to extensive grilling concerning his exact whereabouts between 5:30 and 7 P.M. on the day his wife had been killed.

Bergen finally changed his story. He now stated that he had not returned and remained at Colonial Stores but instead had paid a call upon a young woman he had met while getting a massage at a slenderizing salon. He said that he called her, set up an appointment, and arrived at her apartment at approximately 6 P.M. Bergen further stated that he and the young woman had sexual relations twice, that he paid her for her services, and that he left her apartment just before 7 P.M.

When asked why he had neglected to tell this particular part of his story two years before, Bergen said, "I think it is fairly obvious. It's not the sort of thing that you want to become common knowledge if it isn't absolutely necessary. I had hoped that it wouldn't have to come out, not realizing how this time element, it's been changing and everything now from what people are telling me and so forth, that it would be really necessary to pin myself down so close."

One could readily understand if not sympathize with Bergen's reluctance to publicize his indiscretions, but at the same time it was difficult to reconcile his statements when confronted with the strong denial of the young woman.

She cooperated fully with the authorities and, while denying any intimacies with Bergen, set forth in an affidavit that he had been at her residence at approximately 9 P.M. and not between 6 and 7 P.M. as he had stated.

Mel Abrams, upon being reinterviewed, now admitted that he could have been mistaken as to the time of Bergen's departure from Stillpass on the date in question.

So Bergen had attempted to set up and establish two different alibis covering his whereabouts from 5:30 to 7 P.M. on the evening of his wife's death—and both had now been destroyed.

While this of itself did not prove the truth or falsity of Mrs. Klumpp's statement concerning Bergen's involvement, it did, from a negative angle, raise grave doubts when coupled with Bergen's refusal to take two separate sodium amytal tests formerly agreed to.

Where the evidence at the trial precluded Bergen's presence at the scene of the crime, it now had been established that it not only was a possibility but a strong probability that Mrs. Klumpp had once again been corroborated.

Thousands upon thousands of man-hours had been devoted to the reinvestigation of the Klumpp case. Cold trails were reopened and explored, witnesses were examined and reexamined and then examined yet again in an attempt and hope that some new detail might come to light. The entire reinvestigation had been made by experienced men whose approach was at all times objective and whose goal was that justice might prevail.

I don't suppose that in the annals of crime a case has been more thoroughly investigated or more effort put forth than was expended by the Ohio State Patrol in its reinvestigation of the Klumpp case.

It would appear that at long last we were going to break the Klumpp case wide open but we were once again doomed to frustration and bitter disappointment, for the prosecutor lifted Bergen right off the hook.

One would think that, in view of the disclosures set forth in the report and in the interest of justice, Hover would take some immediate action against Bergen, but sure of his position and the support of the news media, he refused to budge.

His reaction to the report was not only typical but tragic and startling. He denied that Bergen had committed perjury and simply dismissed the other facts established by the report as adding nothing to the case.

He stated that his office had once again questioned Bergen for a period of three hours and that this interrogation had only reaffirmed his belief in Bergen's innocence. Besides, he stated, Cincinnati police had subjected Bergen to polygraph tests, which they announced he had passed with flying colors.

The prosecutor washed his hands of the affair and refused to proceed against Bergen.

The report was received by the public with mixed emotions. Many voiced their individual opinions by writing to newspapers, and the newspapers in turn published varied missives under "Reader's Views." While one letter would criticize DiSalle unmercifully, the next would castigate Hover for his failure to proceed against Bergen.

Again there was a lull in the Klumpp case. The election was ap-

proaching and with DiSalle running for reelection as Governor and
Hover aspiring to the Court of Appeals Bench, each one's time was
consumed in promoting his individual candidacy. Finally, Election
Day arrived, and when the ballots had been counted Rhodes had defeated DiSalle by some 400,000 votes and Hover had been elected to
the Court of Appeals.

"Time is running out," I told Anne the night the election results
came in. "With DiSalle's defeat, he has only eight weeks left in
office. I'm certain the next Governor wants no part of the mess. There
won't be any hope of executive clemency or anything. We've lost."

"You've covered every angle?" she said. Her voice was sad.

"There's only one left," I said. "A personal letter to DiSalle."

I wrote to the outgoing Governor. I did not plead. I respected the
law and the man too much for that. I set forth clearly and concisely
what I considered the facts of the case and the dead end it had reached.
These were not the alleged "facts" presented by the prosecutor to the
jury, they were the true facts as I knew them. These were the facts
that had never once been ruled upon by any appellate court. It was a
foregone conclusion that DiSalle would turn my letter over to the
parole board for advice and recommendation. Another hearing was
set. Again Hover and I went through the little charade that we had
come to know by heart.

The whole thing was wasted motion, for the board immediately
voted to reject my request. Its viewpoint was without delay forwarded
to the Governor and the final decision was back where it had started—
right in DiSalle's lap.

At DiSalle's request the parole board had issued a subpoena for
William Bergen to testify in Columbus at the Klumpp hearing. Bergen
had moved to Maryland and, when served with the board's subpoena,
retained lawyers and thereby gave notice that he would contest the
legality of the entire proceedings.

The matter was thrashed out before Circuit Court Judge Walter
Moorman of Montgomery County, Maryland, who granted a motion
to quash the subpoena filed by Bergen's attorneys upon the ground
that it had not been issued by a Court of Record and therefore did
not comply with the mandatory provisions of the Uniform Deposition
Act.

And so we approached the Governor's last day in office.

"He did it!" Ginny cried one day, handing me the telephone. "He did it!"

I took the telephone from her. It was a reporter, telling me that the Governor had finally commuted Mrs. Klumpp's sentence to second degree murder, which guaranteed her a parole hearing in ten years.

"Oh God," I said. "Oh God . . ."

The Governor's announcement of the commutation was accompanied by an eight-page statement, sometimes objective, sometimes subjective, setting forth his reasons for the commutation granted to Mrs. Klumpp. He criticized Hover for his failure to investigate more fully Mrs. Klumpp's story, and called William Bergen, husband of the slain woman, a man whose conduct "has been so reprehensible as to actually disgust the average citizen.

"As far as Edythe Klumpp is concerned," the Governor continued, "there can be no justifiable excuse for her conduct both in the events which transpired before the killing of Mrs. Bergen and for her failure to tell the truth during the period between the discovery of the body and her subsequent conviction.

"But under our system of government and almost fanatical devotion to equal justice, we do not heap the entire punishment on one while excluding another who also admitted not telling the truth. I feel in all fairness, the continued incarceration of Edythe Klumpp for a minimum of ten years would be punishment for her indiscretions, misdeeds, and her failure to tell the truth."

Then referring to Bergen, the Governor said: "There possibly are many people like William Bergen, but not many have with such complete callousness told of the infidelity to a wife he claimed he loved. This is the same man who in a boasting vein told of conquest after conquest while he was living with his wife and while he was living with Mrs. Klumpp."

The Governor further said that Bergen admitted that he lied while on the witness stand and said the only evidence to contradict Mrs. Klumpp's story that he was with her at the time of the slaying was his own unsupported statement "given after two attempts to establish an alibi had failed.

"Having lied twice, having on two occasions indicated his will-ingness to testify, then having backed away at the last moment, how much can be really believed? How much reliance would a jury place upon his testimony had they known what he had told the highway patrol?"

And subsequently the Governor said: "Were I of a disposition which would enable me to easily turn off the voice of inner conscience, I would have decided long ago that the embarrassment, the frustra-tions, and the abuse arising from this matter were too high a price to pay for one life, or even the incident of unequal justice."

In conclusion, the Governor noted that his decision would not be a "satisfactory solution to the prosecuting attorney or to Mrs. Klumpp's attorney, but I think it more closely represents justice, as imperfect as the solution may be, in view of the fact that the informa-tion at hand is still incomplete."

Regardless of how one might feel about other portions of Di-Salle's statement, it was unanimous that his decision to commute Mrs. Klumpp's sentence to second degree murder pleased no one.

As far as the public was concerned, some argued that the Gov-ernor had gone too far, while others insisted that he should have given Mrs. Klumpp her freedom. The prosecutor was indignant and Mrs. Klumpp was disappointed. I thought then and I feel now that if DiSalle had commuted her sentence to time served it would have satisfied the most bloodthirsty of our citizens and at the same time have appeased those who believed in her innocence. I wasn't satisfied with the commutation, but there wasn't much I could do about it. My main objection was that while the law provided a mandatory parole hear-ing in ten years, it did not guarantee Mrs. Klumpp's freedom at that time, for the parole board could refuse to release her and continue her case for a period of years. At the expiration of that continuance, the board could once again refuse her a parole and again continue her case to some future date.

She, because of her conduct and untrue statements before and during her first trial, had not exactly endeared herself to the parole board; nor would these indiscretions enhance her chances with future parole boards.

It is unfortunate that DiSalle did not commute Mrs. Klumpp's sentence to time served and by one stroke of the pen close the matter once and for all. There can be no doubt but that his decision was a compromise and I don't like compromises in criminal cases.

I had not voted for DiSalle and in fact did not know him until the Klumpp case. Actually, I shouldn't criticize him for not freeing Mrs. Klumpp. But for his intervention, Mrs. Klumpp would have gone to her death in the electric chair and the real facts would never have been disclosed, for electrocution is so final. During the time I was endeavoring to save Mrs. Klumpp's life and the later developments that followed her commutation, I had the opportunity to study and evaluate DiSalle. One seldom meets a man who—regardless of public opinion, pressure, and censure, or political future and ambition—has the fortitude to carry on the tradition of our forefathers and measure up to the ideals we profess rather than practice the realism we find expedient at the moment. It may well be that DiSalle, because of his decisions in the Klumpp case, was responsible for his own political obituary; but at the same time he demonstrated a devotion to duty and a fearless approach in the administration of justice seldom shown by public officials.

The key, in my opinion, to the entire Klumpp case was the polygraph tests given by the Cincinnati police to William Bergen and later relied upon by Hover to sustain his inexorable stand. The police announced that as a result of the tests they were satisfied that Bergen was innocent and therefore dismissed him as a suspect in his wife's death.

To begin with, the results of polygraph tests are not admitted as evidence in any court within the United States for the reason that said tests have been found by experience to be highly unreliable. The polygraph or lie-detector machine is a psychological weapon employed by police and prosecutors in their constant war against crime. It has in some cases wrung reluctant confessions from stubborn suspects, but on the other hand it has cleared and set free guilty parties who know how to "beat" the machine or who were given passing grades by operators not skilled enough to read the results correctly.

Extensive hearings on the use of the polygraph were held in 1964 by the subcommittee of the Committee on Government Operations of the House of Representatives under the chairmanship of Congressman John E. Moss of California, after the propriety of conduct of some of the government's polygraph operators was questioned. When those hearings were concluded, the subcommittee issued a scathing report in which it said there is no such thing as a "lie detector." This view coincides with that of J. Edgar Hoover, director of the Federal Bureau of Investigation, who in connection with the Jack Ruby investigation made this comment:

"It should be pointed out that the polygraph, often referred to as "lie detector,' is not in fact such a device . . . the FBI feels that the polygraph technique is not sufficiently precise to permit absolute judgments of deception or truth without qualifications."

It was unfortunate that the police or prosecutor at the time of the original investigation of Louise Bergen's death had depended exclusively upon the results of a questionable lie detector in their clearing of Bergen. Had they, while the case was "hot," made a thorough investigation of Bergen's whereabouts at the time of his wife's death, he would have been proven a liar without an alibi and a prime suspect.

The fact that he had on two occasions endeavored and failed to fix an alibi for the hours covering his wife's death would be more than sufficient reason for the police and prosecutor to demand of him an explanation and motivation for his sinister actions.

In addition to Bergen's lie detector results and Mrs. Klumpp's confession there was another angle that, in my opinion, played a big part in Hover's attitude and his continued refusal to change his mind concerning the facts and Bergen's involvement in his wife's death. Approximately two years before the Klumpp case I had defended a meter reader by the name of Robert Lyons who had been charged by Hover with first degree murder in the death of Audrey Pugh. Following a trial of some months' duration, Lyons had been found Not Guilty. Hover, following Lyons's acquittal, stated publicly that he made some mistakes during the trial and that I had taken advantage of those mistakes. I feel that he made up his mind that there would be no repetition of the Lyons case and that this fact in a great measure accounted for his refusal to deviate one iota from the "facts" as related by Mrs. Klumpp in her original statement to the police. I will say one thing for Hover: he was consistent. Even when face to face with embarrassing misplaced evidence, the proven perjury of Bergen, or the establishment of the burning of the body during the night when Bergen had testified he was with Mrs. Klumpp, Hover did not budge.

So that is the Klumpp case as I knew it and lived it.

DiSalle and Hover for more than a year participated in a running brawl. The conflict between the two men was reflected by the articles and editorials appearing in many newspapers while the battle raged. The news media had a field day duly recording the charges and countercharges hurled back and forth by the contestants. As a result, the public became so indoctrinated with and confused by the diversity of opinions expressed and the subjective interpretations advanced that the facts became of secondary importance and, owing to the turmoil, almost unrecognizable.

It is my belief that since a jury had convicted Mrs. Klumpp of first degree murder, decreeing her death, and because a Governor later commuted her sentence to life and then reduced the charge to second degree murder, the public has a right to know the facts on which he based his decisions and to determine whether he, as has been charged, usurped our jury system or, to the contrary, was justified in his action.

Over ten years have now passed since that hot night in July when I sat alone in a courtroom where, a short time before, a jury had returned a verdict sending my client, a woman, to her death in the electric chair. I still remember the frantic telephone call I had received before the Klumpp verdict advising me that Frank Poindexter had been found Guilty of first degree murder at Hamilton, Ohio, and had also been sentenced to death.

Sitting there in tomb-like silence with death as my only companion had been an experience I will never forget. I had learned what it meant to sit on death's doorstep with Osiris at my side.

The fact that both Mrs. Klumpp's and Poindexter's lives were ultimately saved in no way eased the hell I had lived through that night and the months that followed.

Former Governor DiSalle is practicing law in Washington, D.C. He recently wrote a book, *The Power of Life or Death,* in which he devotes considerable space to the Klumpp and Poindexter murder cases.

Hover and Schoettmer are dead.

Bergen at last report had married a nineteen-year-old girl and was still living in Maryland.

Mrs. Klumpp has since August, 1959, been an inmate of the

Women's Reformatory at Marysville, Ohio. At a parole hearing in December, 1968, Mrs. Klumpp's case was continued for a period of three years.

You will find me practicing law at the old stand.

A little older, a little wiser, perhaps, but still shaking my head in wonder and disbelief when I try to reconcile Mrs. Klumpp's incarceration with the known facts.

It just doesn't jell worth a damn.

CHAPTER 14
"and in conclusion..."

The souvenirs of this office—and of my life—suddenly seem too many. I could ramble on for ages, citing this trial or that. Here I sit, becalmed. How can I sum up all this and give it some central meaning? How can anyone sum up his life and give it that? I, who have saved clients from the adventure of death, have myself stood at its door, teetering between the world and that vague sweet mystery beyond. This was when I had cancer. I thought I was going to die. The doctors themselves told me that probably the time was up. And there I was, in that hospital bed, so high on Demerol I seemed to be floating about the room. I'd fall asleep, sleep an hour, and then wake up to pick up the thread of conversation. Nights were the worst. I would ask the nurse to raise the blind. I'd look up at the night sky. I wasn't trying to find any supernatural power but I had done a lot of reading—astronomy and so forth—in my life. I got to thinking that light, traveling for billions of years, reaches us long after the original light itself has probably winked out forever. I got to thinking about the universe and how our sun is one of the dinkiest, and how our galaxy is dimestore stuff compared to others, and I came to the conclusion that there had to be something bigger than I was. Corny admission but true. I was less than a piece of sand. It was there, in that hospital room, that I decided that more than ever I would try to be a better person and a better lawyer, helping anyone I could with my small skills, no matter what the public thought. That's why we never turn anyone away at our office. If they have no money, we still sit there and talk to them. That was the new psychology I formed in that hospital room, when I looked out at the stars and thought I was dying.

And that is the way I have lived ever since.

But this does not sum me up.

Let me try another way.

I became a bridge champion almost by default. Toward the end of the 1920's I had a friend who belonged to the Cincinnati Businessman's Club, which he wanted me to join, and I got a junior membership. This was around 1932 and 1933 when the Depression was at its height and business was at its worst. Everybody had all the time in the world. There was this one chap who was vice-president of a big construction company. I wanted his business. To get to know him better I played bridge with him because bridge was what he favored. I lost about one hundred dollars a week for nearly eight weeks in those games. I was borrowing from everybody so I could pay my debts. I knew I had to take some action or I'd be wiped out. Well, in those days Whitehead was the bridge authority, so I got one of his books. For days on end I studied. It wasn't long before I managed to hold my own at the bridge table. In about three months, I started to win, sometimes one hundred dollars a day.

Bridge, because it was a scientific game, fascinated me. With its mathematical probabilities it was a challenge hard to resist. Continuing to study the game, I read every article on bridge I could get my hands on. Together with Charles Porter, I entered the Western Open Bridge Tournament in Cleveland. This contest is comparable to golf's Western Open. We won the pair championship. Shortly after, Charlie and I—together with Jeff Glick and Aaron Frank of Cleveland— entered and played in the American Bridge League's championship tournament held annually at Asbury Park, New Jersey. Although teams from all over the world competed in its many events, the blue-ribbon event was the Knock Out Team of Four. In this event, we reached the finals. We mutually agreed to play the finals in New York City. We were pitted against—of all people!—Eli Culbertson's team. For two days both teams were nose and nose, slugging it out at the Ritz. We won—and were the first Midwest four ever to do so!

Soon I found myself giving lessons and lectures on bridge instead of law. I was invited, expenses paid, to all national tournaments. If I had wanted to, I could easily have become a bridge bum. But I was getting too involved in the game to suit me. I was getting calls from New York and California, sometimes at three in the morning, to settle this or that bridge question. So I talked things over with Charlie Hall, who was a great bridge player. We decided to write our own bridge book. As it turned out, *I* wrote the book. We called it *Winning Contract and the Hall System* because, by then, I had made up my mind to stay in law. As a result of the book, though, teams came from everywhere to play us. Charlie and I were backed by a group of businessmen. The stakes were high—plenty high. I actually played in one game that lasted twenty hours and in those twenty hours fifteen thousand dollars changed hands! But it all boiled down to one thing: I was getting to be known more for the practice of bridge than the practice of law.

So one day I was at the Cincinnati Club where members of the Phoenix Club gathered, playing bridge, and I decided to heck with it. There I was that Saturday afternoon. Everybody else had left. I had, then, no obligations. I looked outside at the August afternoon and I said, "I think I'm wasting my time here smoking, drinking, gambling. I'm going to get out of here." A fellow sitting in the room said, "What else besides cards would you do on a Saturday afternoon?" What else? I went right downstairs—not because of what he had said but because of the collective thing—and I resigned. After the first five Saturdays, I didn't know what else there was to do. I'd leave the office, walk the streets, go to a movie for ten minutes, get out and be itching to get back into the card game—and then all of a sudden a certain peace descended on me as if I had become unshackled and I was no longer tied to this thing called bridge. I used to play six nights a week. I haven't played cards for almost twenty years now.

Or should I sum up these years by telling about the time I was invited to address the law students at the University of Cincinnati—and the invitation was quickly withdrawn by the then dean because I practiced criminal law? I did the next best thing. I invited the students to the Gibson Hotel, rented a ballroom, paid for it myself, and also paid for the booze the fledglings consumed. Their thirst for knowledge was as unbelievable as the subsequent bar tab.

Perhaps I should sum up my days another way. After the Pugh murder case in which I defended Robert Lyons, I was called upon to defend an Arthur Burns in Lawrenceburg, Indiana. Burns, along with an associate, had been charged with the hammer slaying of a seventy-three-year-old truck stop attendant. Upon hearing the story Burns told, I was convinced of his innocence, and the case went to trial.

The prosecuting attorney was Crawford Peters, known far and wide as "Happy" Peters. About a year before our case came to court, he had been elected prosecuting attorney for Dearborn County, Indiana, his campaign advertising reading:

ELECT "HAPPY" PETERS
PROSECUTING ATTORNEY FOR
DEARBORN COUNTY
HE'S BACK ON THE WAGON

And back on the wagon he was. The natives knew "Happy" well and were familiar with his bouts with John Barleycorn. But "Happy" had made a commendable effort, and the good people of that pleasant Indiana county took him at his word and, come Election Day, had rewarded him with the votes.

From the beginning of our trial it was evident that "Happy" had prepared his case well. His demeanor was that of the outraged protector of society, demanding his pound of flesh, settling for nothing less than my client's conviction. But "Happy" saved his big guns for his final argument—and leveled them point-blank at me.

In 1967 a fabulous television personality in the Midwest announced her retirement from the air. She was Ruth Lyons, who in the course of thirty years, first on radio, then on television, had acquired millions of devoted fans in Ohio, Indiana, and Kentucky—as well as way beyond. Come noon every weekday, housewives of those states tuned in her program and for ninety minutes held communion with their broadcast friend and idol. Ruth Lyons was more than a television personality. She was an institution.

To "Happy," one Lyons was the same as another: whether Ruth or Robert (the meter reader I had acquitted of murder). "Happy" stood before the jury and poured it on thick. His hair was disheveled. So was his suit. So was his shirt. So was his tie. Perspiration trickled. He was in fine form as he brayed, "Don't let this city slicker"—pointing at me—"come here to Hoosierland and pull the wool over your eyes. Don't let his suave tactics and honeyed words lead you down the path to a miscarriage of justice. If he tries one more criminal case against me, he'll have to give up his criminal career. *Because there sits the lawyer who for thousands of dollars acquitted Ruth Lyons of murder!"*

The packed courtroom howled. "Happy" looked bewildered. The laughter grew louder. There was no stopping it. The bailiff couldn't gavel it to silence. Judge Lester Baker looked at the scene, shrugged, and motioned me to the bench.

"Mr. Hopkins," he said. "I will entertain a motion for a mistrial."

"Your Honor," I said, "someone else will have to make the motion because I—with all due respect to you—wouldn't try this case over again if you gave me the courthouse."

At last the bailiff got the crowd silenced. "Happy" continued his final arguments.

And always, from the spectators, came titters.

The fire and tension had gone from the trial. Replacing it was an atmosphere of gaiety and good fellowship. The jury returned a verdict finding my client Not Guilty.

When I reached Cincinnati I called Ruth and thanked her for helping me get the Not Guilty verdict.

"Think nothing of it, Foss," she said. "I'm glad to help out a good friend any time. Just call me when I'm needed."

That's Ruth—always neighborly.

But I have belabored you, my friends, much too long with these items of my life. Fifty years ago I began to practice law. Five hundred and fifty-six murder cases later, I am still at it. Do I plan to retire? Men should not retire *from* something but *to* something. And what is sweeter than the practice of law? Let my suggest only this: the afternoon you call my office in need of my help and I do not respond, I will not be retired.

I will be dead.